SUNBEAM RAPIER, ALPINE 1955–65 AUTOBOOK

Workshop Manual for
Sunbeam Rapier 1 1955–58
Sunbeam Rapier 2 1958–59
Sunbeam Rapier 3 1959–61
Sunbeam Rapier 3A 1961–63
Sunbeam Rapier 4 1963–65
Sunbeam Alpine 1 1959–60
Sunbeam Alpine 2 1960–63
Sunbeam Alpine 3 1963–64
Sunbeam Alpine 4 1964–65

by

Kenneth Ball G I Mech E

and the

Autopress team of Technical Writers

AUTOPRESS LTD   GOLDEN LANE   BRIGHTON   BN1 2QJ   ENGLAND

The AUTOBOOK series of Workshop Manuals covers the majority of British and Continental motor cars.

For a full list see the back of this manual.

CONTENTS

ISBN 0 85147 181 1

First Edition 1969
Second Edition, fully revised 1970
Reprinted 1972

© Autopress Ltd 1971

Printed in Brighton England for Autopress Ltd by G Beard & Son Ltd

ACKNOWLEDGEMENT

My thanks are due to Rootes Motors Ltd. for their unstinted co-operation and also for supplying data and illustrations.

I am also grateful to a considerable number of owners who have discussed their cars at length and many of whose suggestions have been included in this manual.

Kenneth Ball G I Mech E
Associate Member Guild of Motoring Writers
Ditchling Sussex England.

INTRODUCTION

This do-it-yourself Workshop Manual has been specially written for the owner who wishes to maintain his car in first class condition and to carry out his own servicing and repairs. Considerable savings on garage charges can be made, and one can drive in safety and confidence knowing the work has been done properly.

Comprehensive step-by-step instructions and illustrations are given on all dismantling, overhauling and assembling operations. Certain assemblies require the use of expensive special tools, the purchase of which would be unjustified. In these cases information is included but the reader is recommended to hand the unit to the agent for attention.

Throughout the Manual hints and tips are included which will be found invaluable, and there is an easy to follow fault diagnosis at the end of each chapter.

Whilst every care has been taken to ensure correctness of information it is obviously not possible to guarantee complete freedom from errors or to accept liability arising from such errors or omissions.

Instructions may refer to the righthand or lefthand sides of the vehicle or the components. These are the same as the righthand or lefthand of an observer standing behind the car and looking forward.

CHAPTER 1

THE ENGINE

1:1 Description

The engine fitted to all models covered by this manual is a straightforward four cylinder overhead valve unit and the instructions given will apply to all models. Variations will be mentioned as necessary, but detail changes in specification will be found in Technical Data in the Appendix.

Some parts of the engine are interchangeable with parts from other engines made by the Rootes Group, but many parts may look similar but are in fact quite different and it is most important to refer to the appropriate parts list when ordering replacements.

The basic engine as fitted to this group of models is to be found in the Rapier Series I and has a capacity of 1390 cc. The bore and stroke are 76.21 mm and 76.2 mm respectively, and the standard compression ratio is 8:1. For certain export markets hollow crown pistons are used which lower the ratio to 7:1. For purposes of identification the letters H and L are added after the chassis number.

These engines are fitted with whitemetal lined big-end shell bearings, and it should be noted that they cannot be bored out to the larger bore of the Series II engine.

For Rapier Series II the capacity is increased to 1494 cc, with a bore of 79 mm and the stroke remaining at 76.2 mm. The compression ratio is increased to 8.5:1 for the standard or high version, but remains at 7:1 for the low.

The steel shells of the big-end bearings are lined with copper/lead and coated with indium to carry the greater loads of the larger engine. There are also increases in the inlet and exhaust valve head sizes for which the diameter is enlarged by 1.58 mm. The size of the cylinder block has also been suitably enlarged.

The same 1494 cc engine is fitted to Rapier III and Alpine I models, but the standard compression ratio was increased to 9.2:1.

With the introduction of Rapier Series II there were also certain minor changes in the engine mountings which do not affect the maintenance requirements.

For the Alpine Series II and onwards and Rapier IV cars the bore size was increased to 3.21 inches (81.5 mm) giving a capacity of 1592 cc. At the same time the diameter of the crankshaft big-end journals was increased and also the big end and little end diameters. The pistons for these engines had the gudgeon pin bores offset towards the maximum thrust side.

To deal with the increased power of the larger engine the output of both the water pump and the oil pump was increased.

Certain detail changes have been made since the introduction of the 1592 cc engine as follows:

From chassis number B3062665 and B9117425
Lighter flywheels and larger inlet valves are used.

From chassis number B3062757 and B9117862
Inlet and exhaust valve stems are chrome plated.

On Alpine Series IV onwards
An improved type piston with closer running clearance and a twin outlet cast iron exhaust manifold are fitted.

The two cutaway drawings in **FIGS 1:1** and **1:2** show very clearly the layout. Overhead valves inclined at an angle of $4\frac{1}{2}$ deg. from the vertical in the aluminium cylinder head are operated by pushrods actuated by a camshaft mounted low down on the off side of the engine driven by a spring tensioned chain from the front end of the crankshaft. An almost vertical shaft driven by skew gears from the camshaft operates the distributor at its upper end, and at the lower end the oil pump located in the crankcase.

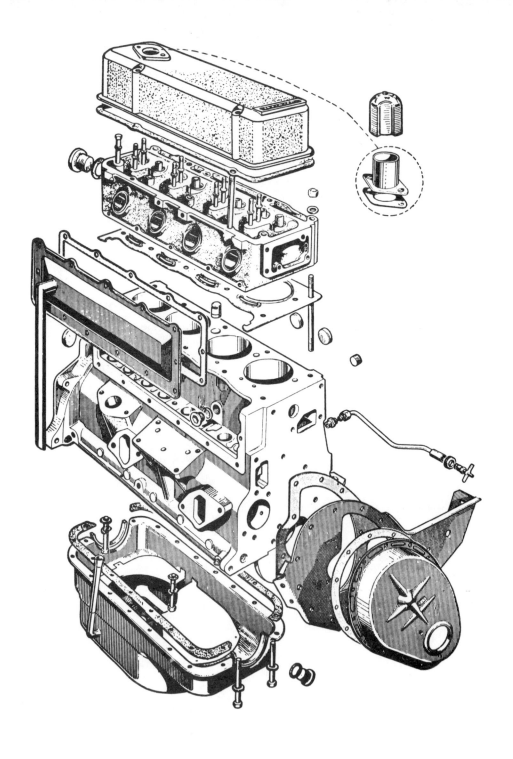

FIG 1:1   Cutaway view of engine and associated parts

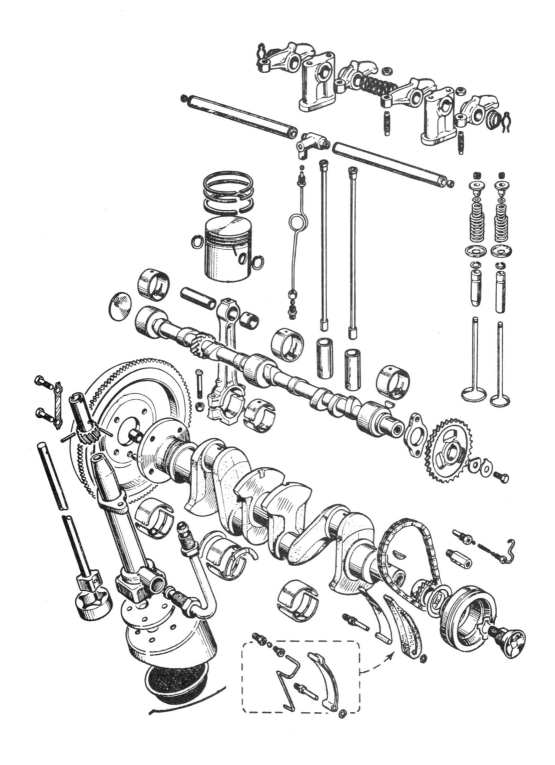

FIG 1 : 2   Exploded view showing working parts

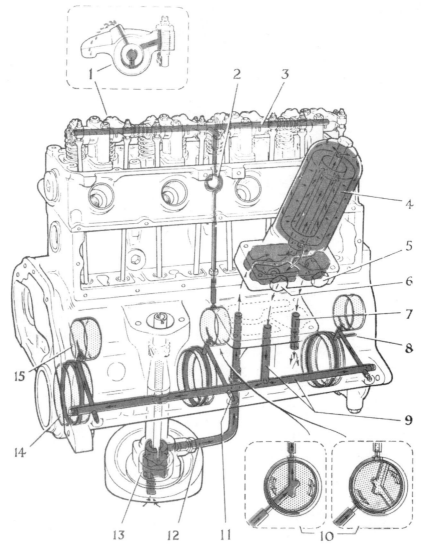

FIG 1:3 Cutaway view showing oil circulation

Key to Fig 1:3   1 Valve rocker oilways   2 Oil feed pipe   3 Oil feed to rocker shaft   4 Full flow oil filter
5 Oil pressure relief valve   6 Filter bypass valve   7 Oil pressure relief valve discharge hole   8 Oil feed to timing chain
oil feed pipe   9 Oil gallery and feed from filter   10 Cross section through camshaft centre journal showing drilling in journal
used to control oil feed to rocker gear   11 Connection point for oil warning light switch or oil pressure gauge   12 Oil feed
from oil pump to filter   13 Oil pump   14 Main bearings   15 Camshaft bearings

The oil, drawn from the sump in the crankcase through a gauze filter, is forced through an external fullflow filter to oilways in the main bearing support webs and all main and camshaft bearings. The oil supply for the overhead valve gear is taken from the centre camshaft bearing at a reduced pressure obtained by the metering device shown inset 10 in **FIG 1:3** and returns by gravity to the sump and so lubricates the tappets.

A pressure relief valve in the oil filter body casing allows surplus oil to return to the sump when pressure exceeds the normal figure of 50 lb/sq in. There is also a bypass valve which opens if the filter becomes blocked.

1:2 Overhauling methods

Before commencing to describe the various operations which the owner-driver is likely to undertake it may not be out of place to draw his attention to the need to observe certain rules in preparation and procedure which will enable him to produce a satisfactory result.

At all times the operator must see that all his equipment and the parts with which he is working are kept clean and should have available adequate supplies of clean rag and paper and also space to store in correct order the various components as he removes them, and marking them in order to ensure their eventual replacement in the same positions as those originally occupied.

It is important to use the correct grades of lubricant etc. as recommended by the manufacturer as the use of unauthorized types may cause damage in use. This applies also to such materials as hydraulic fluid used in the clutch and brake operating systems.

Included in the Appendix at the end of this manual is a section headed 'Hints on maintenance and overhaul' and it is suggested that those who are not skilled engineers may be assisted by reading it before starting work.

1:3 Removing engine

Most operations which become necessary in normal use may be performed without removing the engine from the car, but when removal is needed the following procedure should be followed, and is carried out with the gearbox attached to the engine.

Disconnect the battery. Drain the cooling system and remove the radiator. Drain the sump and gearbox. Remove the propeller shaft. Disconnect the exhaust at the Y junction (Alpine) or at the exhaust manifold flange (Rapier).

Unbolt the clutch operating cylinder without disconnecting the fluid pipe. Disconnect speedometer and the electrical lead to the overdrive solenoid (if fitted). Remove the rear mounting cross member after taking the engine weight. On Series I Rapier cars remove the changespeed shaft and disconnect the gear selector cable to which access may be obtained through the removable floor cover. On later cars, after removing the floor covering it is necessary to remove the gearbox cover and the gearshift lever. Disconnect overdrive switch on top of the gearbox (if fitted). Disconnect thermometer lead from the element terminal. Fuel pipe from the pump. Tachometer drive below the distributor. Oil pressure pipe connection. LT feed wire at SW terminal on the coil.

Disconnect the heater water feed pipes at the cylinder and water pump, dynamo and starter leads, throttle and choke controls. On Series I Rapier only there is an engine tie rod to be removed. Care must be taken when refitting the engine that this tie rod is correctly adjusted before starting the engine.

Remove outer exhaust manifold and scuttle bracing tube (Alpine).

Unbolt the oil filler from the rocker cover. Disconnect engine from mountings.

After checking that all connections between the engine and frame have been broken lift out the engine.

1:4 Lifting and replacing cylinder head

Disconnect the battery. Drain the cooling system. Remove the air cleaner, top radiator hose and overflow pipe. Remove the rocker cover. Pull out snap connector from the thermometer bulb. Disconnect the sparking plug leads and remove the coil.

Remove the screws securing the tappet side cover to the cylinder head. Remove the oil feed pipe to the rocker shaft.

Disconnect heater pipe (if fitted). Remove eight nuts securing the rocker shaft to the cylinder head.

Remove rocker gear and pushrods leaving tappets in place, marking the pushrods for replacing in the same order.

Disconnect fuel pipe connections and throttle control.

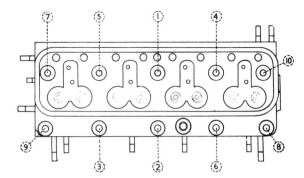

FIG 1:4 Cylinder head showing order for loosening and tightening nuts

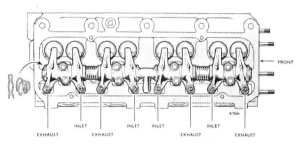

FIG 1:5 Plan view showing rocker gear assembly

FIG 1:6 Method of adjusting valve rocker clearance

Alpine:

Disconnect the inlet and exhaust manifolds at the cylinder head. Slacken off the two exhaust manifold clips at the Y connection. Remove the inlet manifold complete with carburetters, and pull exhaust back pipes clear of the cylinder head.

SEALING RING

FIG 1:7 Valve spring cup showing position of sealing ring

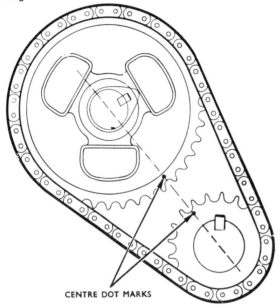

CENTRE DOT MARKS

FIG 1:8 Diagram showing timing marks correctly aligned

Rapier:

This cylinder head may be lifted off without removing the manifolds and carburetters after disconnecting the exhaust pipe at its flange joint.

Remove eight bolts and two nuts and washers and lift off the cylinder head.

To refit the cylinder head reverse the above procedure ensuring that all joint faces are clean and that the new gasket is fitted with the TOP uppermost. Note that gaskets stamped P.103887 are for use on Series I Rapier engines only. For Rapier Series II cylinder head gaskets stamped P.114478 were introduced, and these must always be fitted to these engines and may, if necessary, be used on the earlier cars. Do not displace the tappet cover gasket when lowering the head.

The cylinder head bolts should be tightened to the torque figure given in Technical Data and in the order shown in **FIG 1:4** before tightening the tappet side cover screws.

Assemble the components on the rocker shaft as shown in **FIG 1:5** locating the standards on each shaft to allow the oil feed holes to face downwards. Note that the rockers are offset. Each rocker shaft assembly is fitted with its open end towards the oil feed T piece, which is then inserted between the two shafts with its elbow facing the pushrods.

The other ends of the shafts are plugged.

The rocker shafts are grooved and located by the rocker standard studs nearest to the valves. The grooves should be located on the side nearest the valves.

Adjust the valve clearances as follows:

No. 1 exhaust is adjusted when No. 4 exhaust is fully open.
No. 2 inlet is adjusted when No. 3 inlet is fully open.
No. 3 exhaust is adjusted when No. 2 exhaust is fully open.
No. 1 inlet is adjusted when No. 4 inlet is fully open.
No. 4 exhaust is adjusted when No. 1 exhaust is fully open.
No. 3 inlet is adjusted when No. 2 inlet is fully open.
No. 2 exhaust is adjusted when No. 3 exhaust is fully open.
No. 4 inlet is adjusted when No. 1 inlet is fully open.

The method of adjusting the clearance is shown in **FIG 1:6.** Slacken the locknut, turn the screw until the correct clearance is obtained. Tighten the locknut and re-check.

The correct valve clearances are:

Inlet .012 inch and Exhaust .014 inch with the engine hot.

Start up and run the engine until thoroughly warmed up.

Allow to cool and when cold retighten the cylinder head.

Warm up again and reset the valve clearances.

1:5 Servicing the head

Having removed the cylinder head as described in the previous section plug all waterways and the exposed area of the tappet chamber with clean rag. Scrape the carbon from the combustion chambers and remove the valves. Using a spring compressor remove the split coned cotters. Release the spring and lift off the cup and dual valve spring. Remove the valve. Mark all valves to ensure correct reassembly.

Examine the valves for pitting, burning, cracking or distortion and replace any found to be faulty. Those valves whose condition is good may be ground in by using the following procedure, which should also be used when fitting new valves or when the head seats have been recut.

With a small amount of valve grinding paste on the seat —fine grade if the surfaces are very good, otherwise medium grade and finishing with fine—place the valve on its seating and by means of a suction grinding tool rotate the valve from side to side and occasionally lifting to a new position until both seats have a smooth grey matt finish. Clean all traces of paste from both surfaces.

Any valve too badly marked for satisfactory treatment as above but too good to scrap may have its seat cut to the standard angle of 45 deg. This is best done by a service station as also is the recutting of similarly damaged head seats unless the necessary cutting tools are available.

Head seatings which are beyond recutting may be restored by having inserts fitted. This also should be left to the service station.

If the valve guides are found to be worn they may be renewed but as both removal and fitting require the uniform heating of the cylinder head to a temperature of 200°C (390°F) the operator is advised to take the work to his service station.

Before refitting the valve springs they should be checked against the dimensions given in Technical Data and if any are found to be below the correct length they should be discarded. If either spring of a pair is defective, both inner and outer springs should be replaced. Replace also any faulty valve sealing rings as any deterioration here can cause oiling up of the sparking plugs. (see **FIG 1 : 7**).

When removing the carbon from the piston crown it is always advisable to leave a ring of carbon adjacent to the cylinder bore as this helps to preserve a good seal and to conserve oil. This may be achieved by inserting an old piston ring of the correct size into the bore on top of the piston and then with a blunt tool removing the carbon within the ring. It must be stressed that when removing carbon from aluminium parts such as cylinder head or pistons on no account should abrasives or emery cloth be used.

Having attended to these operations the cylinder head may be reassembled and refitted as described in **Section 1 : 4**.

1 : 6 Servicing the timing gear

1 Drain and remove the radiator as detailed in **Chapter 4**.
2 Slacken the generator mounting screws and remove the fan belt. Unscrew the crankshaft jaw nut and pull off the combined crankshaft pulley and damper (two tapped holes are provided). Remove all screws and nuts holding the timing cover and lift off the cover and oil seal.
3 Remove the split pin and plain washer from the tensioner pivot pin (see **FIG 1 : 2**) and lift off the tensioner blade. Remove fixing bolt, tab washer, and plain washer from the front end of the crankshaft and remove the oil thrower in front of the crankshaft sprocket. Carefully lever off both camshaft and crankshaft wheels together with the chain.
4 To refit the timing gear. Set Nos. 1 and 4 pistons to TDC (see **FIG 1 : 7**) so that the key is to the top of the crankshaft (see **FIG 1 : 8**). Fit the chain to the two wheels so that the timing dots are in line as shown. Turn the camshaft until the key lines up with the keyway in the camshaft wheel and press both wheels home. Replace the camshaft sprocket fixing bolt and washer and a new lock washer.
5 Replace the oil thrower on the crankshaft. Refit the chain tensioner and timing cover. The front face of the timing cover is bolted to a pedestal bolt and the free end of the tensioner blade rests on the inside of the timing case. The remaining parts are replaced in the reverse order to their removal.

If excessive wear is found in either of the sprocket wheels or in the chain do not renew the one item but fit a new set of wheels and chain.

The camshaft sprockets on Rapier Series II engines may be identified by a circular groove machined on the rear face just below the bottom of the teeth. These wheels are also used on later cars and may, if necessary, be used on Rapier Series I.

1 : 7 Removing the camshaft

1 Disconnect the electrical leads and remove the distributor, bracket, and driving shaft (see **Chapter 3**).
2 Drain and remove the sump and oil pump (see **Sections 1 : 8 and 1 : 9**).
3 Remove the tappets. Remove the rocker cover, rocker shaft assemblies, and pushrods. Drain the oil filter and remove the container and element. Remove the

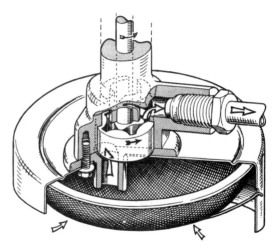

FIG 1 : 9 Cutaway view showing oil circulation through pump

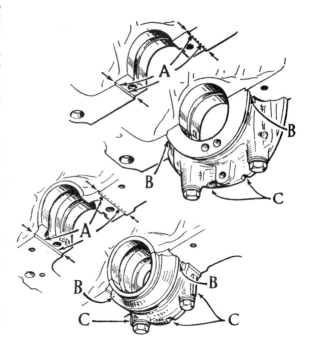

FIG 1 : 10 Diagram of main bearings showing identification marks for correct replacement of bearing caps and cork joints

ignition coil. Remove the screws securing the side cover and lift it off. Take out the tappets and mark for correct refitting.
4 Remove the fuel pump (see **Chapter 2**).
5 Remove the radiator (see **Chapter 4**).
6 Remove the timing cover, timing wheels and chain.
7 Remove two setscrews and take off the camshaft thrust plate. Withdraw the camshaft.

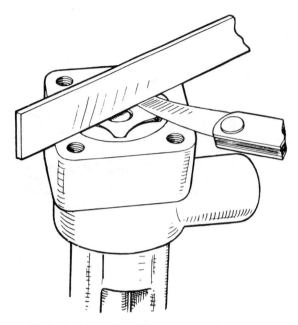

FIG 1:11   Measuring oil pump rotor end clearance

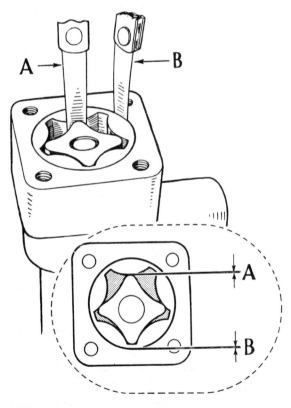

FIG 1:12   Measuring oil pump rotor side clearances

8 Refitting is a reversal of this procedure. Instructions for the correct timing of the camshaft and the distributor will be found in their respective sections.

9 After replacing the timing wheels the camshaft end float should be checked. End float must not exceed .002–.003 inch (.050–.076 mm). Oversize thrust plates are available if required.

1:8 Removing sump and oil strainer

Drain the oil from the sump by removing the plug on the lefthand side.

Undo eighteen bolts and lower the sump from the crankcase.

Remove the spring clip from the oil pump shroud and withdraw the gauze. Wash in petrol or paraffin. Do not dry with a fluffy rag (see **FIG 1:9**).

Replacing sump:

As the sump face is in line with the horizontal axis of the crankshaft main bearings a semi-circular cork joint is used between the front and rear main bearing caps and the sump in addition to the normal face joints at each side as shown in **FIG 1:10**.

The semi-circular cork joints should be fitted to the front and rear main bearing caps after fitting the cylinder block two bottom face side joints. There are two thicknesses of the semi-circular cork joints, .180 to .190 inch or .150 to .160 inch. (4.5 to 4.88 or 3.8 to 4.0 mm). **These joints are not interchangeable.** The thin joint has replaced the thick joint and is recognized by its colour dyed ends. Where thin joints are used the bearing caps have a casting recess, or cast protrusions as shown in **FIG 1:10** by the letter C. The identification used on the front main bearing caps can be seen with the sump in position. A small number of these bearing caps are without casting marks and have rough ground grooves as illustrated.

When the identifying marks are seen on the front and rear main bearing caps the thin cork joint must be used.

Both ends of the cork joints must be square and come up to the ends of the two side joints.

All sump joints should be fitted dry except when working from underneath when the side joints have to be stuck to the cylinder block bottom face. A small quantity of quick setting compound should be applied to the ends of all joints at the points B to ensure a satisfactory oil seal in the corners.

The centre sump bolts should be fitted first, and all bolts should be progressively tightened.

1:9 Servicing the oil pump

To remove:

Remove the distributor cap and turn the engine until the distributor is pointing to No. 1 firing position and the crankshaft pulley pointer lines up with the timing cover pointer at TDC. Remove the distributor.

Remove the sump.

Disconnect the oil delivery pipe from the pump and from inside the crankcase. Undo the two setscrews at the pump locating flange and remove the pump.

To dismantle:

Remove the gauze filter. Remove four hexagon headed

screws securing the base plate to the pump body. Lift out the outer rotor ring. Clean all traces of oil from inside the pump body and rotors. Replace the outer rotor.

Check the following clearances:

1 End clearance between the inner and outer rotor ring and the pump body. The maximum and minimum clearances are .003 and .001 inch (.076 and .025 mm) when measured as shown in **FIG 1:11.**

2 Side clearances as shown in **FIG 1:12.** The maximum and minimum clearances are as follows:

A .006 and .001 inch (1.52 and .025 mm).
B .008 and .005 inch (.20 and .127 mm).

If the maximum clearance is exceeded a replacement pump should be fitted.

To refit:

Ensure that the engine is at TDC with No. 1 piston in the firing position.

Replace the oil pump so that the distributor driving slot in the oil pump drive is positioned as shown in **FIG 1:13.**

No jointing of any kind is used between the pump face and the cylinder casting.

Replace the gauze. Refit the sump, and fill with the correct grade of engine oil.

Refit the distributor and check the ignition timing as detailed in **Chapter 3.**

1:10 Removing clutch and flywheel

Remove the gearbox complete with bellhousing as instructed in **Chapter 6.**

Remove the setscrews securing the clutch cover to the flywheel, slackening off evenly all round. Remove the clutch assembly and driven plate. Knock the flywheel tabwashers clear of the setbolts. Remove the setbolts and pull off the flywheel from the crankshaft flange.

The starter ring is shrunk on to the flywheel and in the event of excessive wear on the teeth the complete flywheel and ring may be returned to the manufacturers for reconditioning or, if the necessary equipment is available, the starter ring may be replaced as follows:

Support the flywheel assembly, with the starter ring on top, in a suitable container by means of three or four metal blocks under the starter ring. Pour in sufficient cold water to submerge the lower part leaving the starter ring exposed.

Heat the starter ring evenly with a welding torch in order to expand it and allow the flywheel to drop out. Remove the flywheel from the water and dry.

Before fitting a new starter ring ensure that the mating faces are clean and smooth.

Heat the new ring evenly to 220°C (428°F) and place in position on the flywheel with the chamfered sides of the teeth to the clutch side of the flywheel. Make sure that the ring is completely over the securing lip and bedding against its locating face.

On cooling the ring will contract and be firmly secured to the flywheel.

Replacement of the flywheel is the reverse of the removal procedure taking care to observe the correct torque loading figures given in Technical Data. Check for run out at the outer edge of the flywheel clutch facing which must not exceed .003 inch (.076 mm). Use new locking washers.

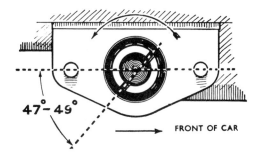

FIG 1:13 Distributor driving slot correctly positioned in oil pump drive

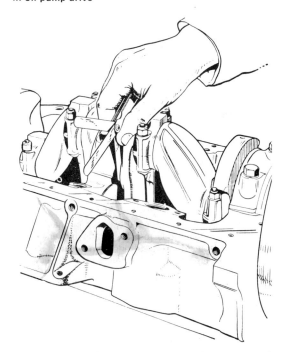

FIG 1:14 Measuring crankshaft end float

1:11 Pistons and connecting rods

The big-end bearings used on Rapier Series I engines consist of steel shells with whitemetal linings. On the Series II engines and subsequently indium coated copper/lead bearings are fitted and it is essential that the correct type be fitted as replacements.

To remove:

Remove the cylinder head. Remove the sump.

Remove the self locking nuts securing the big end bearing caps and remove the caps complete with the bottom half of the big end bearings, carefully marking both cap and rod for correct refitting.

Scrape any carbon from the rim of the cylinder bore and withdraw the pistons and rods from above.

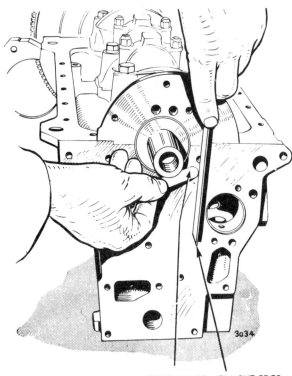

FEELER GAUGE   STRAIGHT EDGE

FIG 1:15 Checking front main bearing cap alignment

To replace:

Reverse the above procedure ensuring that the oil squirt holes in the rods just above the big ends face to the righthand side viewed from the rear.

Tighten all nuts to the torque figure given in Technical Data, but do not use the same self-locking nuts if they can be screwed on with the fingers.

1:12 Pistons, rings and gudgeon pins

Gudgeon pins:

To remove the gudgeon pin take out the circlips, scrape away any carbon in the piston bosses, warm the assembly and push out the pin. Tight gudgeon pins should never be driven out of a cold piston.

Reassembly is the reverse of the above, but new circlips of the correct size should always be used.

The correct fit for the gudgeon pin is that it should be a finger push fit in the piston and just free enough in the little end bush for the rod to fall by its own weight when held horizontally at a temperature of 21°C (70°F).

The diameters of the three grades of gudgeon pins are given in Technical Data.

Piston Rings

The top compression ring is chromium plated with the word VACROM etched on a side face. It may be fitted either way up.

The second compression ring must be fitted with the widest face marked TOP uppermost.

A slotted type scraper ring is fitted in the third groove.

On the earliest Series I Rapier engines there is no fourth ring groove in the piston. On later cars when the four groove piston was used the bottom groove was left vacant. The latest Series I cars and all Series II have a scraper ring fitted here.

On Rapier Series III and Alpine Series I the fourth groove is used only after the car has covered a very considerable mileage.

All later cars are fitted with pistons having three rings only.

Before fitting new rings it will be necessary to remove the glaze from the bores by using a dummy piston wrapped with a sheet of fine emery paper and worked up and down in the bore and at the same time rotated in each direction. Mask off the bottom of the cylinder to prevent any particles from dropping into the crankcase. Wash down and dry thoroughly.

The correct piston ring gap (see Technical Data) can be measured by placing a piston about one inch down the bore and pressing the new ring down on to it and inserting a feeler gauge between the ends. If necessary the ends of the ring may be filed to give the correct gap.

Fit the rings in their grooves so that the gaps are spaced out around the piston and are not in line above each other.

Pistons:

On the top face of each piston and on two machined bosses at each end of the cylinder block on the lefthand side there are stamped grade letters to indicate the diameter of the pistons and the bores, and in production pistons are fitted to bores having similar grade letters.

There are four grades and the difference between each grade letter is .0004 inch (.010 mm). The diameter difference between piston and bore having similar grade letters is the required clearance for the piston.

The grade diameters for cylinder bores and pistons are listed in Technical Data.

If it is required to fit a new piston under service conditions the following procedure should be followed:

Measure the cylinder bore diameter and from the size obtained subtract the correct piston clearance and from this dimension choose a suitable grade of piston. Example (1494 cc engine dimensions used).

Bore size as measured 3.1116 inches.

3.1116 — .0018 = 3.1098 inches.

The nearest piston size to 3.1098 inches is Grade C and this therefore is the correct size to fit.

1:13 Crankshaft and main bearings

Removing:

If required the main bearing shells can be removed for inspection or renewed, provided the crankshaft main bearing journals are not worn, without removing the crankshaft from the engine. The procedure is as follows:

Drain out the engine oil and remove the sump and oil pump.

Slacken all main bearing fixing bolts one or two turns. Starting at one end of the crankshaft remove the bottom main bearing cap and the corresponding top half bearing by pushing it round the crankshaft journal with a thin piece of metal. Replace the bottom bearing and cap to support the crankshaft before proceeding to remove the next main bearing cap.

The main bearing shells for these engines are white metal lined and are interchangeable. They are available in standard size and undersizes as detailed in Technical Data.

Replacing:

Top half bearings are replaced in a reverse manner to that described for removal. Note the following:

1 Ensure that the locating lips engage correctly in their respective recesses.

2 Bearings are stamped according to their sizes and on renewal the same size must be fitted except when an undersize crankshaft is fitted. In such cases the correct undersize bearings must also be fitted.

3 Particular attention must be paid to cleanliness of all mating surfaces and the oil return thrower recess in the rear main bearing housing.

4 Before replacing the front and rear main bearing a very small quantity of a non-setting jointing compound should be applied to the sides of the cylinder block recess into which the bearing caps locate (see **FIG 1:10**).

5 Ensure that the front main bearing cap is pulled up against the timing case before fully tightening the front main bearing cap bolts.

As each bearing is tightened up the crankshaft should be turned to ensure that it is free. The correct torque figures will be found in Technical Data.

Crankshaft end thrust is taken by two semicircular steel washers having whitemetal thrust faces across which are cut two vertical oil grooves. The thrust faces are fitted towards the crankshaft thrust faces and may be removed by pushing them around the crankshaft centre journal after taking off the centre main bearing caps.

Endfloat of the crankshaft can be checked by using feeler gauges as shown in **FIG 1:14.** The correct end-float is given in Technical Data together with other relevant dimensions.

Oversize thrust washers, .005 inch (.127 mm), are available for use with crankshafts which have had the thrust faces reground at each end of the centre main bearing journal.

To remove crankshaft:

Remove the engine from the car. Remove the cylinder head, pushrods and tappets. Remove the timing wheels and chain. Remove the engine front plate and sump. Remove connecting rods and pistons as described above.

Remove the clutch (see **Chapter 5**) and flywheel.

Remove the main bearing caps.

Lift out the crankshaft.

Crankshafts having oval or scored journals should be replaced by factory reconditioned units. These are available in the undersizes given in Technical Data, also available are corresponding oversize main and big-end bearings.

The maximum permissible undersizes for regrinding crankshafts are given in Technical Data. Not more than .005 inch (.127 mm) may be removed from each thrust face at the ends of the crankshaft centre journal.

To refit crankshaft:

Check that the oilways are clear. This is best done by forcing paraffin through them and is particularly important if there are any signs of a run bearing.

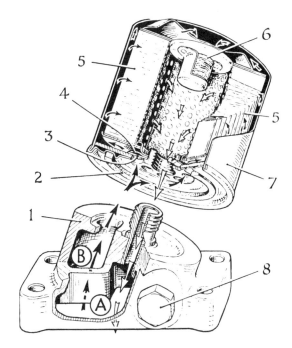

FIG 1:16 Cutaway view of the internal construction of the throw away type oil filter

Key to Fig 1:16   1 Adaptor casting   2 Rubber joint ring
3 and 4 Anti-drain valve   5 Filter element   6 Bypass valve
7 Filter casing   8 Oil pressure relief valve

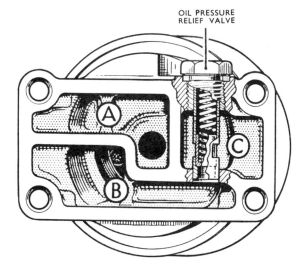

FIG 1:17 Underside view of filter adaptor casting showing position of relief valve

Place the crankshaft in position checking that the top halves of the main bearings and thrust washers (centre) are correctly fitted into the crankcase.

Fit the lower halves of the bearings together with the main bearing caps.

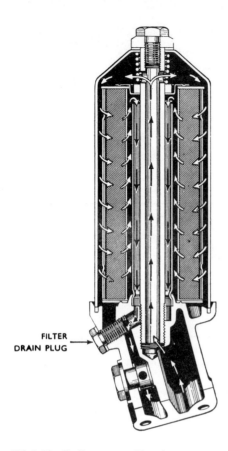

through the screwed spigot to compartment A in the adaptor casting. From it passes to the engine main oil galleries.

The entry ports on the underside of the filter are covered by a flexible anti-drain valve 3 and 4 which prevents the oil from draining out when at rest.

A piston type relief valve in compartment C (see **FIG 1:17**) opens to admit all excess oil from compartment B when the pressure exceeds approximately 60 lb/sq in. (4 kg/sq cm). This excess oil returns to the engine sump.

A bypass valve 6 is fitted inside the throw-away filter unit and opens in the event of the filter element becoming blocked and allows the oil to pass directly to the engine bearings. The bypass valve opens when there is a pressure difference of over 7 lb/sq in. above and below the valve.

The filter unit should be changed every 6000 miles or 10.000 km and may normally be removed by hand unscrewing in an anticlockwise direction.

Before fitting the new filter clean the joint face on the adaptor casting and smear the joint ring 2 with engine oil. Screw the filter into position until it just touches the joint face on the adaptor casting then **screw one third of a turn only by hand.**

Run the engine and check for leaks. Top up the sump if necessary.

All other models

The renewable element type of oil filter fitted to the remaining cars covered by this manual is shown in **FIGS 1:18** and **1:19**.

Oil from the pump flows into compartment B and through the hollow bolt which secures the filter element into the filter casing. The oil then passes from the outside through the element to the inside then upwards on the inside of the element and down through the steel tube into the compartment A which feeds the main oil gallery. The steel tube inside the filter prevents the oil from draining out when the engine is not running.

The plunger type pressure relief valve in compartment C opens to allow excess oil to return to the sump when the pressure exceeds approximately 50 lb/sq in. (3.5 kg/sq cm).

The bypass valve, which normally closes a port connecting compartments A and B, opens if the element becomes blocked and passes the oil directly to the engine.

The pressure relief valve has a hexagonal head and is screwed into the front of the filter body casting. The bypass filter is similar and is screwed into the rear of the body casting.

To renew the filter element. Drain the filter by means of the drain plug (see **FIG 1:18**). Remove the centre bolt and withdraw the element. After fitting a new element run the engine and check for leaks. Top up the sump if necessary.

FILTER DRAIN PLUG

FIG 1:18 Earlier renewable element type oil filter showing oil circulation

Replace the main bearing cap bolts. Check that the front face of the front main bearing cap is in alignment with the machined front surface of the cylinder block (see **FIG 1:15**).

Tighten bolts to the correct torque and check endfloat as described above.

Lubricate all running surfaces with engine oil when assembling.

1:14 External oil filter

On all models the oil filter is of the fullflow type in which all the oil from the pump is filtered on its way to the engine bearings, but on some cars the filtering element alone is removable from its casing for renewal while on other models the whole filtering unit is thrown away and replaced by a new one.

Alpine III and IV. Rapier IV:

These cars are fitted with oil filters of the throw away type as illustrated in **FIG 1:16**. The adaptor casting 1 is bolted on the righthand side of the cylinder block.

Oil from the pump enters compartment B and passes through eight portholes into the filter body 7 and through the filter element 5 to the centre as shown, and thence

1:15 Reassembling the engine

Instructions for reassembly and refitting the many component parts of the engine have been given in the same sections of this chapter which detailed their removal and dismantling, so that it should not be necessary to do more than remind the operator of the correct sequence in which these operations should be carried out and to mention any points of importance which might either be overlooked or need to be emphasized.

Before commencing work make sure that all tools and equipment required for the task are available and that new gaskets and washers, which are produced in complete kits, have been obtained. The necessity for absolute cleanliness must also be stressed even to the avoidance of fluffy rags from which fragments can obstruct the oilways. Ensure also that all rubbing surfaces are well lubricated before assembly.

First refit the crankshaft and the main bearings in the cylinder block having checked that the oilways are clear and being careful to observe the torque loading figures given in Technical Data and also the permissible amount of end float allowed (see **Section 1 : 13**).

Refit the flywheel assembly (see **Section 1 : 10**) which must be carefully checked for true running and security. Use new locking washers and measure the runout.

When replacing the clutch as instructed in **Chapter 5** it is essential that the internal splines on the driven plate hub should not be assembled dry and if a new plate, which will have waterproof grease applied as packed, is not to be fitted the operator should apply a small quantity.

When fitting the clutch driven plate a gearbox stem wheel may be used as a mandrel for the correct location when the clutch cover is fitted. This is most important in ensuring the correct alignment of the gearbox primary shaft with the clutch plate and the spigot bearing. Note also that the smaller boss of the driven plate hub faces towards the flywheel. Tighten the six securing screws progressively and evenly.

Refit the gearbox and bellhousing taking great care not to tilt the assembly in any way as this would place excessive strain on the clutch plate.

Instructions for refitting the connecting rods and the pistons have been given in **Section 1 : 11** but the operator is again reminded of the necessity to ensure that when the original parts are being refitted they must be fitted in the same positions exactly as before.

The camshaft together with the timing wheels and chain are next fitted, observing very carefully the procedure for securing the proper timing given in **Section 1 : 6,** and checking the camshaft end float before replacing the oil thrower, chain tensioner and timing cover.

Replace the crankshaft pulley and damper, and refit the fan belt the adjustment for which is detailed in **Section 4 : 2.**

Replace the oil pump and the distributor drive as described in **Section 1 : 9.**

Replace the tappets and pushrods.

Refit the cylinder head assembly complete, using a new gasket and observing the correct order for tightening the head nuts and bolts to the required torque figure.

Replace the rocker gear and adjust the rocker clearances remembering that they will need to be reset after the cylinder head has been finally tightened down after running the engine. This procedure is fully described in **Section 1 : 4.**

Alpine:

On these cars the inlet and exhaust manifolds cannot be fitted to the cylinder head until the head has been replaced in position.

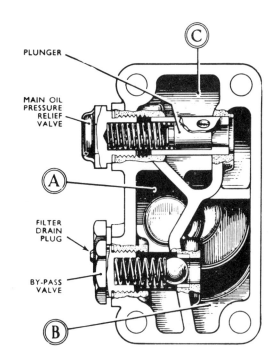

FIG 1 : 19 Underside view of filter base showing pressure relief valve and bypass valve

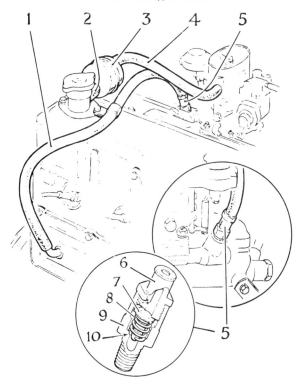

FIG 1 : 20 Modified closed crankcase ventilation system

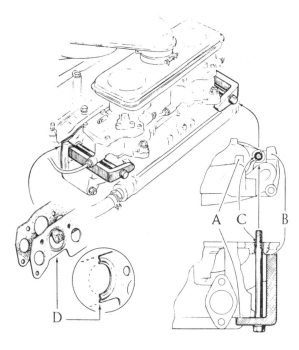

FIG 1:21 Details of modified joint and manifold clamps

Rapier:

The cylinder head on these cars may, if desired, have the manifolds and carburetters attached before refitting the head.

Refit the distributor to its driving shaft and re-set the timing as detailed in **Chapter 3.**

1:16 Replacing the engine in the car

This operation is carried out by reversing the procedure detailed in **Section 1:2.** The operator is again advised to inspect carefully all lifting gear, jacks and supports and to guard against possible failure.

Before connecting any of the bolts holding the engine to the frame examine the flexible mountings for softness or deterioration and replace if there is any doubt as to their condition.

Having secured the engine and gearbox to the frame and attached all the controls and connections as detailed the engine and gearbox should be filled with the correct grade of oil. Fill the cooling system with water.

Bleed the clutch hydraulic system and check for correct operation (see **Chapter 5**).

Carry out a final inspection of all connections and joints for loose ends or leaks. Start the engine and check again after running at operating temperature for a few minutes.

1:17 Modifications

Closed crankcase ventilation system.

For cars supplied to those countries where regulations forbid the discharge of crankcase fumes directly to the atmosphere a modified system of crankcase ventilation is used as illustrated in **FIG 1:20.** Reference to the drawing will make the method of operation clear.

At idling speed when manifold depression is high enough to draw the regulator valve 7 on to its seat 10, the crankcase fumes are drawn into the carburetter through the pipes 2 and 4 and the flame trap 3.

As the throttle opens and the inlet manifold depression decreases the spring 8 lifts the regulator valve off its seat and allows the crankcase fumes to be drawn from the tappet cover through the pipe 1. Ventilation air for the crankcase under these conditions is drawn through the pipe 4.

Servicing:

The regulator valve should be removed, dismantled and cleaned in paraffin every 6000 miles or 10,000 km. The flame trap should be washed at the same time and turned upside down to dry. Hoses should be examined for fouling or damage.

If the valve or its seat are found to be worn a new assembly should be fitted. A damaged or corroded spring should be renewed.

Testing:

Refit the valve unit but leaving off the hose. Start the engine. At idling speed the valve should be firmly on its seat and further pressure from above with a thin rod should not affect the engine performance.

To check that the valve opens correctly insert a piece of thin wire about $1\frac{1}{2}$ inches long into the inlet end of the unit then if the engine speed is suddenly increased the test wire will be seen to lift about 2 or 3 mm.

If the correct operation is not obtained a new spring should be fitted.

Inlet manifold joint:

A modified joint for the inlet manifold on Rapier III cars and later has been introduced under the Part No. 5220646 and consists of two pieces: (1) A Cemjo gasket with an internal steel strengthening frame. (2) A steel slipper joint.

The gasket is fitted first to the cylinder head and then the slipper with the raised corrugations facing outwards as shown in **FIG 1:21.**

Do not use any jointing compound. Only use once.

Ensure that the manifold face is not distorted, and if necessary it must be filed flat.

Inlet manifold leaks. Rapier IIIA:

To deal with particularly bad cases of air leaks at the inlet manifolds of these cars the manifold clamps shown in **FIG 1:21** have been introduced under Part Nos. 1208798 and 19406481. Two of each are required per car. They cannot be fitted to Rapier III engines.

Remove carburetters and inlet manifolds. Remove the exhaust manifold and file the unfinished bosses B so that they are flat and parallel to the gasket face.

Clean off both manifold faces and the joint face on the cylinder head.

Check the face of the inlet manifold against a surface plate and if necessary have it faced up.

Check, and if necessary file down, to ensure that the

inside length of the longest arm of each clamp is the same. In some instances it may be necessary to file metal off the inlet manifold bosses A in order to make a proper face for the clamps to contact.

Bolt up both manifolds to the cylinder head without any joint.

Assemble both clamps in position and use sheet metal between the inlet manifold and the clamps so that the clamp is parallel to the clamp bolt when tightened to 25 to 28 lb ft, check that at least .020 inch (.50 mm) clearance exists at C between the long bolts and the semi-circular holes at each end of the inlet manifold. If necessary the manifold should be filed to give the required clearance.

Remove each clamp and measure the thickness of each set of packing material used between each clamp and the inlet manifold with a micrometer. Record these as front and rear readings.

Remove both manifolds. File the front boss of the exhaust manifold so that it is reduced in thickness by the amount of the front reading. File the rear boss to reduce its thickness by the amount of the rear reading.

Fit the inner and outer new type joints (see above and **FIG 1 : 21**). Replace the manifolds tightening the long $\frac{3}{8}$ inch bolts to 25 lb ft and the $\frac{5}{16}$ inch bolts to 14 lb ft, check that the clamps fit correctly at A and B and are parallel to the long holding bolts and that the centre bolt is not bottoming in the cylinder tapped hole.

Replace the carburetters and tune in the normal manner.

1 : 18 Fault diagnosis

(a) Engine will not start

1 Defective coil
2 Faulty distributor capacitor (condenser)
3 Dirty, pitted or incorrectly set contact breaker points
4 Ignition wires loose or insulation faulty
5 Water on sparking plug leads
6 Corrosion of battery terminals or battery discharged
7 Faulty or jammed starter
8 Sparking plug leads wrongly connected
9 Vapour lock in fuel pipes
10 Defective fuel pump
11 Overchoking
12 Underchoking
13 Blocked petrol filter or carburetter jets
14 Leaking valves
15 Sticking valves
16 Valve timing incorrect
17 Ignition timing incorrect

(b) Engine stalls

1 Check 1, 2, 3, 4, 10, 11, 12, 13, 14, 15 in (a)
2 Sparking plugs defective or gaps incorrect
3 Retarded ignition
4 Mixture too weak
5 Water in fuel system
6 Petrol tank vent blocked
7 Incorrect valve clearances

(c) Engine idles badly

1 Check 2 and 7 in (b)
2 Air leak at manifold joints
3 Slow running jet blocked or out of adjustment

4 Air leak in carburetter
5 Over rich mixture
6 Worn piston rings
7 Worn valves stems or guides
8 Weak exhaust valve springs

(d) Engine misfires

1 Check 1, 2, 3, 4, 5, 8, 10, 13, 14, 15, 16, and 17 in (a) and 2, 3, 4, and 7 in (b)
2 Weak or broken valve springs

(e) Engine overheats

See chapter 4

(f) Compression low

1 Check 14 and 15 in (a). 6 and 7 in (c), and 2 in (d)
2 Worn piston ring grooves
3 Scored or worn cylinder bores

(g) Engine lacks power

1 Check 3, 10, 13, 14, 15, 16 and 17 in (a), 2, 3, 4 and 7 in (b), 6 and 7 in (c) and 2 in (d)
2 Check (e) and (f)
3 Leaking joint washers
4 Fouled sparking plugs
5 Automatic advance not operating correctly

(h) Burnt valves or seats

1 Check 14 and 15 in (a), 7 in (b), 2 in (d). Also check (e)
2 Excessive carbon around valve seat and head

(j) Sticking valves

1 Check 2 in (d)
2 Bent valve stem
3 Scored valve stem or valve guide
4 Incorrect valve clearance

(k) Excessive cylinder wear

1 Check 11 in (a). See Chapter 4
2 Lack of oil
3 Dirty oil
4 Piston rings gummed up or broken
5 Badly fitting piston rings
6 Connecting rods bent

(l) Excessive oil consumption

1 Check 6 and 7 in (c) and check (k)
2 Ring gaps too wide
3 Oil return holes in piston choked with carbon
4 Scored cylinders
5 Oil level too high
6 External oil leaks
7 Ineffective valve stem oil seals

(m) Crankshaft and connecting rod bearing failure

1 Check 2 in (k)
2 Restricted oilways
3 Worn journals or crankpins
4 Loose bearing caps
5 Extremely low oil pressure
6 Bent connecting rod

(n) Internal water leakage

See Chapter 4 Cooling System

(o) Poor circulation

See Chapter 4 Cooling System

(p) Corrosion

See Chapter 4 Cooling System

(q) High fuel consumption

See Chapter 2 Fuel System

(r) Engine vibration

1 Loose generator bolts
2 Fan blades out of balance
3 Mounting rubbers loose or ineffective
4 Exhaust pipe mountings too tight
5 Misfiring due to faulty ignition

CHAPTER 2

THE FUEL SYSTEM

2:1 Fuel Pump. Description

The fuel pump used on all models covered by this manual is an A.C. mechanically operated unit and is mounted on the righthand side of the engine. It incorporates a gauze filter inside a glass bowl and is driven by an eccentric on the camshaft. In order that the pump may provide a supply of fuel when the engine is not running a hand primer is fitted.

The pump is shown in section in **FIG 2:1** and reference to this drawing will make the following description of its operation quite clear.

As the camshaft revolves an eccentric 7 actuates the fuel pump rocker arm 6 pivoted at 8 which pulls the pullrod 11 together with the diaphragm 13 downwards against the pressure of the spring 12 thus creating a depression in the pump chamber 15. Fuel is thus drawn from the tank into the glass bowl by way of the pump intake 3 and after passing through the filter gauze 17 and the inlet valve 1 it enters the pump chamber 15.

On the return stroke the pressure of the spring pushes the diaphragm upwards forcing fuel from the chamber through the outlet valve 16 and outlet 14 to the carburetters. When the carburetter bowls are full the floats will shut the needle valves thus preventing any flow of fuel and the daiphragm will be held downwards against the pressure of the spring until the carburetters require further fuel and the needle valves open.

The rocker arm operates the connecting link 9 by making contact at 5 thus allowing idling movement of the rocker when there is no movement of the fuel pump diaphragm. The spring 4 keeps the rocker arm in constant contact with the eccentric to eliminate noise.

To gain access to the filter gauze for cleaning purposes first remove the glass bowl after slackening the securing screw and swinging the fixing clamp to one side. The washer 2 and the filter can then be removed from the main casting.

The hand primer 10 is used when, for any reason, the carburetter float chamber or the pump bowl has become empty. A few pulls upward of the hand primer on these occasions will fill the float chamber with fuel and ensure an easy start without prolonged use of the starter and consequent drain on the battery. Excessive use of the hand primer will not overfill the carburetter as the design of the pump frees the primer when the float chambers are full.

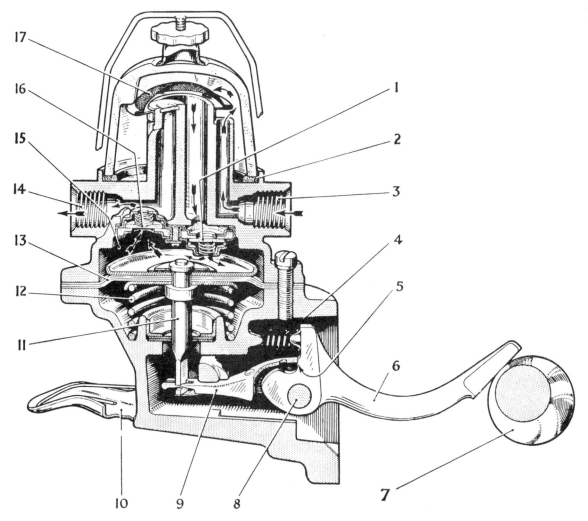

FIG 2:1 Sectional view of fuel pump

2:2 Routine maintenance

The only maintenance required on the fuel pump is the occasional cleaning of the filter gauze which is removed as described in **Section 2:1.** The gauze should be washed in clean petrol and replaced before refitting the washer. On no account should a fluffy rag be used for cleaning or drying the filter.

When refitting the washer see that it is in good condition and that the seating is clean. Do not overtighten the screw when securing the glass bowl.

At the same time as the filter is removed for cleaning it is as well to check the tightness of the two nuts holding the pump to the crankcase and the six screws securing the two halves of the pump housing.

Possible causes of poor operation apart from air leaks at the two joints just mentioned are loose or broken springs, a defective diaphragm, or worn or sticking valves, but before removing and dismantling the pump first check

the following points:
1 That the fuel tank is not empty and that all unions are tight.
2 That the filter is clean and the washer in good condition.
3 The action of the pump with the delivery pipe to the carburetter disconnected. For this test disconnect the delivery pipe at the carburetter and with the engine switched off turn the engine over a few times. There should be a spurt of fuel at each working stroke of the pump, i.e. every two revolutions of the engine.

2:3 Removing and dismantling

Disconnect the fuel pipes at the pump and remove the two nuts holding the pump to the crankcase. Lift away the pump noting carefully the number of joints between the pump and the crankcase.

Before commencing to dismantle the pump—using **FIG 2:2** for reference—thoroughly clean the exterior and make a mark across the two flanges of the pump housing as a guide when reassembling. Remove the six setscrews 11 and separate the two halves of the main casting.

Turn the diaphragm and pullrod assembly 13 through an angle of 90 deg., when it may be removed from its securing slot in the connecting link 20 and withdrawn. **Do not attempt to separate the four diaphragm layers.**

Remove one circlip 24 and withdraw the rocker arm pin. The rocker arm 22 together with the connecting link 20, spring 21, and washers 19 may now be removed.

Withdraw the valve retainer screw 10 from inside the upper casting and remove the retainer plate 9 valve assemblies 7 and valve retainer gasket 8.

Thoroughly clean all parts in paraffin. The diaphragm assembly should be renewed if there are any signs of cracking or hardening. Valve assemblies cannot be dismantled and should be renewed if at all defective. All gaskets and joints should be renewed as a matter of routine, including the fabric oil seals on the diaphragm pullrod 17 and the valve retaining joint 8.

The diaphragm spring 14 seldom requires replacement, but, if necessary, ensure that the replacement has the same identification colour as the original.

Very little wear may be tolerated on the parts of the fuel pump and any doubtful part should be renewed.

2:4 Reassembly

Replace the valves, retainer and retainer gasket and secure with the two screws. The valves must be re-assembled in the pump as shown in **FIG 2:1**.

Assemble the link packing washers, rocker arm and rocker arm spring in the body. Insert the rocker arm pin through the hole in the body, at the same time engaging the packing washers, link and rocking arm, and then spring the retaining clips into the grooves at each end of the pin, the rocker arm pin should be a tap fit in the body.

Place the diaphragm spring in position in the pump body. Place the diaphragm assembly over the spring and centre the upper end of the spring in the lower protector washer. Press downwards on the diaphragm, at the same time turning the assembly to the left so as to engage the slots on the pullrod with the fork in the link, then turning the assembly a quarter turn to the left thus setting the pullrod in its working position in the link and permitting the alignment of the holes in the diaphragm with those in the pump body flanges.

When first inserting the diaphragm assembly into the pump body the locating tab on the outside of the diaphragm should be in the position shown in **FIG 2:3**. After the assembly has been given the quarter turn to the left the tab should be in the position indicated by the dotted outline.

The sub-assemblies of the pump may now be put together as follows:

Push the rocker arm towards the pump until the diaphragm is level with the body flanges.

Place the upper half of the pump into the position shown by the mark made on the flanges before dismantling.

Replace the cover screws and spring washers and tighten just sufficiently to engage the washers.

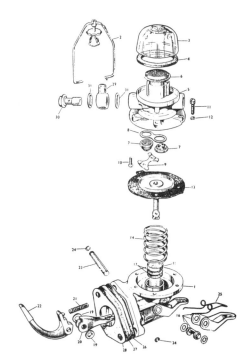

FIG 2:2 Exploded view of fuel pump

Key to Fig 2:2 1 Body 2 Glass cover retainer
3 Glass bowl 4 Bowl gasket 5 Cover 6 Filter gauze
7 Valve 8 Valve gasket 9 Valve retaining plate
10 Valve retainer screw 11 Screw No. 10 U.N.F.
12 Washer $\frac{3}{16}$ inch spring 13 Pull rod and diaphragm
14 Diaphragm spring 16 Priming lever 17 Oil seal washer
18 Oil seal retainer 19 Rocker pin washer 20 Link
21 Return spring rocker arm 22 Rocker arm
23 Rocker arm pin 24 Rocker arm pin circlip
25 Primer spring 26 Joint pump to insulator
27 Heat insulator 28 Insulator to cylinder block joint
29 Outlet union 30 Banjo bolt 31 Fibre washer

Before finally tightening the screws push the rocker arm towards the pump using a length of tube about 4 inches long slipped over the end of the rocker arm so as to hold the diaphragm at the bottom of its stroke. Hold in this position and tighten the screws alternately. After assembly the edges of the diaphragm should be flush with the two flanges. Any appreciable protrusion indicates incorrect fitting and attention should be paid to maintaining inward pressure on the rocker arm while tightening the securing screws.

Replace the filter gauze and cork seating gasket in position and replace the glass bowl as previously described.

2:5 Testing

The pump should be tested after assembly and before refitting to the engine and in the absence of a bench testing rig this may be carried out as follows:

Flush the pump by immersing it in a pan of clean paraffin and working the rocker arm about six times, then empty the pump by continuing to operate it while held above the bath.

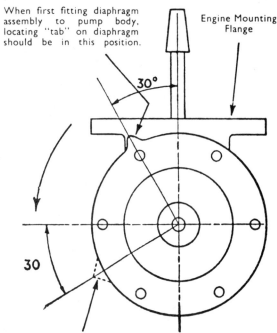

When first fitting diaphragm assembly to pump body, locating "tab" on diaphragm should be in this position.

Engine Mounting Flange

30°

30

After engaging notches in bottom of pull rod with slot in link and turning quarter turn to the left, tab on diaphragm should be in this position.

FIG 2:3   Diagram for correct fitting of diaphragm

With the pump still held clear of the liquid place a finger over the inlet union and work the rocker several times. Upon removing the finger a distinct noise should be heard which will indicate that the pump has developed a reasonable degree of suction.

To check the delivery side of the pump place a finger over the outlet union and press the rocker arm inwards. Hold the air which has been drawn into the pump chamber under compression for a few seconds while the pump is held submerged in the pan of paraffin and watch the flanges clamping the diaphragm for any signs of air leaks.

Refitting the pump to the engine by reversing the removal procedure, taking care to ensure that the rocker arm is correctly positioned. Run the engine for a few minutes and examine the pump and pipe unions for fuel leakage.

Excessive fuel pump pressure, which may cause flooding and heavy fuel consumption, may be remedied by fitting additional packings between the pump and the cylinder block. Conversely too much packing can cause fuel starvation.

2:6 Stromberg DIF 36 carburetter

This carburetter is used on early Rapier Series I cars and is shown in the exploded view of **FIG 2:4**. It is a downdraught unit with a double venturi system, an accelerator pump for increased fuel supply on sudden throttle opening and a bypass or power jet which is mechanically brought into operation at near full throttle openings only.

Before any tuning adjustments can usefully be made to a carburetter it is essential to ensure that the unit itself is in good order and that the various engine services are all correctly adjusted.

After thoroughly cleaning the outside of the carburetter, proceed to dismantle it as follows:

Refer to **FIG 2:4**. Remove the five setscrews 30 securing the float chamber cover taking care not to damage the gasket.

Unscrew the float fulcrum screw 27 and remove the float 26 and the needle valve 24. With a suitable box spanner remove the needle valve seating.

Remove the accelerator pump assembly 40.

Unscrew and remove in order the bypass valve 48, the pump feed valve 45, the pump discharge ball valve 43 and the pump jet plug 47. The pump discharge jet may now be unscrewed.

Unscrew and lift out the idle tube 36.

Remove the main jet plug 33 and washer 34. Unscrew the metering jet 32.

Removal of the main discharge jet is rarely necessary except in the event of damage or complete blockage. If removal is required, screw a tapered tap into the hole in the bottom of the jet and pull the jet downwards. Never attempt to drive it out.

The high speed bleed 39 is removed by first unscrewing and then pushing out with a piece of pointed wood.

Unscrew the idle discharge and progression hole plugs with a screwdriver.

Separate the throttle valve body 1 from the main body 18 and lift out the large venturi 16 and the thick gasket 19. The fast-idle cam operating rod 65 will need to be disconnected.

Wash all parts in clean petrol and dry with non-fluffy cloth. Ensure that all jets are of the correct sizes and free from any obstruction by blowing through with compressed air. Never use wire for this purpose, and do not attempt to alter a jet by reaming out to a larger size.

The carburetter is reassembled by reversing the above operation. If the main discharge jet 35 has been withdrawn it is important to ensure that the positioning grooves are correctly located.

2:7 Tuning adjustments

Float level:

The fuel level in the float chamber must be checked while the engine is idling and the car standing on level ground.

Remove the float chamber cover and with a suitable gauge measure the level from the top face of the float chamber. The correct reading should be between $\frac{23}{32}$ and $\frac{25}{32}$ inch (18.25 and 19.84 mm).

If the fuel level is outside these limits remove the float and the float arm and adjust the setting by very carefully bending the float arm by using two pairs of pliers. Bending the float upwards will raise the level and vice versa.

Slow-running adjustment:

This adjustment must be made when the engine is at working temperature.

Adjusting the throttle stopscrew 11 controls the engine speed, and the mixture strength required to give the most even slow-running is obtained by adjustment of the idle needle valve 37.

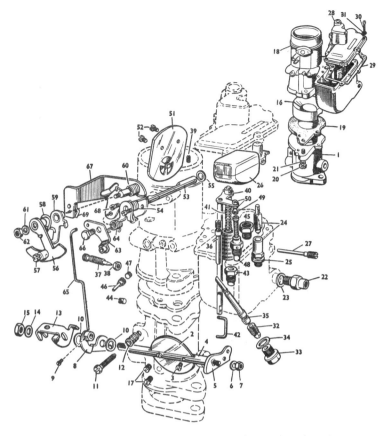

FIG 2:4 Exploded view of Stromberg DIF 36 carburetter

Key to Fig 2:4 1 Throttle valve body 2 Throttle valve 3 Throttle valve spring 4 Throttle lever stem
5 Pump lever 6 $\frac{3}{16}$ inch shakeproof washer—pump lever 7 Nut—pump lever 8 Lever—fast-idle rod
9 Screw—fast-idle rod 10 Washer—fast-idle lever 11 Micro screw—throttle stop lever 12 Micro screw spring—
throttle stop lever 13 Throttle lever 14 $\frac{5}{16}$ inch shakeproof washer—throttle stem to lever 15 Nut—throttle stem to lever
16 Venturi 17 Plug (over idle discharge holes) 18 Main body 19 Gasket—throttle body to main body
20 Screw—throttle body to main body 21 $\frac{5}{16}$ inch spring washer—throttle body to main body 22 Union adapter—
petrol intake 23 Fibre washer—petrol intake 24 Needle valve and seating 25 Needle valve seating washer 26 Float
27 Fulcrum screw—float 28 Chamber cover—float 29 Gasket—float chamber cover 30 Screw—float chamber cover
31 $\frac{5}{16}$ inch spring washer—float chamber cover 32 Metering jet 33 Plug—metering jet 34 Gasket—metering jet
35 Main discharge jet 36 Idle tube 37 Idle needle valve 38 Locknut—idle needle valve 39 High speed bleed
40 Pump rod and piston assembly 41 Piston spring 42 Pump link 43 Pump discharge valve 44 Pump plug
45 Pump check valve 46 Pump discharge jet 47 Plug (over discharge jet) 48 Bypass valve 49 Pushrod—bypass valve
50 Pushrod nut—bypass valve 51 Air horn valve (choke) 52 Screw—air horn valve 53 Air horn stem 54 Spring—
air horn stem 55 Stem end washer—air horn stem 56 Cam lever 57 Spring—choke cable 58 Spring—cam lever
59 Floating lever—cam 60 Spring, floating lever 61 Washer—cam and floating lever tube holder 62 Nut—cam and floating
lever tube holder 63 Cam follower 64 Spring cam following 65 Fast-idle rod 66 Fulcrum screw 67 Tube holder c/w stud
68 Screw—tube holder to body 69 Clip—choke cable

By combining the two settings an even tick-over will be obtained with the carburetter just off the rich condition.

Fast-idle setting:

This adjustment is required to ensure adequate throttle opening to prevent the engine from stalling after the choke control has been pushed home and before the engine is fully warmed up. The mechanism when correctly adjusted provides for the choke control to act as a hand throttle for the first half inch of travel before the choke commences to close.

Refer to **FIG 2:5**. Slacken off the setscrew at the throttle end of the fast-idle rod and insert a $\frac{3}{64}$ inch drill between the throttle valve and the body as shown.

Hold the choke in its fully closed position and re-tighten the adjustment setscrew. Remove the drill, close the choke control and check the throttle butterfly opening.

Bypass tappet adjustment:

This is the setting which determines the throttle position at which the bypass or power jet commences to supply the extra fuel supply needed at full throttle. In order to carry out this operation it is necessary to remove the carburetter from the engine in order to gain access to the throttle butterfly valve.

Remove the float chamber cover.

Insert a $\frac{9}{32}$ inch drill between the butterfly valve and the throttle body in line with the idle discharge holes and close the butterfly lightly upon it.

Check that the bypass tappet or pushrod 49 is just engaging the bypass valve 48.

The correct setting is obtained by rotating the nut 50 as shown in **FIG 2:6** in the appropriate direction. Note also the supporting thumb to prevent undue strain on the accelerator pump mechanism.

Accelerator pump:

The accelerator pump link 42 is normally connected to the inner hole in the pump lever 5, but in certain conditions when an increased supply is required it may be moved into the outer hole.

2:8 Zenith carburetter

Alpine models I, II and III (early) are fitted with twin Zenith WIP 36 carburetters with separate gauze type air intake filters.

Rapier models III and IIIA are fitted with twin Zenith WIA 36 carburetters which have a single oil bath air cleaner. Both are of the downdraught type and will be described together as the only difference is that a bypass valve and jet system on the type WIA which supplies increased amounts of fuel at wider throttle openings is blanked off on the type WIP.

Both types have an accelerator pump to provide extra fuel when the throttle is suddenly opened and to prevent starvation at such times.

The drawing **FIG 2:7** shows the internal layout of components and passageways and in conjunction with the exploded view given in **FIG 2:8** should make the following description of the carburetter's operation and construction quite clear.

The rich mixture required for starting from cold is obtained by pulling out the choke control knob which operates the choke butterfly, and at the same time opens the throttle to the correct starting position.

Slow-running is controlled by the throttle stop screw and the volume control screw. Clockwise movement of the former will open the throttle and increase the engine speed and vice versa. Clockwise rotation of the volume control screw will weaken the mixture and unscrewing it will make the mixture richer. The method for obtaining the correct combination of these two controls is given in **Section 2:12**.

The fuel supply over the middle and upper ranges is controlled by the main jet and the throttle butterfly valve, assisted in the type WIA by the bypass valve and jet which are automatically brought into operation by the lowered manifold depression at wide throttle openings.

2:9 Maintenance

Apart from the very occasional cleaning of the jets the only maintenance necessary is the servicing of the air intake silencers and cleaners.

Alpine:

These gauze intake filters should be removed occasionally and cleaned by washing in paraffin. After cleaning

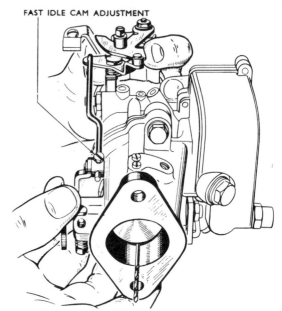

FAST IDLE CAM ADJUSTMENT

FIG 2:5   Setting fast-idle adjustment

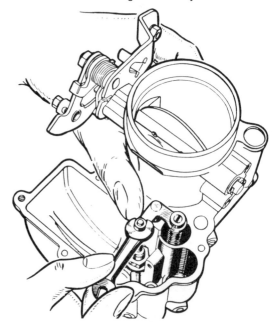

FIG 2:6   Adjusting bypass tappet

they should be blown dry or alternatively allowed to drain dry.

Rapier:

Under normal conditions, such as those obtaining in the United Kingdom, the oil bath cleaner needs to be serviced every 3000 miles (5000 km) but in territories where dust is prevalent this distance may be halved with advantage.

Refer to **FIG 2:9** and after slackening the clip on the

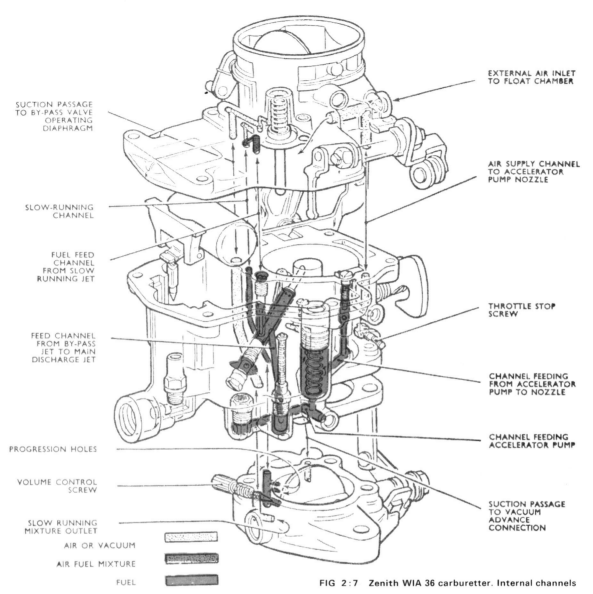

SUCTION PASSAGE
TO BY-PASS VALVE
OPERATING
DIAPHRAGM

SLOW-RUNNING
CHANNEL

FUEL FEED
CHANNEL
FROM SLOW
RUNNING JET

FEED CHANNEL
FROM BY-PASS
JET TO MAIN
DISCHARGE JET

PROGRESSION HOLES

VOLUME CONTROL
SCREW

SLOW RUNNING
MIXTURE OUTLET

AIR OR VACUUM

AIR FUEL MIXTURE

FUEL

EXTERNAL AIR INLET
TO FLOAT CHAMBER

AIR SUPPLY CHANNEL
TO ACCELERATOR
PUMP NOZZLE

THROTTLE STOP
SCREW

CHANNEL FEEDING
FROM ACCELERATOR
PUMP TO NOZZLE

CHANNEL FEEDING
ACCELERATOR PUMP

SUCTION PASSAGE
TO VACUUM
ADVANCE
CONNECTION

FIG 2:7 Zenith WIA 36 carburetter. Internal channels

hose connecting the top of the air box to the air cleaner undo the thumb screw in the centre and lift off the cover. Remove the oil bath container.

Swill the filter gauze, which is attached to the cover, in paraffin and either blow dry or allow to drain thoroughly.

Clean out the oil bath and refill with clean engine oil up to the level mark.

Replace the oil bath container, refit the filter cover with the gauze and tighten the thumb screw.

Tighten the clip on the hose connection on the air box above the carburetters.

2:10 Dismantling

Before a carburetter is dismantled it should be thoroughly cleaned externally.

Remove the split pin, washer and pin from the connecting link on the accelerator pump operating cam.

Remove six cheese-headed screws holding the top of the carburetter to the carburetter body. Lift out the float. The float needle is attached by a clip.

Remove four cheese-headed screws holding the throttle body and lift out the venturi after removing its locating screw.

Remove the metering jet, which also holds the main jet in position. This may fall out unaided, but it is not necessary to remove the main jet for cleaning as it can be blown through in position.

Remove the slow-running or idle jet. Remove the accelerator pump check valve (this has a fine gauze cover).

On WIA carburetters remove the bypass valve. The bypass jet which is fitted into the bottom of the bypass valve body must not be removed.

Remove the shouldered cheese-headed screw retaining

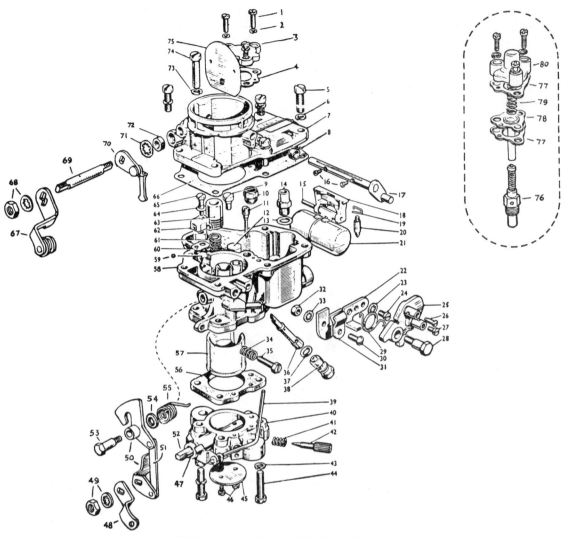

FIG 2:8 Exploded view of Zenith carburetter

Key to Fig 2:8 1 Cover screw 2 Spring washer 3 Cover 4 Cover joint 5 Screw $\frac{1}{4}$ inch BSF x $\frac{3}{4}$ inch cheese head
6 Washer $\frac{1}{4}$ inch spring 7 Float chamber cover 8 Spring controlling automatic opening of choke 9 Accelerator pump
piston retaining screw 10 Accelerator pump check valve 11 Idle jet 12 Blanking plug (WIP carburettor only)
13 Joint (gasket)—needle valve seating 14 Needle valve seating 15 Float pivot 16 Screw, special—butterfly to spindle
17 Choke spindle complete with lever 18 Float pivot bracket 19 Clip—needle valve 20 Needle valve 21 Float
22 Bracket assembly—control cable 23 Washer $\frac{7}{16}$ inch shakeproof 24 Screw No. 10 UNF x $\frac{7}{16}$ inch, fillet head
25 Cam lever—choke control 26 Screw securing choke control cable 27 Screw, special—fast-idle rod to swivel
28 Screw—choke control lever swivel 29 Spring—choke control lever 30 Screw 2 BA x $\frac{1}{2}$ inch, cheese head
31 Clip 32 Nut 2 BA 33 Washer $\frac{7}{16}$ inch shakeproof 34 Slow running speed screw spring
35 Slow-running speed adjusting screw 36 Main discharge jet 37 Sealing ring—metering jet 38 Metering jet
39 Floating lever complete with rod 40 Carburetter throttle body 41 Slow-running volume control screw spring
42 Slow-running volume control screw 43 Washer $\frac{1}{4}$ inch spring (throttle body to main body) 44 Screw $\frac{1}{4}$ inch BSF
x 1 inch cheese head (throttle body to main body) 45 Throttle butterfly 46 Screw—butterfly to spindle
47 Bearing—floating lever 48 Throttle lever (throttle spindle) 49 Nut and shakeproof washer (throttle spindle)
50 Stop plate complete with link and cam 51 Link, attached to stop plate and cam 52 Throttle spindle 53 Shouldered bolt
54 Washer 55 Cam return spring 56 Heater insulator—throttle body to main body 57 Choke tube (venturi)
58 Main body 59 Accelerator pump discharge ball valve 60 Accelerator pump discharge nozzle gasket
61 Accelerator pump piston spring 62 Accelerator pump discharge nozzle 63 Accelerator pump piston
64 Nozzle retaining screw gasket 65 Accelerator pump discharge nozzle retaining screw 66 Float chamber cover gasket
67 Accelerator pump operating roller and lever 68 Nut and shakeproof washer 69 Accelerator pump operating spindle
70 Accelerator pump internal operating lever complete with pushrod 71 Washer $\frac{7}{16}$ inch shakeproof 72 Nut
73 Washer $\frac{1}{4}$ inch spring 74 Screw $\frac{1}{4}$ inch BSF x 1$\frac{1}{2}$ inch, cheese head 75 Choke butterfly
76 Bypass valve and jet (WIA carburetter only) 77 Diaphragm gaskets (WIA carburetter only) 78 Diaphragm and plunger
(WIA carburetter only) 79 Diaphragm return spring (WIA carburetter only) 80 Diaphragm cover (WIA carburetter only)

the accelerator pump piston in its bore. Lift out the piston and its return spring.

While holding the carburetter in a vertical position remove the cheese-headed screw securing the accelerator pump discharge nozzle. Remove the nozzle and its paper joint and note that a small steel ball without a spring is fitted below the nozzle securing screw. This ball is the accelerator pump delivery valve and is removed by inverting the carburetter.

On WIA models remove three screws securing the diaphragm cover and the diaphragm with its return spring.

The carburetter is now dismantled sufficiently for cleaning.

All jets and orifices are carefully calibrated and must not be cleaned with wire or other hard material nor, if a change of jet size is necessary, should any attempt be made to alter the old one.

Clean all parts with petrol and all passages with compressed air.

A list of jet sizes and other specifications is given in Technical Data.

2:11 Reassembly

The procedure for reassembling the carburetter is a reversal of the dismantling described in the previous section and will be simplified by reference to the exploded view in **FIG 2:8**. Close attention should be given to the following points:

1 The top cover joint should be renewed to ensure that no air leaks into the slow running passage ways.
2 The joints on each side of the bypass valve operating diaphragm should be renewed.
3 On WIA carburetters the diaphragm spring must seat squarely in the metal cup on the top of the diaphragm when the cover is replaced.
4 The small gasket below the accelerator pump discharge nozzle should be renewed.
5 The synthetic rubber sealing ring fitted in the groove around the metering jet just above its hexagon head must be renewed if not in good condition.
6 The accelerator pump delivery valve ball must be replaced before inserting the discharge nozzle screw. This ball must not be tapped or forced on to its seat. If this is done it may jam into the hole immediately below the seating.

A little jointing compound should be used on the heat insulator faces when refitting the throttle body to the main carburetter body.

2:12 Tuning and synchronization

Before undertaking a description of the various adjustments which may be made to obtain the best results it must be stressed that in addition to the requirement that all the carburetter parts be clean and unworn the condition and adjustment of the remainder of the engine must also be in first class order e.g. valve gear, ignition system, fuel supply, etc.

Synchronization of throttles and slow-running

Refer to **FIG 2:10**. Loosen the clamp bolt 3 to allow the independent movement of each throttle, and unscrew both throttle stop screws 2 until both throttles are in the fully closed position and the screw ends clear of their

FIG 2:9 Oil bath air cleaner

abutments. Holding the throttles in the closed position tighten the clamp bolt.

Screw in the front carburetter throttle stop screw until it just touches and then screw in a further one and a half turns.

Screw in the volume control screw 1 or the slow-running air control screw 4 by hand. Do not use a screwdriver. Then screw back the screw 1 three-quarters of a turn, or screw 4 one and quarter turns in an anti-clockwise direction.

When the engine is hot adjust the screws 1 or 4, as applicable, on the front carburetter to give the smoothest idling. Then adjust the rear carburetter in a similar manner. Readjust the front carburetter if necessary.

The correct idling speed of approximately 850 rev/min should now be secured by adjustment of the front throttle stop screw 2 and at the same time resetting the screws 1 or 4 if necessary. It should be noted that the idling speed is set by the throttle stop screw 2 and the mixture strength by the screws 1 or 4.

When the idling speed is correct adjust the rear carburetter throttle stop screw until it just touches its abutment.

A check must now be made to see that the rear carburetter does not reach its full throttle stop before the front. The throttle stops may be filed if necessary.

A further test of synchronization may now be made by listening through a cardboard tube to the intake hiss as the engine speed is increased to about 1000 rev/min. The sound from both carburetters should be the same and the clamping bolt should be loosened and the throttles adjusted to obtain this condition. If such an adjustment is made, ensure that both throttle stop screws come against their stops when idling.

Throttle setting for starting

Refer to **FIG 2:11**. This drawing illustrates the adjust-

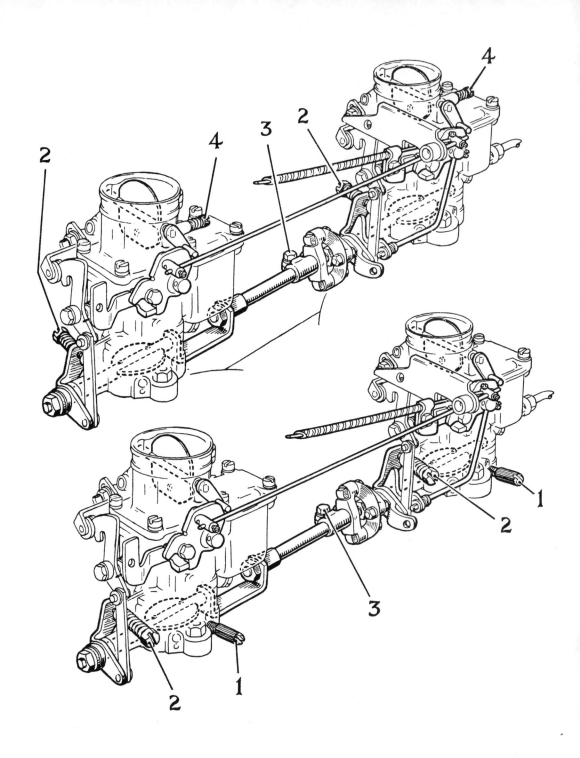

FIG 2:10   Synchronizing the throttles and slow-running

Key to Fig 2:10   1 Volume control screw (not fitted if 4 is used)   2 Slow-running speed adjustment screw
3 Coupling yoke clamp bolt   4 Slow-running air adjustment screw (not fitted if 1 is used)

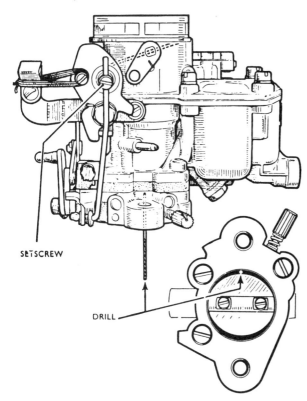

SETSCREW

DRILL

FIG 2:11   Setting the throttle fast-idle position

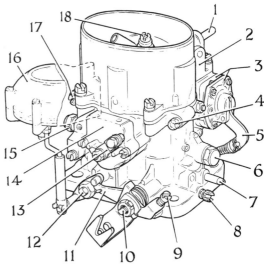

FIG 2:12   Solex B.32 P.A.I.A. carburetter. External view

Key to Fig 2:12   1 Fuel inlet   2 Float chamber cover and carburetter top body   3 Accelerator pump   4 Primary throttle barrel pilot jet (slow-running jet)   5 Accelerator pump operating lever   6 Primary throttle barrel main jet holder   7 Vacuum advance connection   8 Slow-running volume control screw   9 Slow-running speed adjustment   10 Primary throttle   11 Overriding lever   12 Secondary throttle   13 Starter assembly operating lever   14 Starter assembly   15 Secondary throttle barrel main jet holder   16 Secondary throttle operating unit   17 Secondary throttle barrel pilot jet (not slow-running)   18 Carburetter top body centre fixing screw

ment provided for ensuring that the throttle is set to the best position for cold starting when the choke is fully closed.

Slacken off the setscrew and tie the operating cam in the full starting position. Insert a No. 70 drill or a piece of wire 0.7 mm dia. between the throttle and the carburetter body as shown and tighten the setscrew.

Release the choke operating cam. Check by operating the choke control and observing that the throttle opens to the position as measured.

Accelerator pump adjustment:

The purpose of the accelerator pump is to overcome the temporary fuel shortage on snap throttle openings and is constructed with a two position slot in the operating arm whereby a choice of pump stroke length is available.

The operating arm is normally fitted with the fulcrum shaft in the nearest hole to the crank arm. In this position the short pump stroke is given.

To change to the long stroke and increase the amount of fuel delivered the fulcrum shaft is moved to the hole farthest from the arm crank.

Carburetter faults:
Excessive fuel consumption:

(a) Check that the choke is not held partly closed.
(b) Ensure that there are no fuel leaks at the inlets or

joint faces and that all the jets are fully tightened.
(c) Check the rubber sealing ring on the main jet.
(d) On WIA carburetters check that the bypass valve is not sticking or leaking. Check that the gaskets are not allowing air leakage. Check the condition of the diaphragm.
(e) Check that the jets are of the sizes specified.

Bad slow-running:

(a) Check the synchronization of the throttles and the slow-running adjustments just described. If this is not effective check the following possible causes.
(b) Check that the idle jet is not blocked.
(c) Ensure that all the slow-running passages are clear.
(d) Check the joint between the top part of the carburetter and the float chamber for possible air leaks.
(e) Apply a little jointing compound to the faces of the heat insulator joint.
(f) Check the condition of the tapered end of the slow-running volume control screw and its spring.
(g) Examine the throttle spindle for wear.

Difficult starting:

(a) Check fuel pump operation and float chamber level.
(b) Ensure that the choke butterfly closes completely.
(c) Check that the throttle opens to the fast-idle position for starting.
(d) Examine the choke control for failure to remain in the

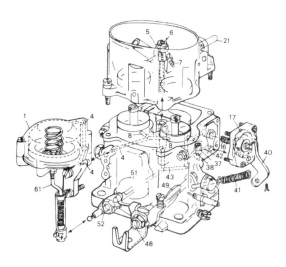

FIG 2:13 Solex carburetter. View showing accelerator pump and secondary throttle systems

closed position after setting. If the choke creeps back when released it can be stiffened up by slightly bending the inner cable.

(e) Difficulty in starting when hot is usually caused by an over-rich mixture and, provided that there is not a constant flooding, will normally be overcome by gently opening the throttle wide and holding it so when operating the starter.

Poor top speed performance:

(a) Ensure that the throttle butterfly is opening fully.

(b) On WIA carburetters see that the bypass jet is clear and is of the specified size. To do this the bypass valve must be removed from the float chamber, but no attempt made to separate the jet orifice cup from the valve body. The jet number is stamped on the hexagon of the body.

(c) Check the fuel supply to the float chamber. Low output pressure from the fuel pump may cause starvation under full throttle conditions.

2:13 Solex carburetter

Alpine models III (late) and IV and Rapier IV are fitted with a Solex carburetter type B.32 P.A.I.A. This is a twin choke and twin throttle barrel unit which overcomes certain disadvantages on single choke carburetters when engine outputs are increased beyond moderate ratings particularly if it is required to provide economy and good part throttle performance. On this Solex carburetter one barrel is tuned to give good economy at intermediate throttle openings and the other to give maximum performance when operating in conjunction with the first.

The primary throttle is operated over its whole range by the movement of the accelerator pedal. The action of the secondary throttle is automatic and depends on the position of the primary throttle and the amount of suction in the primary throttle choke tube.

The secondary throttle operating unit 16 in **FIG 2:12** consists of a diaphragm and spring connected by a cranked rod and ball joint to the secondary throttle 12 spindle lever, while an internal passage connects the vacuum side of the diaphragm with cross drillings in the choke tubes. This is illustrated in **FIG 2:13**.

The secondary throttle is prevented from opening by the lever 11 in **FIG 2:12** until the primary throttle is at least two thirds open. Then, if the requisite suction is created, the diaphragm will lift and open the secondary throttle, these actions are shown in **FIG 2:14**.

In order to provide the extra fuel required for immediate response to sudden openings of the throttle an accelerator pump is provided as shown at 17 in **FIG 2:15** which also shows the operating lever 40 and the rod 45 linking it to the primary throttle lever.

2:14 Maintenance and slow-running adjustment

The only maintenance required apart from servicing the air filter is to ensure that the jets are not obstructed. The jets may be easily removed from the exterior of the body and, on removal, provide ready made holes to drain off any sediment which may have collected in the float chamber. On no account should any wire be used to clear a jet.

The air cleaner is shown in section in **FIG 2:16** and is removed by loosening the clip on the carburetter end of the joint connecting the air cleaner to the carburetter, and removing the two bolts securing the fixing strap to the supporting bracket.

Release the clips 1 and withdraw the cleaner end 3. Remove the wing nut 4 and washer. Lift off the element end plate 5 and element 7. Remove the two joint rings 6.

The element should normally be renewed every 12,000 miles (20,000 km) but should be blown free of dust every 3000 miles (5000 km). At the same time all dust should be blown out of the cleaner housing 2 and the interior wiped clean. It is important that the filter is used dry. It must never be oiled.

To refit an element place the joint rings 6 on the cleaner end cover 3 and the element end plate 5. Place the element in position, refit the end plate and replace the wingnut and washer.

Replace the assembly into the air cleaner casing taking care not to catch the element positioning tabs.

Refit the cleaner by reversing the removal procedure noting that the seam joint in the cleaner housing rests in the slot provided in the support bracket.

Slow-running adjustment:

This is the only adjustment which should be required in normal use and is carried out as follows:

Adjust the slow-running speed adjustment screw 9 in **FIG 2:12** to give an engine idling speed of 850 rev/min.

Adjust the slow-running volume control screw 8 so that the engine is running evenly with the screw rotated as far anti-clockwise as possible. Readjust the engine speed if necessary with the speed adjustment screw 9.

When this procedure is finished the engine should be running evenly at 850 rev/min just off the 'hunting' or rich idling condition. This is obtained by having the volume control screw 8 rotated anticlockwise as far as possible consistent with even running at the idling speed.

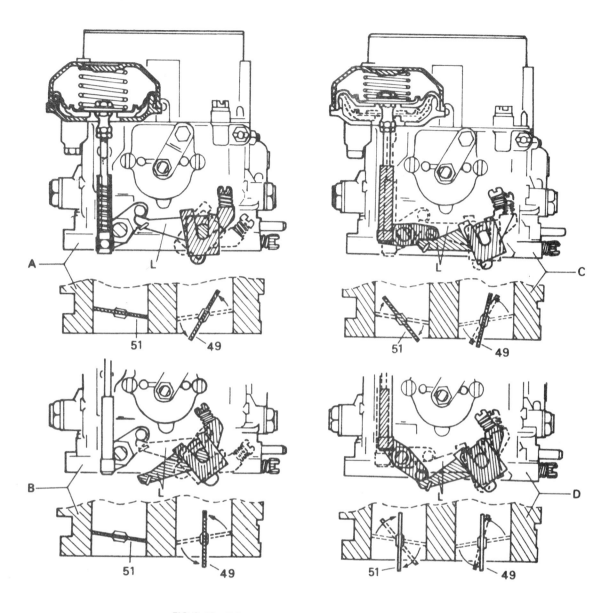

FIG 2:14 Primary and secondary throttle movements

Key to Fig 2:14
A Primary throttle (49) movement during which secondary throttle (51) is always closed
B Primary throttle operating range, when engine speed is too low to provide the necessary suction in the primary throttle choke tube, to actuate the secondary throttle operating unit   C & D Primary throttle (49) movement needed when sufficient suction exists in the primary choke tube to open the secondary throttle (51)   (C) half way, (D) fully open

2:15 Removing and dismantling

Remove the air cleaner (see **Section 2:14**).

Remove the fuel pipe and the vacuum advance pipe from the carburetter.

Disconnect the choke control inner and outer cables, and the throttle operating shaft at the carburetter.

Remove four nuts and washers and lift off the carburetter.

Blank off the flange on the inlet manifold to prevent the entry of any foreign matter.

Having removed the carburetter the operator will find no difficulty in further dismantling if reference is made to the very comprehensive exploded view given in **FIG 2:17**. Many of these parts can be removed and replaced without removing the carburetter from the engine.

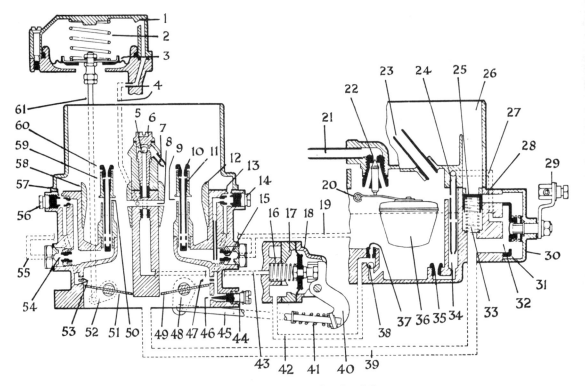

FIG 2:15 Solex carburetter. Sectional diagram

Key to Fig 2:15   1 Secondary throttle operating unit housing   2 Diaphragm return spring   3 Secondary throttle operating unit diaphragm   4 Depression feed passage and passage restrictor   5 Accelerator pump delivery ball valve   6 Accelerator pump delivery assembly   7 Accelerator pump delivery nozzle   8 Drilling in choke tubes connected to passage 4   9 Primary throttle barrel main spraying orifices   10 Primary throttle barrel air correction jet   11 Primary throttle barrel emulsion tube   12 Primary throttle barrel choke tube   13 Primary throttle barrel pilot jet air bleed   14 Primary throttle barrel pilot (slow-running) jet   15 Primary throttle barrel main jet   16 Accelerator pump diaphragm return spring   17 Accelerator pump diaphragm   18 Accelerator pump end cover   19 Feed passage to primary barrel main jet   20 Float lever pivot pin   21 Fuel intake connection to float chamber   22 Float needle valve and seat   23 Internal air vent to float chamber   24 Starter fuel feed dip tube   25 Starter assembly air control piston   26 Carburetter top body   27 Fuel passage to starter disc valve   28 Air passage   29 Starter assembly operating lever   30 Starter assembly cover housing   31 Starter assembly disc valve   32 Passage in starter disc valve   33 Starter device piston return spring   34 Starter well   35 Starter jet   36 Float   37 Jet controlling accelerator pump output (by bleed back to float chamber)   38 Accelerator pump intake non return valve   39 Starting mixture feed passage   40 Acceletator pump operating lever   41 Accelerator pump operating spring   42 Feed passage to accelerator pump   43 Delivery passage from accelerator pump   44 Slow running volume control screw   45 Accelerator pump operating link rod   46 Slow-running outlet in primary throttle barrel   47 Bypass (progression) holes in primary throttle barrel   48 Primary throttle lever   49 Primary throttle   50 Secondary barrel main spraying orifices   51 Secondary throttle   51 Secondary throttle   52 Secondary throttle operating lever   53 Secondary throttle barral bypass (progression) holes   54 Secondary barrel main jet   55 Feed passage to secondary barrel main jet   56 Secondary throttle barrel pilot (progression) jet   57 Air bleed to pilot jet in secondary barrel   58 Secondary barrel choke tube   59 Secondary throttle barrel emulsion tube   60 Secondary throttle barrel air correction jet   61 Secondary throttle operating rod

2:16 Reassembly

The operation of reassembling the carburetter will be greatly assisted by reference to **FIG 2:17** which shows clearly the positions of the component parts. Particular attention should be given to the following:

1 In view of their similarity care must be taken to ensure that the pilot jets 72 and 75, main jets 28 and 77, and choke tubes 11 and 15 are fitted in their correct positions. See Technical Data.

2 The choke tubes are held in position by the two pointed setscrews and locknuts 73 and 74. They are located by narrow slots in their narrow ends.

3 Do not omit the joint 70 between the secondary throttle operating unit body 69 and the carburetter main body.

4 Note the small rubber sealing ring on the vacuum passage between the secondary throttle operating unit cover 83 and the body 69.

5 A brass dowel locates the vacuum drilling (4 in **FIGS 2:13** and **2:15**) in the carburetter body and the secondary throttle operating unit. There is a small drilling through this dowel which must be clear if the unit is to function correctly.

6 The lever 60 must be assembled to the starter assembly disc valve, 58 spindle so that they take the relative

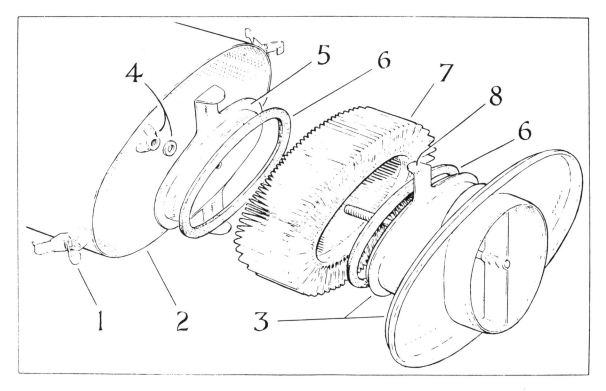

FIG 2:16   Air cleaner element assembly

positions shown in **FIG 2:17**.

7 The lever 42 and items 34 to 45 must be assembled on the primary throttle spindle in the positions as shown in **FIG 2:17**.

8 Ensure that the outer end of the lever 42 fits below its roller contact on the secondary throttle operating lever 50.

2:17 Tuning the Solex carburetter

The operator is already aware that no carburetter tuning can be effective until and unless the remainder of the engine and its services are in correct adjustment. Having now ensured that the carburetter is correctly assembled and adjusted and the specified jets in use there is little to be done by way of tuning.

Tuning for slow-running has been explained in **Section 2:14**.

Choke control setting:

Release the setscrews holding the choke control outer and inner cables and push the outer cable into its fixing abutment as far as possible and tighten its securing screw.

Push the starter assembly operating lever 60 against the operating stop farthest from the outer cable fixing.

Position the choke control so that the knob is $\frac{1}{8}$ inch from the full in position and tighten the setscrew securing the outer cable at the lever end.

Pull the choke control outwards as far as possible and check that the lever comes up against the other stop nearest to the outer cable fixing position.

Push the choke control fully inwards and check that the lever comes up against the farther stop.

Secondary throttle stop setting

This very important adjustment prevents the secondary jet system from supplying fuel when the primary system alone is sufficient. It also ensures that the secondary throttle cannot stick in the closed position. The carburetter must be removed from the engine. Refer to **FIGS 2:15** and **2:18**.

1 Clean the exterior and carefully remove any deposits in both throttle bores.

2 Release the operating rod 61 from the ball joint on the secondary throttle operating lever 52.

3 Hold the primary throttle 49 in the fully open position by inserting a short length of $\frac{1}{2}$ inch diameter rod between the open throttle and the bore.

4 Adjust the secondary throttle stop shown in **FIG 2:18** so that there is .002 inch (.05 mm) clearance between the throttle butterfly plate 51 and its bore **at each side** of its diameter at right angles to the throttle spindle. If the clearances are unequal the throttle plate fixing screws should be slackened and the plate centralized as the clearances are checked. Retighten the screws when similar clearances are obtained.

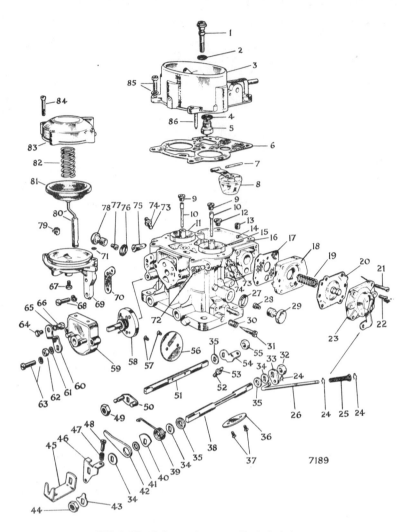

FIG 2:17 Solex carburetter. Exploded view

Key to Fig 2:17   1 Screw and accelerator pump ball valve assembly   2 Fibre washer   3 Top body and float chamber cover
4 Needle valve assembly washer   5 Float needle valve assembly   6 Joint—top body to main body   7 Float pivot pin
8 Float   9 Air correction jets   10 Emulsion tubes   11 Secondary throttle choke tube   12 Starter jet
13 Accelerator pump bleed back jet   14 Accelerator pump intake ball valve   15 Primary throttle choke tube
16 Carburetter main body   17 Joint—accelerator pump to main body   18 Accelerator pump body
19 Accelerator diaphragm return spring   20 Accelerator pump diaphragm (membrane)   21 Accelerator pump fixing screw
22 Accelerator pump cover fixing screw   23 Accelerator pump cover and lever assembly   24 Wire type circlip
25 Accelerator pump lever operating spring   26 Accelerator pump operating rod   27 Fibre washer
28 Main jet—primary throttle barrel   29 Main jet holder   30 Volume control adjustment spring
31 Slow-running mixture volume control screw   32 Lever retaining nut   33 Accelerator pump operating lever
34 Shoulder spacing washer   35 Nylon sealing washer   36 Primary throttle   37 Primary throttle fixing screws
38 Primary throttle spindle   39 Return spring, secondary throttle return lever   40 Spring positioning plate   41 Lever bearing
42 Lever—secondary throttle release and return   43 Lock washer   44 Nut—primary throttle operating lever
45 Primary throttle operating lever   46 Primary throttle abutment plate   47 Slow-running speed adjustment screw spring
48 Slow-running speed adjustment screw   49 Secondary throttle lever nut   50 Secondary throttle operating lever
51 Secondary throttle spindle   52 Secondary throttle closed position stop screw   53 Stop screw locknut
54 Secondary throttle stop plate   55 Stop plate fixing nut   56 Secondary throttle   57 Secondary throttle fixing screws
58 Starter assembly disc valve   59 Starter assembly body   60 Starter assembly operating lever   61 Spring washer
62 Lever fixing nut   63 Starter assembly fixing screw and spring washer   64 Choke cable to lever fixing screw   65 Circlip
66 Lever pivot—choke inner cable   67 Fixing screw—choke control outer cable   68 Fixing screw and spring washer—
secondary throttle operating unit   69 Secondary throttle operating unit body   70 Joint—secondary throttle operating unit
to carburetter main body   71 Small rubber sealing ring   72 Pilot jet—primary throttle barrel
73 Fixing screws for choke tubes   74 Fixing screw locknuts   75 Pilot jet—secondary throttle barrel   76 Fibre washer
77 Main jet—secondary throttle barrel   78 Main jet holder   79 Ball joint clip   80 Connecting rod and spring loaded ball joint
81 Secondary throttle operating diaphragm (membrane)   82 Diaphragm return spring   83 Secondary throttle operating unit cover
84 Cover fixing screw   85 Fixing screw and spring washer—carburetter top body   86 Dip tube—starting fuel circuit

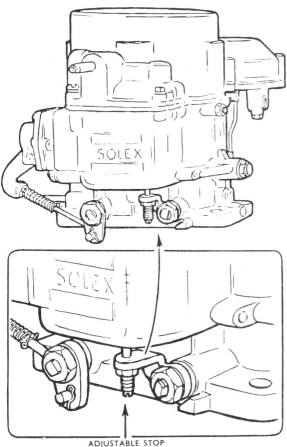

FIG 2:18   Secondary throttle stop adjustment

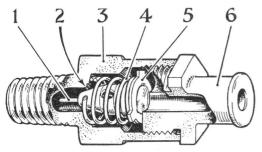

FIG 2:19   Crankcase ventilation regulator

5 Refit the carburetter and adjust the slow-running as already described.

Secondary throttle operating rod:

This rod 61 is adjusted at the diaphragm end so that the ball joint end lines up with the ball on the secondary throttle lever 52 when the secondary throttle is closed and the diaphragm 3 is at the bottom of its stroke.

Carburetter faults:

Excessive fuel consumption:

First check that there are no fuel leaks in the system from the fuel tank to the carburetter and that all carburetter joints and assemblies are tight.

(a) Ensure that the correct sizes of jets etc. as specified in Technical Data are fitted and that they are all tight in their holders.
(b) Check that the choke operating cable is correctly adjusted with the operating lever against its back stop and the control $\frac{1}{8}$ inch from the full 'IN' position.
(c) Ensure that the face of the disc 31 in FIG 2:15 in the starter assembly is seating correctly and that the surfaces are clean and smooth.
(d) Ensure that the float needle and seat assembly 22 is clean and tight in the body and that the joint washer is undamaged. Renew if faulty.

Poor high speed performance:

(a) Ensure that the primary throttle is opened fully when the accelerator pedal is pressed down as in normal use.
(b) Check the operation of the secondary throttle for full and free movement in each direction.
(c) Check the setting of the secondary throttle stop screw.
(d) Check these points in the secondary throttle operating unit: The diaphragm is in good condition. The joint between the unit and the carburetter body is air tight. The passages 8 and 4 between the choke tube and the diaphragm upper faces are clear. Clear the drilling in the brass locating dowel. If necessary the unit may be removed and tested by mouth suction through the brass dowel or by immersing in water and observing any air bubbles when the diaphragm is moved.
(e) Check that both main jets 15 and 54 are of the correct size and are not obstructed.

Poor slow-running:

If the adjustments described in Section 2:14 are not effective check the following points:
(a) Ensure that the carburetter and manifold joints are not leaking.
(b) Check the crankcase ventilation regulator and clean if necessary.
(c) Remove and blow through the slow-running pilot jet 14.
(d) Remove the slow-running volume control screw 44 and jet 14 and blow through the passage ways.

Poor acceleration:

This is most likely to be caused by faulty operation of the accelerator pump. After checking that the small circlips on the accelerator pump operating link rod 45 are in place, examine the accelerator pump assembly in the following order: Remove the screw and delivery ball valve 5. Remove the jet 37 and ball valve 38 in the float chamber. Remove the four brass screws securing the acceletator pump and the circlip on the outer end of the operating rod, and lift off the accelerator pump assembly.

Remove two brass screws and lift off the end cover 18 to inspect the diaphragm 17. Renew if faulty.

Blow through the passages 42 and 43.

Replace the intake ball valve 38 and jet 37.

Reassemble and refit the accelerator pump noting that when refitting the diaphragm 17 it should be pressed against the back stop on the operating lever side before tightening the two screws holding the pump cover plate to the pump body. This ensures that the diaphragm can move effectively over its whole range.

Difficult starting:

Check the choke control operation to ensure full movement of the choke operating lever.

Remove the carburetter top body 26 and float 36 and examine the starter jet 35 for blockage. Sediment here may also indicate a need to clean the fuel pump filter.

Check the movement of the starter air control piston 25.

Flat spots:

Assuming that the operator has attended to the settings and adjustments already described any flat spots will usually be caused by blockages in the bypass (progression) holes in the primary 47 or secondary 53 throttle barrels. These may be cleared by applying compressed air to either the slow-running jet location after removing the jet 14 or the secondary pilot jet 56 location.

2:18 Crankcase ventilation regulator

The purpose of this regulator is to prevent the emission of crankcase fumes directly into the atmosphere by drawing them into the inlet manifold. It must also control the amount of such air admitted according to the engine speed and throttle opening, otherwise the carburetter settings will be upset, particularly those for slow-running.

FIG 2:19 shows the internal arrangement and operation of the regulator. At small throttle openings with high inlet vacuum the valve 5 is drawn against its seat 2 in the outlet (induction manifold) end of the body 3 against the pressure of the spring 4. This restricts the flow to the quantity which passes through the drilling in the valve. The 'jiggle' pin 1 prevents the small hole from becoming blocked.

As the engine speed increases the spring lifts the valve off its seat and allows an increased flow through the unit and provides the crankcase ventilation required under driving conditions.

Servicing:

The unit should be removed, dismantled by unscrewing the inlet end 6 from the body, and cleaned in paraffin every 6000 miles (10,000 km). If any of the components appear to be worn or corroded, particularly the spring, they should be renewed.

The connecting rubber pipe should be washed clear of sludge, and also the breather filter located on the engine tappet cover.

When reassembling make sure that the spring is correctly located and that the valve is not tilted in the body.

2:19 Air cleaner. Fibre pad type

On some cars an air cleaner of the type shown in **FIG 2:20** is fitted. The filter element is a flat oil wetted fibre pad.

The element should be removed every 12,000 miles (20,000 km) and discarded. Access is obtained by releasing the four spring clips and the clip holding the filter to the carburetter intake. The new prepared element

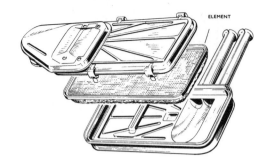

FIG 2:20 Air cleaner. Fibre pad type

2:20 Fault diagnosis

(a) Leakage or insufficient fuel delivered

1 Air vent in tank obstructed
2 Fuel pipes blocked
3 Air leaks at pipe connections
4 Fuel pump filter blocked
5 Pump gaskets faulty
6 Pump diaphragm defective
7 Pump valves sticking or seating badly
8 Fuel vapourizing in pipes due to heat

(b) Excessive fuel consumption

1 Carburetter(s) need adjusting
2 Fuel leakage
3 Choke control sticking
4 Dirty air cleaner
5 Excessive engine temperature
6 Brakes binding
7 Tyres under-inflated
8 Idling speed too high
9 Car overloaded

(c) Idling speed too high

1 Rich fuel mixture
2 Carburetter controls sticking
3 Slow-running screws incorrectly adjusted
4 Worn carburetter butterfly valve

(d) Noisy fuel pump

1 Loose mountings
2 Air leaks on suction side or at diaphragm
3 Obstruction in fuel pipe
4 Clogged pump filter

(e) No fuel delivery

1 Float needle stuck
2 Air vent on filler pipe obstructed
3 Pipe line obstructed
4 Pump diaphragm stiff or damaged
5 Inlet valve in pump stuck open
6 Bad air leak on suction side of pump

CHAPTER 3

THE IGNITION SYSTEM

3:1 Description

The ignition system comprises a high-tension induction coil and a combined distributor, contact breaker, and automatic timing control assembly driven at half engine speed from the camshaft. Included also is a vernier control which provides an easy means of making small adjustments by hand to the ignition timing in order to obtain the best performance from various grades of fuel and to compensate for changes in engine condition.

The spring loaded governor weights of the automatic timing control mechanism are mounted on the distributor driving shaft below the contact breaker and are linked by a lever action to the cam of the contact breaker. Under the centrifugal force imparted by rising engine speed the weights swing outwards against spring pressure to move the contact breaker cam and so advance the timing of the spark as required for high speed running.

A vacuum operated timing control is also fitted which is connected by a small pipe to the inlet manifold. Under part throttle conditions with a high degree of vacuum in the manifold the spring-loaded diaphragm is pulled towards an advanced ignition position, but with a reduced vacuum such as that obtaining under hill climbing conditions at wide throttle openings the spring returns the diaphragm assembly to the required retarded position.

These mechanisms may be seen in the exploded view of the distributor given in **FIG 3:1**.

3:2 Routine maintenance

Very little maintenance work is required and consists of keeping the assembly clean and in correct adjustment and the little lubrication as follows (refer to **FIG 3:2**):
1 A smear of grease or oil on the cam and the pivot post.

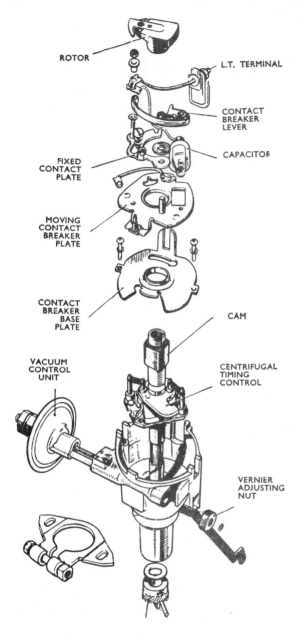

ROTOR

L.T. TERMINAL

CONTACT
BREAKER
LEVER

CAPACITOR

FIXED
CONTACT
PLATE

MOVING
CONTACT
BREAKER
PLATE

CONTACT
BREAKER
BASE
PLATE

CAM

VACUUM
CONTROL
UNIT

CENTRIFUGAL
TIMING
CONTROL

VERNIER
ADJUSTING
NUT

FIG 3:1   Exploded view of distributor

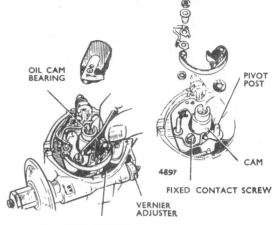

OIL CAM
BEARING

PIVOT
POST

CAM

4897

FIXED CONTACT SCREW

VERNIER
ADJUSTER

OIL TIMING CONTROL

FIG 3:2   Contact breaker maintenance

Cleaning the contact breaker:

The moulded distributor cap should be cleaned inside and out with a soft dry cloth with particular attention to the spaces between the metal electrodes. Ensure that the carbon brush moves freely in its holder.

If the contact points are dirty or pitted they should be cleaned with a very fine carborundum stone or emery cloth and wiped with a petrol moistened cloth. To do this the contact breaker lever should be lifted off after first removing the nut, washer, insulating piece, and connection from the spring anchor post. Check the free movement of the contact breaker on its pivot and polish the pin with fine emery cloth if necessary. Clean and lubricate.

Adjusting the contact breaker points:

After cleaning and refitting check the setting of the gap between the contact breaker points with a feeler gauge after turning the engine until one of the cams has opened the points to the maximum extent. This gap should measure .015 inch.

If any adjustment is required slacken the screw securing the fixed contact plate and adjust its position to give the correct gap. Tighten the screw.

3:3 Distributor removal

Disconnect the HT leads from the sparking plugs noting their positions and the HT lead from the coil. Remove the distributor cap.

Turn the engine until the timing mark on the crankshaft pulley is opposite the TDC pointer on the timing case (see **FIG 3:3**). The distributor should be pointing to the No. 1 firing position.

Disconnect the low-tension lead from the distributor body and the vacuum pipe.

Remove the two set bolts securing the aluminium distributor housing to the crankcase and withdraw the whole assembly.

Note the position of the slots in the oil pump drive shaft (see **FIG 3:4**).

2 A few drops of oil through the gap at the edge of the contact breaker plate to lubricate the centrifugal advance mechanism.

3 A few drops of oil to the cam bearing spindle which is exposed by lifting off the rotor arm as shown. Do not remove the screw as there is clearance to allow the oil to pass.

4 Take care that no oil gets on the contact breaker plate or the points.

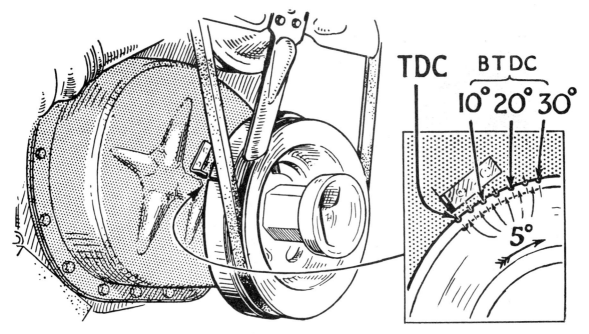

FIG 3:3   No. 1 cylinder TDC pointer. Insert shows BTDC timing marks

3:4 Dismantling the distributor

Refer to **FIG 3:1**. Lift off the rotor arm. Disconnect the vacuum unit link to the moving contact breaker plate and remove the two screws at the edge of the contact breaker base. Lift off the complete contact breaker assembly. Remove the circlip on the end of the micrometer timing screw and turn the micrometer nut until the screw and the vacuum unit are freed. Take care not to lose the ratchet and coil type spring under the micrometer nut.

The complete shaft assembly and centrifugal timing control can now be removed. This assembly is dismantled by unscrewing the screw inside the cam and removing the cam assembly which will enable the weights and springs of the centrifugal timing control to be lifted off the action plate.

The contact breaker assembly is dismantled by removing the nut, insulating piece, and connections from the pillar on which the spring is anchored. Slide off the terminal moulding. Lift off the contact breaker lever and the insulating washer beneath it. Remove the screw securing the fixed contact plate together with the spring and plain washers and take off the plate. Withdraw the screw securing the capacitor and contact breaker earth lead. Dismantle the contact breaker base assembly by turning the base plate in a clockwise direction and pulling to release it from the moving plate.

If the shaft is slack in the body, the long bearing bush should be pressed out and a new bush fitted after allowing it to stand in engine oil for twenty four hours.

3:5 Reassembly and replacement

After complete dismantling proceed as follows:

1 Place the distance collar over the shaft, smear with oil, and fit it into its bearing.
2 Refit the vacuum unit into its housing and replace the springs, milled nut and circlip.
3 Reassemble the centrifugal timing control. Place the cam and cam foot assembly over the shaft, engaging the projection on the cam foot with the weights and fit the securing screw.
4 Smear the contact breaker base plate with oil, fit and secure the moving plate and refit into the distributor body. Engage the link from the vacuum unit. Refit the two base plate securing screws, one of which also secures the earth lead.

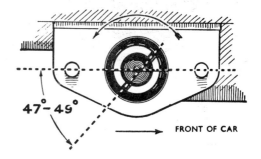

FIG 3:4   Correct timing position of distributor drive

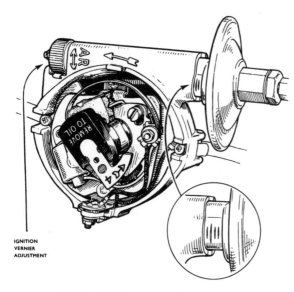

FIG 3:5   Distributor vernier control

FIG 3:6   Fitting HT cables to distributor cover

5 Refit the capacitor. Place the fixed contact plate into position and secure lightly with one plain and one spring washer.

6 Replace the insulating washers etc, on the pivot post and on the pillar holding the contact breaker spring. Refit the contact breaker lever and spring.

7 Slide the terminal block into its slot.

8 Replace the low-tension and capacitor connectors on to the insulating piece and fit them on the pillar holding the contact breaker spring. Refit the washer and nut ensuring that the eyelets do not foul the cover or the vacuum advance mechanism.

9 Set the contact gap to 0.015 inch and tighten the securing screw.

10 Refit the rotor arm and the cover.

Refitting:

The distributor is refitted by reversing the removal procedure. The operator is again reminded of the necessity to ensure that the timing indications are as shown in **FIGS 3:3** and **3:4** before commencing the operation.

If the plug leads have been removed from the distributor cover ensure that they are replaced in the correct firing order of 1, 3, 4, 2. The rotor rotates in an anticlockwise direction seen from above.

3:6 Retiming

Refer to **FIG 3:3** and the timing instructions in Technical Data. Turn the engine forward by hand until the TDC line on the crankshaft pulley is the required distance before the pointer on the timing case.

Set the vernier control to the midway position (two divisions showing on the scale. **FIG 3:5**.).

Remove the distributor cap and connect a 12-volt bulb between the LT terminal and earth.

Disconnect the vacuum advance pipe to avoid possible strain.

Slacken the distributor clamp screw and turn the body of the distributor anticlockwise as far as possible.

Switch on the ignition and turn the distributor slowly clockwise until the bulb lights which indicates that the points have just opened. Tighten the clamp screw.

Check the setting by turning the engine twice and observing the position of the pointer when the bulb lights again.

Switch off. Remove the bulb. Refit all parts.

Stroboscopic timing:

When this method of timing is employed the engine speed should be set at 1000 rev/min to avoid confusion caused by the automatic advance mechanism at the recommended slow-running speed of the engine.

3:7 HT Cables

When a high-tension cable shows signs of deterioration it should be replaced by new 7 mm rubber covered ignition cable.

To make the connections to the terminals in the distributor cover remove the cover and slacken the screws on the inside of the moulding and pull out the old cables. Having cut the new cables to the correct length push one end firmly into the hole after smearing it with silicone grease and tighten the screw. The screw will pierce the rubber insulation and make a sound contact with the cable core (see **FIG 3 : 6**).

To connect a new cable to the ignition coil pass the cable through the knurled moulded nut, bare about $\frac{1}{4}$ inch at the end of the cable, thread the wire through the brass washer which has been removed from the old cable, and bend back the strands as shown in **FIG 3 : 7**. Screw the nut into the terminal.

3:8 Sparking plugs

The sparking plugs should be regularly removed for inspection and cleaning. Examination of the condition of the electrodes will often give valuable information as to such tuning settings as fuel mixtures and ignition timing.

The normal deposit on the electrodes should be brown or greyish tan in colour. A white or yellowish deposit is also quite normal in an engine which has been used for long spells of steady driving or town work. Cleaning and setting the gap to the recommended .025 inch is all that is needed.

Deposits of wet black sludge indicate oil fouling caused by oil entering the combustion chamber past worn rings or pistons, or worn valves and guides. A hotter type of plug may be effective but in severe cases an engine overhaul may be required.

Dry, black and fluffy deposits are caused by petrol fouling resulting from incomplete combustion. This may be due to running with an excessively rich mixture or use of the choke. Long periods of idling or slow speed running will also cause these symptoms as also will defective ignition giving incomplete combustion.

Plugs having a white or blistered appearance have been overheating. The cause here may be inefficient cooling, incorrect ignition timing, or over long periods of high speed running. Attention to the engine should cure the trouble, but it may be found helpful to fit plugs of a cooler running type.

The plugs should be cleaned on an air blast machine and tested under pressure after attending to the electrodes. These should be filed clean and level and set to the correct gap. Always adjust the gap by bending the side electrode, never the centre element. Before replacing in the engine clean the screw threads with a wire brush, taking care to avoid the centre electrode and insulator.

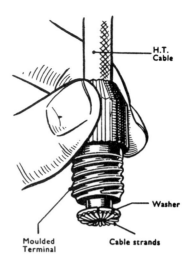

FIG 3 : 7   Fitting HT cable to terminal nut

3:9 Fault diagnosis

(a) Engine will not fire

1 Battery discharged
2 Distributor points dirty or out of adjustment
3 Distributor cap dirty, cracked or tracking
4 Carbon brush in distributor cap not contacting rotor
5 Faulty cable or loose connection in low-tension circuit
6 Distributor rotor arm cracked
7 Faulty coil
8 Broken contact breaker spring
9 Contact points stuck open

(b) Engine misfires

1 Check 2, 3, 5 and 7 in (a)
2 Weak contact breaker spring
3 High-tension plug or coil cables cracked or perished
4 Sparking plug loose
5 Sparking plug insulation dirty or cracked
6 Sparking plug gap incorrect
7 Ignition timing too far advanced

CHAPTER 4

THE COOLING SYSTEM

4:1 Description
4:2 Maintenance
4:3 Water pump removal
4:4 Water pump dismantling

4:5 Water pump reassembling
4:6 Thermostat removal and testing
4:7 Water temperature gauge
4:8 Fault diagnosis

4:1 Description

On all models covered by this manual the cooling water is circulated round the engine by an impeller type pump mounted on the front of the cylinder block and driven by a belt from the crankshaft, which also drives the generator. The radiator fan is bolted to the front of the pump driving pulley. Water is drawn from the bottom of the radiator and after passing through the engine it reaches a thermostatically operated valve, mounted on the front of the cylinder head, which remains closed while the engine is cold and returns the water directly to the pump intake without passing through the radiator. Some coolant water also circulates from the rear of the cylinder head through the induction manifold jacket to the intake side of the pump.

As the engine warms up, the water quickly reaches a preset temperature at which the thermostat valve opens and passes the water through the radiator. The thermostat operating temperatures are given in Technical Data.

The radiator filler cap incorporates a spring-loaded relief valve which, in addition to preventing undue loss of water, by allowing a pressure to build up in the system, increases the temperature at which the water will boil and so increases the operating efficiency of the engine. The relief valve operating pressures for the various models are given in Technical Data (see **FIG 4 : 1**).

Alpine I and II:

On these cars a cross-flow radiator is fitted. With this type the water is drawn from the bottom of the righthand (offside) tank of the radiator and, after passing round the engine, enters the thermostat housing and, when the valve is open, flows into an aluminium header tank bolted to the top of the housing.

From the header tank the water passes to the upper end of the lefthand (nearside) tank of the radiator through the top hose.

Alpine III and Rapier models:

A vertical type radiator is used on these cars. Water is drawn from the lower end of the radiator through the bottom hose and passes round the engine to the thermostat and, at working temperatures, direct to the upper end of the radiator through the top hose.

4:2 Maintenance

Periodically, and depending on the water which has been used, it will be necessary to flush out the entire cooling system to remove any sediment which may have accumulated.

Remove the filler cap and open the two drain cocks. One under the offside of the radiator and the other on

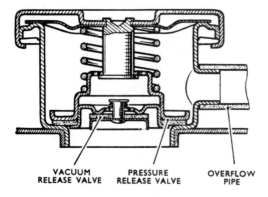

FIG 4:1 Sectional view of radiator filler cap

VACUUM RELEASE VALVE PRESSURE RELEASE VALVE OVERFLOW PIPE

the front of the nearside part of the engine front bearer plate. Turn both taps anti-clockwise to open. If a heater is fitted set the temperature control to 'HOT'.

When the water has finished running out the system should be flushed by means of a hose pipe inserted in the filler orifice. Heavier accumulations of sediment which may not be able to pass downwards through the water passages may frequently be removed by back-flushing whereby the hose pipe is applied to the bottom outlets and the water forced upwards to the filler and carrying out the sediment in that direction. Where, due to the type of water that may have been used, there is scale or furring in the water passages it may be desirable to use a proprietory cleansing compound between flushing out and refilling. This must be used according to the makers instructions.

To avoid the possibility of the cooling system freezing under winter conditions it is recommended that an anti-freeze mixture of the ethylene-glycol type be added. Owing to the difficulty in completely draining the heater system it is essential when a heater is fitted to use an antifreeze mixture.

Before adding the antifreeze drain and flush the system. Close the drain cocks. Pour in the correct quantity of antifreeze for the degree of protection required (see the table below) and fill the system with water. If a heater is fitted the control must **not** be in the **hot** position. After filling, run the engine for a few minutes, check the water level and top up if necessary.

The recommended quantities of antifreeze conforming to BS.3151 or BS.3152 are:

Antifreeze % per cent	Starts freezing at	Frozen solid
25	—13°C or 9°F	—26°C or —15°F
33⅓	—19°C or —2°F	—36°C or —33°F
50	—36°C or —33°F	—48°C or —53°F

The belt driving the water pump and the fan should be checked periodically for tension and this is correct when there is ⅝ inch in the centre of the longest run of the belt.

To adjust the tension first slacken off the generator mounting bolts and rotate the generator body until the required tension is obtained. Tighten the bolts and re-check (see **FIG 4:3**).

4:3 Water pump removal

It is first necessary to remove the radiator as follows:

Drain the cooling system and disconnect the top and the bottom water hoses. Remove the bolts securing the radiator to the baffle plates.

Slacken the bypass hose. Remove the thermostat housing.

Slacken the generator mounting bolts and remove the driving belt. Remove the fan blades.

Disconnect the heater hose when fitted.

Remove the four bolts and withdraw the pump.

4:4 Water pump dismantling

A sectional view of the water pump is given in **FIG 4:2**. The impellor and fan pulley centre are a press fit on the pump spindle which forms part of a specially constructed shaft and bearing unit.

It is important not to wash the pump at this stage in paraffin, petrol or other cleansing fluid since this would enter the bearing and contaminate the lubricant with which it is packed in manufacture. There is no provision for any further lubrication in service. Cleaning the pump body should be left until the pump has been dismantled.

Remove the bearing locating screw and the counter-sunk bolt and nuts securing the back coverplate. Remove the coverplate and its paper joint.

Support the pump body and press on the spindle at the impeller end. This will bring the impeller against the pump body and allow the spindle to be pressed out of the impeller and housing leaving the water seal in position.

Lift out the water seal.

Examine the spindle and bearing unit. If the bearing shows any sign of wear or roughness the spindle should be pressed out of the fan pulley centre.

Clean and examine the pump body. If there are signs of wear in the bearing bore or the face immediately behind the impeller the housing should be renewed.

The water seal has a carbon face mounted in a rubber housing and held against the machined face on the rear of the impeller by a spring in the housing. If either of these parts are worn or if the pump is leaking they should be renewed.

It is most important to have a smooth flat face, square to the axis of the spindle, on that part of the impeller in contact with the carbon face of the seal.

4:5 Water pump reassembling

Place the bearing unit in the pump body with the larger diameter of the spindle to the front of the housing, lining up the locating hole in the bearing with the threaded hole in the pump body. Replace the bearing locating screw.

Press the largest diameter of the spindle into the pulley centre until the front face of the pulley is positioned as detailed in **FIG 4:2**. This position ensures the correct alignment of the fan pulley with the crankshaft pulley.

Place the thrower disc in its groove on the spindle between the bearing and the seal unit.

Place the water seal on the smaller diameter of the spindle with the carbon face to the rear and push the seal firmly into the housing.

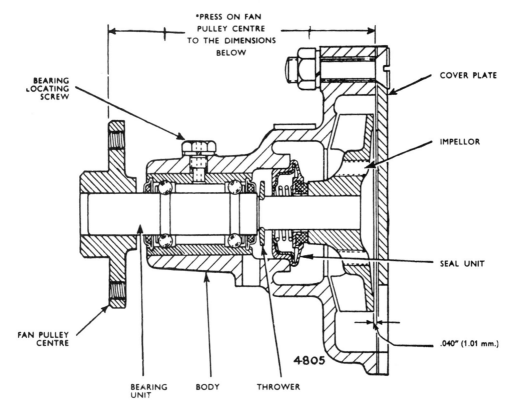

*PRESS ON FAN
PULLEY CENTRE
TO THE DIMENSIONS
BELOW

BEARING
LOCATING
SCREW

COVER PLATE

IMPELLOR

SEAL UNIT

FAN PULLEY
CENTRE

.040" (1.01 mm.)

4805

BEARING
UNIT

BODY

THROWER

FIG 4:2   Sectional view of water pump

Key to Fig 4:2   Alpine I and Rapier III   4.00 to 4.01 inches (101.6 to 101.8 mm)
                    Other models   4.865 to 4.875 inches (121.5 to 123.8 mm)

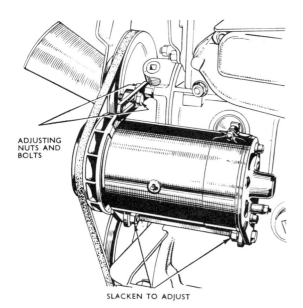

ADJUSTING
NUTS AND
BOLTS

SLACKEN TO ADJUST

FIG 4:3   Generator and fan belt adjustment

Press the impeller onto the shaft until it is in the position shown. Note that there should be a clearance of .040 inch (1.01 mm) between the outer face of the impeller and the coverplate.

Fit the coverplate using a new joint and secure with the countersunk bolt and nut.

4:6 Thermostat removal and testing

The thermostat is located in the thermostat housing at the front end of the cylinder head.

Drain the radiator to below thermostat level.

Disconnect the water hose connection to the header tank on Alpine models I and II, or the water outlet pipe on Rapier models or Alpine III and later.

Remove the two bolts holding the header tank, or water outlet pipe, to the thermostat housing. Remove the header tank, or the water outlet pipe, and lift out the thermostat. If the thermostat valve is found to be open on removal it is defective and must be renewed.

When refitting, which is the reverse of the above procedure, a new joint washer should be used between the header tank, or the water outlet pipe, and the thermostat housing.

To test:

Suspend the unit in a suitable vessel of water together with a reliable thermometer. Heat the water slowly while stirring and observing the thermometer.

The thermostat valve should commence to open and be fully open at the temperatures given in Technical Data for the various models.

A faulty thermostat must be replaced by a new unit and if a replacement is not immediately available the car should be run without it rather than have a faulty unit in service.

4:7 Water temperature gauge

This instrument is electrically operated and consists of two units, the transmitter element in the thermostat housing and the gauge on the instrument panel. A single insulated wire connects these two units and a reading is given only when the ignition is switched on.

Removal of element and gauge:

Drain the radiator to below thermostat level. Disconnect the battery.

Remove the insulated lead from the element terminal. Unscrew and remove the element.

The gauge is removed by disconnecting the two electrical leads and removing two knurled nuts. This frees the instrument which may be removed from the panel.

To test:

Remove the temperature element and immerse it in a suitable container of water together with a thermometer. Earth the outer body of the element to the thermostat housing and switch on the ignition. A comparison of the readings shown by the instrument under test and the thermometer will show if it is reasonably accurate.

4:8 Fault diagnosis

(a) Internal water leakage

1 Cracked cylinder wall
2 Loose cylinder head nuts
3 Cracked cylinder head
4 Faulty head gasket
5 Cracked tappet chest wall

(b) Poor circulation

1 Radiator core blocked
2 Engine water passages restricted
3 Low water level
4 Loose fan belt
5 Defective thermostat
6 Perished or collapsed radiator hoses

(c) Overheating

1 Check all in (b)
2 Sludge in crankcase
3 Faulty ignition timing
4 Low oil level in sump
5 Tight engine
6 Choked exhaust system
7 Binding brakes
8 Slipping clutch
9 Incorrect valve timing
10 Retarded ignition
11 Mixture too weak

(d) Corrosion

1 Impurities in the water
2 Inadequate draining and flushing

CHAPTER 5

THE CLUTCH

5:1 Description

On all models covered by this manual a hydraulic clutch withdrawal mechanism is employed consisting of a master cylinder directly connected to the clutch pedal and a hydraulic pipe coupling to the operating or slave cylinder which in turn is attached by a rod to the clutch withdrawal lever. These components may be seen in **FIGS 5:1** and **5:2**.

Alpine I and Rapier I, II and III:

These cars use an 8 inch single dry plate A-type clutch with a self-lubricating release bearing. The only external adjustment is on the operating piston rod attached to the clutch withdrawal lever and is effected by slackening off the locknut at the back of the fork and turning the piston rod in the desired direction to obtain a free movement at the outer end of the withdrawal lever of $\frac{3}{32}$ inch (2.4 mm). This adjustment may be seen in the inset to **FIG 5:2**.

Alpine II and III, and Rapier IIIA:

These cars are fitted with an 8 inch single dry plate AS (Strap drive) type clutch (see **FIG 5:3**), in which the torque is transmitted from the cover to the pressure plate through three pairs of spring steel straps arranged tangentially so that they can deflect during clutch opetation without disturbing the balance of the assembly and by eliminating friction a reduced operating effort is required. No adjustment at the slave cylinder operating rod is necessary and none is provided. There is, however, a two position adjustment to the pedal, see the inset to **FIG 5:1**, which can be changed by moving the clevis pin 73 securing the master cylinder pushrod 58 into either of the two holes provided in the pedal 46.

Late Alpine III and IV and Rapier IV:

These cars have a diaphragm type clutch which is described in **Section 5:6**.

5:2 Maintenance

Apart from the adjustment for free movement of the clutch pedal which has been dealt with in the previous Section, the only maintenance required in normal use is the regular inspection of the fluid level in the master cylinder reservoir. This should be done every 3000 miles (5000 km) and if necessary fluid should be added to bring the level up to within $\frac{1}{2}$ inch from the top. The addition of fluid should only be necessary at long intervals and any large drop in fluid would indicate a leak which should be traced and rectified.

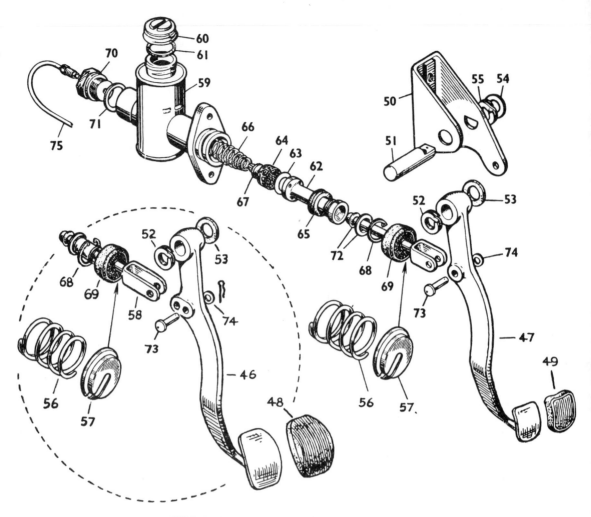

FIG 5:1   Master cylinder and clutch pedal linkages

Inset   Two position adjustment on Alpine II and III

It is important to use only the grade of hydraulic fluid specified for each model. Recommended grades are:

Alpine Girling Fluid SAE Spec. 70 R.3.

Rapier Lockheed Super Heavy Duty Brake Fluid SAE 70 R.3.

Under certain circumstances such as when the clutch withdrawal mechanism has been disturbed, or the fluid level has been allowed to fall very low, it may be necessary to bleed the system to remove any air bubbles. This is carried out as follows:

1 Fill the reservoir with the recommended fluid and ensure that it is kept at least a quarter full throughout the operation. If this is not done air will be drawn in and necessitate a fresh start.

2 Attach a rubber tube to the bleeder screw 40 (see **FIGS 5:2** and **5:3**), on the slave cylinder, allowing the free end to be submerged in a small quantity of fluid in a clean glass jar or other suitable container.

3 Slacken the bleeder screw and depress the clutch pedal slowly, tightening the screw before the pedal reaches the end of its stroke. Allow the pedal to return unaided.

4 Repeat operation 3 until air bubbles cease to appear from the end of the tube in the glass jar.

5:3 Servicing the hydraulic system

Removing the master cylinder:

This works on similar principles to the master cylinder in the hydraulic brake system and its construction and operation can be seen in the sectional view given by **FIG 5:4**.

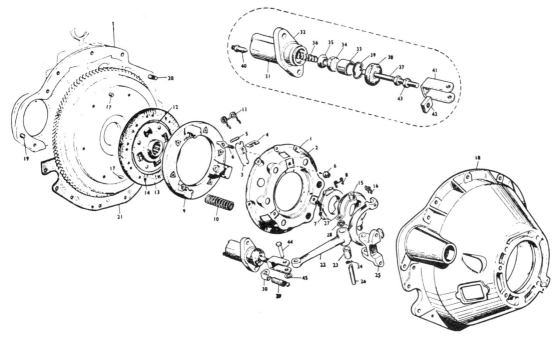

FIG 5:2 Exploded view. Clutch and slave cylinder components

Alpine I and Rapier III

Refer to **FIG 5:1**. Disconnect the pressure pipe 75 from the cylinder barrel and the clevis pin 73 from the clutch pedal. Remove the two fixing bolts and detach the cylinder and pushrod. Unscrew the filler cap 60 and pour the fluid into a clean container. Compress the external return spring 56 and remove the retaining cap 57. Slide the spring off the piston rod.

To dismantle:

Pull back the rubber boot 12 (see **FIG 5:4**), and push the piston 10 down the bore of the cylinder and remove the circlip 13. Withdraw the piston, washer 9, rubber cup 8, retainer 7 and return spring 6. The secondary cup 11 is removed by stretching it over the end of the piston with the fingers only.

To reassemble:

Having renewed any parts showing excessive signs of wear or damage and any perished rubber parts, assembly is carried out as follows, with all parts wetted in hydraulic fluid:

Fit the secondary cup on the piston so that the lip of the cup faces the piston head and see that it is properly seated round the groove. Fit the retainer on the smaller end of the return spring and insert into the cylinder. Insert the main cup into the cylinder, lip foremost, taking care that the lip does not get turned back. Insert the washer 9 in the direction shown. Locate the pushrod 14 or 15 in the piston and press into the cylinder taking care not to damage or displace the secondary cup. Fit the

circlip ensuring that it beds securely in its groove and that the collar in the pushrod is retained by the circlip.

Fill the reservoir with clean hydraulic fluid and test the master cylinder by pushing the piston inwards and allowing it to return under the pressure of the return spring. After a few strokes fluid should flow through the outlet plug 4.

To refit:

Fit the boot 12 on to the cylinder so that the vent hole in the boot will be underneath when mounted on the car. If the old boot is damaged or perished it should be renewed.

Bolt the master cylinder to the mounting brackets. Refit the clevis pin with its washer and splitpin. Check the pedal adjustment on those types where such adjustment is provided. Fill the reservoir with fluid and bleed the system as described in **Section 5:2** and check for leakages while applying a firm pressure to the pedal.

The slave cylinder:

The interior construction of the slave cylinder may be seen in **FIGS 5:2** and **5:3** and it operates similarly to the hydraulic brake wheel cylinder. Inside the main cylinder body 32 is a piston 33, rubber cup 34, cup filler 35, return spring 36, operating rod 37, connected to the clutch withdrawal lever and retained in position by a circlip 39 and a rubber boot 38. It will be seen that on Alpine II and III and Rapier IIIA cars no circlip is fitted, nor is there an adjustment at the fork.

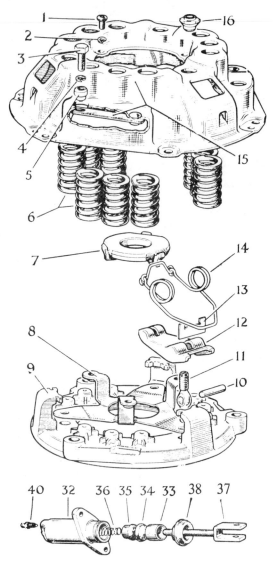

FIG. 5:3 Exploded view. Clutch and slave cylinder

Alpine II and III and Rapier IIIA

To remove and dismantle:

Disconnect the pressure pipe from the slave cylinder 29 when fitted and remove the clevis pin to free the pushrod from the operating lever. Remove the two fixing bolts and lift off.

Clean the exterior of the assembly before pulling back the rubber boot and removing the circlip when fitted. Withdraw the internal parts and clean in brake fluid. It may be found necessary to apply air pressure to the pipe connection in order to expel the internal parts.

To reassemble and refit:

Having cleaned all the pieces and replaced any showing signs of wear, dip them in fluid and reassemble in the following order:

Fit the spring in the cup filler and insert into the bore of the cylinder. Carefully push in the rubber cup and insert the piston, flat face innermost. Refit the circlip (Alpine I and Rapier III). Replace the pushrod and the rubber boot. Replace the two securing bolts and the clevis pin. Refit the external return spring and connect the pressure pipe. Bleed the system as already described in **Section 5:2**).

5:4 Clutch removal and dismantling

It is first necessary to remove the gearbox and bell-housing in accordance with the instructions given in **Chapter 6** of this manual and the operator is again warned of the great care needed to avoid any tilting of the gearbox during removal or replacement nor must he allow any weight to hang on the drive shaft during these operations.

Slacken off evenly the six setscrews holding the clutch cover to the flywheel and remove the clutch assembly and the driven plate.

Examine all parts for wear and note the condition of the friction linings and faces. If the friction faces are badly scored or pitted it may be necessary to replace the flywheel and the pressure plate and if the linings are badly worn or showing the discolouration caused by oil being present the driven plate should be exchanged. The operator is advised not to attempt to fit new linings himself, nor should he dismantle the cover assembly. Either he should give the work to a service agent or fit an exchange unit.

If the release bearing 15 in **FIG 5:2** is worn it may be removed for replacement by removing the spring clips securing it to the withdrawal lever. Always renew the spring clips when reassembling.

5:5 Reassembling and refitting clutch

These operations are performed by reversing the removal procedure.

If a new driven plate is to be fitted it will have a small amount of a waterproof grease applied to the internal splines as supplied. Grease should be applied before assembly if the original plate is to be refitted.

It is most important that the driven plate should be correctly located when the clutch cover is fitted, and this will be facilitated by using a suitable mandrel (a gearbox stem wheel will do for the purpose) fitted through the hub of the plate. Note that the smaller boss of the driven plate hub faces towards the flywheel. This alignment is necessary to allow the gearbox primary shaft to pass through the clutch plate into the spigot bearing in the rear end of the crankshaft.

Replace the clutch cover on the dowels and tighten the six setscrews evenly.

Refit the gearbox and bellhousing in accordance with the instructions given in **Chapter 6**.

Bleed the hydraulic system as detailed in **Section 5:2**.

When a new clutch assembly is obtained it will be seen that there are three small L-shaped 'keepers' which save the necessity of compressing the springs when

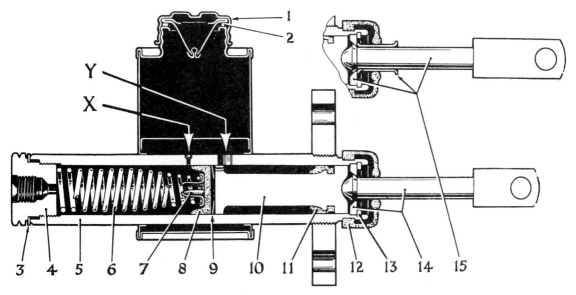

FIG 5:4   Master cylinder. Sectional view

Key to Fig 5:4

1 Filler cup	2 Washer	3 Outlet plug washer	4 Outlet plug	5 Cylinder
6 Return spring	7 Spring retainer	8 Main cup	9 Piston washer	10 Piston	11 Secondary cup
12 Rubber boot	13 Stop circlip	14 Pushrod (Alpine Series I and Rapier cars)	15 Pushrod (Alpine Series II cars)

replacing the cover. These keepers, which are painted in red, must be removed after the fixing bolts have been finally tightened.

5:6 The diaphragm clutch

This type of clutch, which is illustrated in **FIG 5:5**, is fitted to the later cars covered by this manual and is operated by the same hydraulic system as is used with the earlier type clutches. The removal and refitting procedures are also the same.

A copper impregnated graphite release bearing is fitted which is self lubricating and so no attention in this regard is necessary.

The assembly consists of a pressed steel cover 9 and a cast iron pressure plate 4 which are linked together by three flat steel straps 1 and a steel diaphragm spring 7.

This diaphragm spring is pinched between two fulcrum rings 3 which are secured to the cover by the rivets 8.

A release plate assembly 5 is attached to the cover by three spring steel straps, each rivetted at one end to the cover and at the other end to the release plate itself.

Three retractor clips 2 bolted to the pressure plate clip over the rim of the diaphragm to ensure that the pressure plate retracts during cluth disengagement.

During assembly the diaphragm comes under load and is flattened from its original dished profile, and this load applied via the outer fulcrum ring provides the pressure on the pressure plate.

Pressure on the release plate deflects the diaphragm spring away from the pressure plate due to the leverage about the inner fulcrum ring and disengages the clutch. No adjustment is necessary and none is provided.

The clutch driven plate may be removed and replaced as on the earlier models as may the cover assembly, on which again no home servicing should be attempted.

This unit is carefully balanced during manufacture and when any attention becomes necessary a replacement unit should be obtained.

The release bearing is copper impregnated graphite and no lubrication is necessary.

Master cylinder, Rapier IV and Alpine IV:

The hydraulic master cylinder used with the diaphragm spring clutch on these cars is similar to that used on the earlier models, but incorporates a provision for adjusting the clutch pedal free play. This should be .040 inch (1 mm) and is measured between the pedal stem and the pedal stop behind the parcel tray.

To adjust: Push back the pedal return spring and cap and loosen the locking nut on the end of the master cylinder pushrod. Rotate the pushrod until the correct clearance is obtained and retighten the locknut.

Do not attempt to adjust the free play by altering the setting of the pedal stop as this will also affect the brake pedal clearance.

5:7 Fault diagnosis

(a) Drag or spin

1 Oil or grease on driven plate linings
2 Misalignment between engine and gearbox primary shaft
3 Leaking master cylinder, slave cylinder or pipe line
4 Driven plate binding on primary shaft splines
5 Binding spigot bearing of primary shaft
6 Distorted engine backplate
7 Distorted driven plate
8 Distorted or damaged pressure plate or clutch cover
9 Broken driven plate linings
10 Dirt or foreign matter in clutch
11 Air in hydraulic system

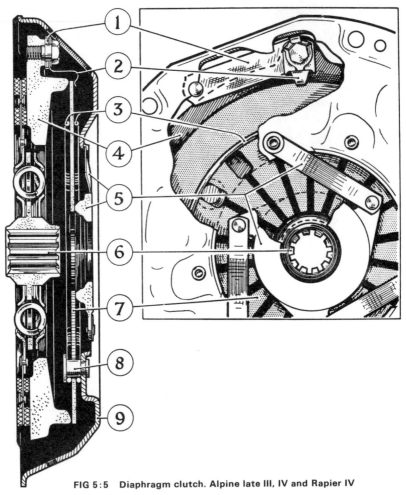

FIG 5:5   Diaphragm clutch. Alpine late III, IV and Rapier IV

Key to Fig 5:5   1 Drive straps   2 Retractor clips   3 Fulcrum rings   4 Pressure plate   5 Release plate
6 Driven plate   7 Diaphragm spring   8 Rivets   9 Coverplate

(b) Fierceness or snatch

1 Check 1, 2, 3 and 6 in (a)
2 Worn clutch linings

(c) Slip

1 Check 1, 2 and 6 in (a)
2 Check 2 in (b)
3 Weak pressure springs
4 Siezed piston in slave cylinder
5 Insufficient clearance at operating lever (where provided)

(d) Judder

1 Check 1, 2 and 6 in (a)
2 Pressure plate not parallel with flywheel face
3 Contact area of driven plate linings not evenly distributed
4 Bent primary shaft
5 Buckled driven plate

6 Faulty engine or gearbox flexible mountings
7 Loose propeller shaft bolts

(e) Rattle

1 Check 3 in (c)
2 Broken springs in driven plate
3 Worn release mechanism
4 Release bearing loose on fork

(f) Tick or knock

1 Worn primary shaft spigot or bearing
2 Worn splines in driven plate hub
3 Faulty release bearing
4 Loose flywheel

(g) Driven plate fracture

1 Check 2 and 6 in (a)
2 Drag and distortion due to gearbox hanging in plate hub

CHAPTER 6

THE GEARBOX

6:1 Description

The gearbox fitted to all models is a fourspeed unit having baulk ring-type synchromesh engagement on the three upper forward ratios, of these second and third employ helical gears and are in constant mesh.

Gearchanging is effected through a floor mounted remote control mechanism which is illustrated and described later in this chapter. (**Section 6:4**).

A factory fitted overdrive is available as an optional extra. It is engaged by a switch mounted on the steering column and controlled by an isolator switch on the gearbox top cover which permits engagement of overdrive in top and third gears only. The overdrive unit is described in **Section 6:7.**

The internal construction of the gearbox is shown in the exploded view given in **FIG 6:1** which also shows the main differences to be found in the earlier and the later cars. The three synchronized gears are engaged by dog clutches while first gear has a sliding gear engagement.

6:2 Maintenance

Maintenance on the gearbox consists in regularly checking the oil level and topping up every 3000 miles (5000 km).

The correct level for the oil is level with the bottom of the filler orifice on the righthand side of the gearbox and which is accessible through a cover in the raised section of the front floor of the car. The grade of oil specified for earlier cars is SAE 30. From Rapier chassis No. B.33100001 and Alpine chassis No. B.94100001 the correct grade is SAE.10W/30.

Every 6000 miles (10,000 km) the gearbox, and overdrive unit when fitted, should be drained and refilled with fresh oil. This is preferably carried out when the oil is warm and more fluid.

At the same interval a few drops of engine oil should be applied to the two lubrication holes in the gearbox top cover for the gearchange mechanism and to the base of the gearlever underneath the rubber grommet.

6:3 Removing gearbox

After positioning the car on a ramp or over a pit proceed as follows:

Disconnect the battery. Drain the radiator and the gearbox. Replace the plug. Remove the top water hose. Disconnect the carburetter throttle linkage.

Alpine:

Remove the floor cover and gearlever. Disconnect the exhaust system from the branch pipes and remove.

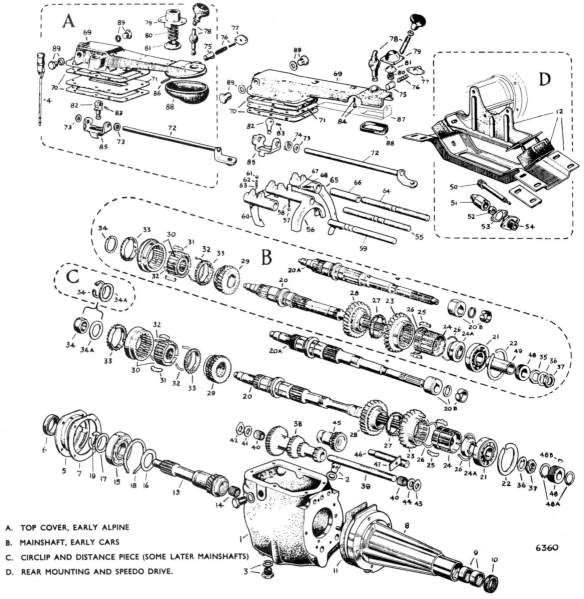

FIG 6:1 Exploded view of gearbox

A. TOP COVER, EARLY ALPINE

B. MAINSHAFT, EARLY CARS

C. CIRCLIP AND DISTANCE PIECE (SOME LATER MAINSHAFTS)

D. REAR MOUNTING AND SPEEDO DRIVE.

6360

Remove the propeller shaft rear coupling bolts, disconnect the coupling and withdraw the shaft rearwards. Support the rear of the engine and detach the rear crossmember from the underframe. Disconnect the speedometer cable and the clutch hydraulic pipe. Remove the lower bellhousing bolts and the bolts securing the clutch slave cylinder. Lower the engine and remove the gearbox crossmember. Remove the starter motor and the upper bellhousing bolts.

Withdraw the gearbox and bellhousing rearwards and downwards.

Rapier:

Remove the rocker cover. It may be necessary to remove the complete rocker shaft when a heater is fitted.

Remove the engine rear lifting brackets. Disconnect the exhaust flange from the manifold and the front hanger bracket.

Remove the propeller shaft rear coupling bolts and withdraw the shaft downwards and to the rear.

Jack up the rear of the engine and remove the bolts securing the rear mounting bracket to the frame.

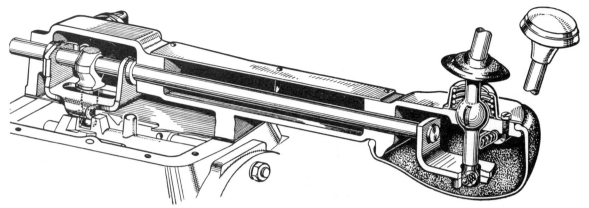

FIG 6:2   Top cover assembly. Early Alpine cars

Disconnect the speedometer cable. Disconnect the hydraulic clutch supply pipe or, on later models, remove the slave cylinder from the bellhousing.

Disconnect the starter cables and remove the motor.

Series I:

Disconnect the rod from the external changespeed lever on the countershaft below the steering column.

Remove the coverplate in the centre of the floor and disconnect the selector cable trunnion. Remove the selector cable complete.

Remove the engine tie bar.

Series IV:

Unscrew the gearlever knob. Remove the ashtray. From behind and above the blower switch remove the wingnut fixing which secures the upper edge of the console to the lower edge of the facia.

Remove the front and the rear gearbox tunnel covers.

Disconnect the wires from the overdrive solenoid—when fitted—and the gearbox isolator switch.

Lower the rear of the engine. Remove the nuts and bolts securing the bellhousing and withdraw the complete assembly downwards and to the rear.

Do not in any way tilt the gearbox during these operations or permit its weight to hang on to the clutch driven plate as the strain so imposed may cause considerable damage.

6:4   Removing top cover and gearchange

This operation may be carried out either with the gearbox in the car or after its removal.

On early models remove the oil level dipstick. No dipstick is fitted on those models with the oil level filler plug.

Unscrew the gearbox top cover bolts and lift off the cover taking care not to damage the paper joint.

The gearlever is removed by sliding up the rubber grommet and loosening the setscrews securing the spring retaining cap to the casing.

Early Alpine cars:

Remove the rubber boot (see **FIG 6:2**), from below the gearlever mounting.

Remove the coverplate with the reverse stop spring

and plunger from the side of the gearlever mounting. Remove the setscrews securing the lever spring retaining cap to the extension casting and take off the cap, spring and cupped washer. Lift out the gearlever. Note the spring loaded ball at the lower end of the lever. This is positively located in its drilling to prevent dropping out during dismantling.

Undo the locking wire from the square-headed bolt securing the internal shift lever to the remote control shaft. Remove the bolt and withdraw the shaft through the rear of the casing. This will also release the safety latch and spacing washers, one at each end of the latch.

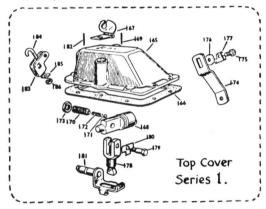

FIG 6:3A   Top cover. Rapier Series I

Rapier Series 1 (see **FIG 6:3A**):

Undo the lockwasher 177 and remove the bolt 175 securing the external gearshift lever 174. Undo the lockwasher 185 and slacken the nut 186 to release the external selector lever 183.

Undo the lockwasher 180, remove the setscrew 179 to release the internal gearchange lever 178.

Great care must be exercised when removing the detent mechanism comprising items 170 to 173 to ensure that their relative settings are not disturbed. Remove the locating pin 169 with a punch and push out the changespeed lever shaft from inside. Do not lose the ball 171 and spring 172 which will be released.

Drive out the pin 182 and push the selector shaft 181

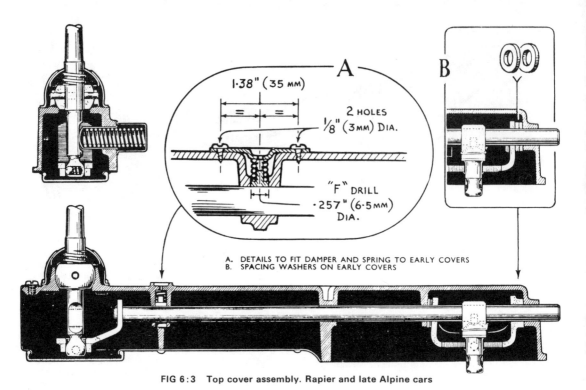

A. DETAILS TO FIT DAMPER AND SPRING TO EARLY COVERS
B. SPACING WASHERS ON EARLY COVERS

FIG 6:3 Top cover assembly. Rapier and late Alpine cars

and lever 178 into the cover.

When refitting this top cover take care not to over-tighten the bolt 179 so that the changespeed lever 178 is free to swing on its shaft.

Items 171 and 172 are refitted through the bore in the cover.

After inserting the pins 182 and 169 peen over the ends of the holes.

Rapier Series II and later and late Alpine cars:

Remove the seven setscrews (see **FIG 6:3**), securing the coverplate and lift off the plate. Remove the two setscrews securing the reverse bias spring plate and remove the plate, bias spring and plunger. Undo the locking wire and remove the screw which secures the selector lever to the operating shaft. Note the position of the safety latch spacing washers.

Slide out the shaft through the rear of the casing. (On later models this will release the damper pad and spring located in the cover.) The safety latch, selector lever and washers will now be freed and may be removed. Note the position of the washers for correct location when reassembling.

The inset 'A' in **FIG 6:3** illustrates a modification to the top cover on early cars for fitting a damper pad and spring if required.

6:5 Dismantling the gearbox

Removing clutch bellhousing:

Extract the springs securing the clutch release bearing and remove the release bearing assembly.

Remove the bolts and washers securing the withdrawal lever bracket to the bellhousing and extract the lever.

Remove the bolts and washers securing the bellhousing to the gearbox. Lift off the bellhousing from the gearbox spigot.

Removing rear cover:

Remove the speedometer pinion and bush. Unscrew two bolts and one nut to remove the rear mounting plate. Remove two bolts and washers and lift the rear cover off the casing. Remove the paper joint.

If the rear bushes are worn or scored a replacement cover complete with bushes should be obtained.

Removing selector shafts and forks

These must be removed towards the rear. (See **FIG 6:1**).

Tap out the reverse selector shaft 64 noting the distance piece 66 at the rear of the selector fork. Tap out the other two selector shafts 55 and 59 and remove the selector forks.

Front cover assembly:

Having removed the top and rear covers and the selectors as described remove the four setscrews securing the front cover 5. Remove the setscrew and washer securing the lock plate 47 and remove the plate by sliding it downwards. By inserting dummy layshaft (details of this tool will be given at the end of this section) move the layshaft 39 rearwards until it is clear of the fixed thrust washer 43 permitting the layshaft cluster to be lowered to the bottom of the casing 1.

Withdraw the front cover assembly, taking care not to lose the needle rollers 14 from the mainshaft spigot bearing.

Remove the fourth-speed baulk ring 33 from the synchrohub 30 marking each part for correct reassembly. Remove the circlip 18 securing the bearing 15 in the front cover and press the stemwheel 13 assembly out of the cover. Remove the circlip 19 securing the bearing and washer 17 and press off the stemwheel. Remove the bearing shield 16 and the oil seal pressed into the cover.

Mainshaft assembly:

On early cars (see inset 'B' in **FIG 6:1**), release the lockwasher 36 and unscrew the nut 37 securing the bearing to the shaft. Remove the distance piece 49 and the speedometer gear 48.

On later cars the nut 37 and washer 38 may be removed after the circlips, speedometer gear 48 and key have been removed.

While supporting the forward end of the mainshaft assembly drive the assembly forward with a mallet until it is free of the rear bearing 21. Holding the second-speed synchrohub assembly 23 to 26 withdraw the mainshaft assembly throuth the aperture in the front of the casing. The second-speed assembly may be lifted out of the top of the casing.

Remove the second-speed wheel 28 and separate the baulk ring from the gear, marking them for later identification.

Secure the mainshaft in a vice using soft metal clamps and remove the front circlip or nut 34. Remove the third- and fourth-speed synchrohub 30 (see also **FIG 6:4**), which is a press fit on the mainshaft. Remove the third-speed wheel 29 and separate the baulk ring from the gear. Remove the third and fourth sliding sleeve. Remove the three short shifting plates 31 and two circlips 32.

(See also **FIG 6:5**). Remove the first-speed wheel 23 from the hub 24 and detach the three long shifting plates 25. Remove the distance piece 24A and withdraw the two circlips 26.

The dummy layshaft tool is made up using a rod $\frac{3}{4}$ inch diameter (19 mm) and $6\frac{1}{2}$ inch long (165.1 mm).

Layshaft assembly

This is withdrawn complete with rollers 40 abutment ring 41 and floating steel thrust washer through the aperture in the front of the casing. Remove the two bronze thrust washers 42 and 43.

The reverse wheel 45 is removed after the withdrawal to the rear of its spindle 46.

The rear bearing may now be pressed out of the casing, but note that if the circlip 22 is removed a new one must be fitted when assembling.

6:6 Gearbox reassembly:

This is the reverse of the dismantling procedure and the operator's attention is drawn to the following points:

As always absolute cleanliness is essential, and all moving parts should be dipped in clean oil before final assembly and checked at each stage for movement. Paper joints, where used, should be renewed and all external screws and bolts should be dipped in a non-setting jointing compound before use.

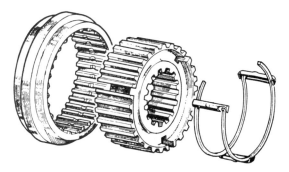

FIG 6:4 Arrangement of 3rd and 4th speed synchrohub

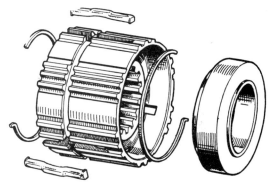

FIG 6:5 Arrangement of 2nd speed synchrohub

If the gearbox has been stripped on account of poor synchromesh the following items should be checked:

The baulk rings, or their replacements, should be examined for grooves and burrs on the cone faces. Examine the slots for the shifting plates for roughness. Check the freedom of movement of the baulk ring on its hub. Examine the cone faces on the gear wheels and if ridges are present fit a replacement. Any roughness should be rubbed down, and a new baulk ring should always be lapped to the synchrohub cone with metal polish.

Insert the reverse wheel and spindle into the casing with the gears to the rear.

Assemble the layshaft assembly and measure the end float between the thrust washers. This should be .006 to .008 inch (.152 to .203 mm) and is adjusted by a selection of the correct thickness of floating thrust washer. The bronze thrust washers (large one to the front) are held in position with thick grease as are the needle rollers, twenty seven at each end of the cluster. After positioning the needle rollers fit the abutment ring in the recess at the front of the cluster and lower the complete cluster with the dummy shaft into the casing and then fit the rear floating steel thrust washer.

Before assembling and fitting the mainshaft assembly the following points should be attended to:

Ensure that the dog teeth of the baulk rings are in good condition and that the grooves in the tapered bore of the rings are clean. See that the gear cone which mates with the baulk ring is free from glazing or ridging.

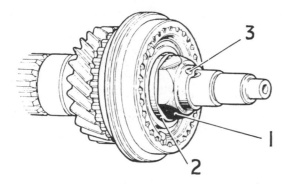

FIG 6:6 Nut and washer securing 3rd and 4th speed synchrohub

Baulk rings and their corresponding cones should be checked for concentricity by rotating the two together after having applied 'blue' to one surface and observing the marking on the other. Check the rings also for distortion by laying on a surface plate. If at any point a .001 inch feeler gauge may be inserted a new ring should be obtained.

Slide the third and fourth sliding sleeve on to the hub and check for easy engagement without excessive play.

Examine the shifting plates for wear particularly at the centre and at the ends.

FIG 6:7 Pressing mainshaft into rear bearing

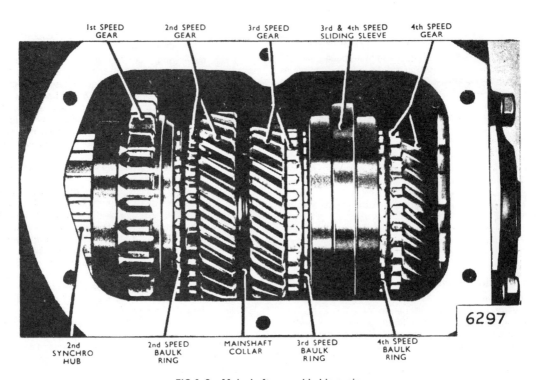

FIG 6:8 Mainshaft assembled in casing

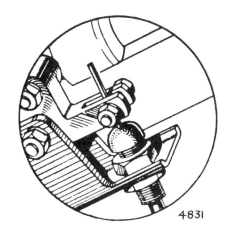

FIG 6:9   Adjusting steering wheel end of selector cable

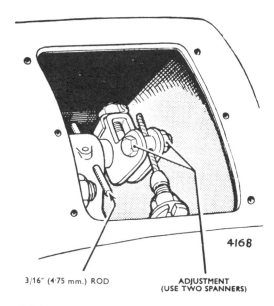

3/16" (4·75 mm.) ROD   ADJUSTMENT
                             (USE TWO SPANNERS)

FIG 6:10   Adjusting selector linkage at gearbox

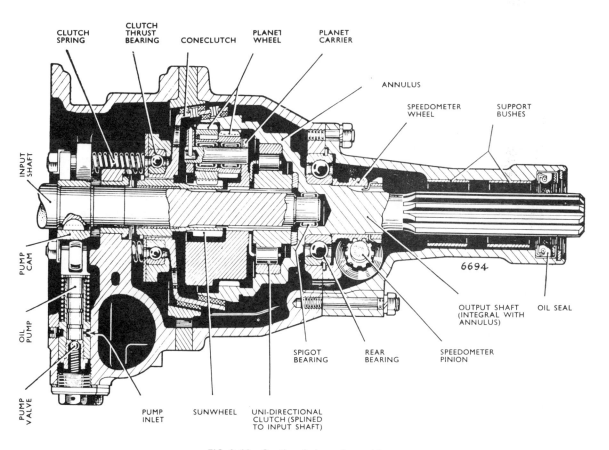

CLUTCH
SPRING

CLUTCH
THRUST
BEARING

CONECLUTCH

PLANET
WHEEL

PLANET
CARRIER

ANNULUS

SPEEDOMETER
WHEEL

SUPPORT
BUSHES

INPUT
SHAFT

PUMP
CAM

OIL
PUMP

PUMP
VALVE

PUMP
INLET

SUNWHEEL

UNI-DIRECTIONAL
CLUTCH (SPLINED
TO INPUT SHAFT)

SPIGOT
BEARING

REAR
BEARING

SPEEDOMETER
PINION

OUTPUT SHAFT
(INTEGRAL WITH
ANNULUS)

OIL SEAL

6694

FIG 6:11   Sectional view of overdrive

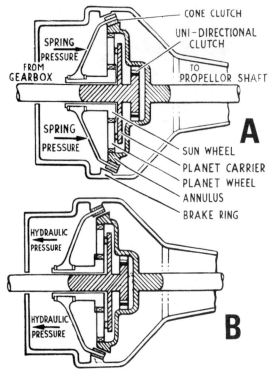

FIG 6:12 Diagrams of overdrive operation

Labels in figure A:
CONE CLUTCH
UNI-DIRECTIONAL CLUTCH
SPRING PRESSURE
FROM GEARBOX
TO PROPELLOR SHAFT
SPRING PRESSURE
SUN WHEEL
PLANET CARRIER
PLANET WHEEL
ANNULUS
BRAKE RING

Labels in figure B:
HYDRAULIC PRESSURE
HYDRAULIC PRESSURE

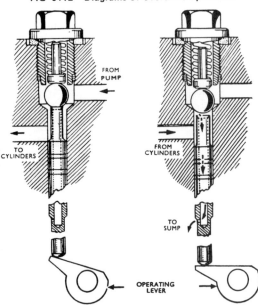

FIG 6:13 Operating valve

Labels in figure:
FROM PUMP
TO CYLINDERS
FROM CYLINDERS
TO SUMP
OPERATING LEVER

Renew the synchro circlips if they are weak or worn and, when fitting, ensure that they are correctly located in the underside of the shifting plates and that the locating hooks are not in the same shifting plate. Note also that the free ends of the circlips follow opposite directions from one another. (see **FIG 6:4**).

The second-speed synchrohub circlips are assembled in a similar manner (see **FIG 6:5**). After assembly test all parts for free movement.

The location of the third and fourth synchrohub on the mainshaft is secured by three different methods. See **FIG 6:1** and insets 'B' and 'C'. When fitted with a spring ring 34 in 'B' the thickest possible ring from the five available grades should be used. When fitted with a circlip and a distance piece 34 and 34A in 'C' the thickest possible distance piece from the four thicknesses available should be used. In each case ensure that the circlip is fully located in its groove in the mainshaft. Always use a new circlip or spring ring.

On later cars the third- and fourth-speed hub is secured by a nut and washer 1 and 2 in **FIG 6:6**. The nut should be tightened to a torque of 80 lb ft and using a suitable punch the flange of the nut should be peened into the indentation in the mainshaft 3. Always use a new nut.

When pressing the mainshaft into the rear bearing take care to line-up the second-speed shifting plates 25 with the slots in the second baulk ring 27 which should be held lightly against its mating cone. Make sure also that the first-speed wheel 23 and the third- and fourth-speed sleeve 30 are maintained in position on their respective hubs 24 and 30.

In order to ensure that the rear main bearing 21 is held firmly against the distance piece 24A place the gearbox on a base as shown in **FIG 6:7** so that the shaft may pass through the notches while the bearing rests on the plate. The shaft is then pressed through the bearing until the distance piece is securely held between the bearing and the second speed hub.

Replace the third and fourth synchrohub on the mainshaft and secure with its circlip or nut 34. Pass the first and second synchrohub and the second-speed wheel assembly down through the top of the casing with the bevelled first-speed teeth to the rear and insert the mainshaft through the front of the casing, passing its rear end through the first and second synchro assembly and the bearing aperture at the rear of the casing.

Fit the rear bearing and press completely into position. On early cars (inset 'B') fit the spacer 49, speedometer gear 38, spacer 35, lockwasher and nut 36 and 37. On cars fitted with the later-type mainshafts fit the lockwasher and nut 36 and 37 then the speedometer gear and circlips 48 and 48A (see also **FIG 6:8**).

Having ensured that the twenty-seven needle rollers are in position in the stemwheel, fit the front cover and stemwheel assembly with the drain hole in the 6 o'clock position. Use a new paper joint.

Invert the gearbox and insert the layshaft spindle from the rear and replace the layshaft cluster ensuring that the thrust washers at each end are correctly positioned. Fit the locking plate 47.

With the gearbox upright fit the third and top, the first and second, and the reverse selector forks. Fit the reverse distance piece 66 and shaft with the long end of the shaft to the front.

Fit the third and fourth, and the first and second selector shafts 59 and 55.

Refit the rear cover with a new paper joint. Refit the rear mounting plate. Check that all the shafts are free and that all the gears can be selected.

Refit the top cover ensuring that the internal selector lever can move freely across the slots in the forks.

6:7 Replacing the gearbox

First replace the clutch bellhousing by reversing the removal procedure given in **Section 6:5**.

The gearbox assembly is refitted in reverse order to the removal instructions given in **Section 6:3** and no difficulty should be experienced.

Adjustment of selector cable:

Rapier Series I prior to chassis No. A3602318:

Refer to **FIG 6:9**. Slacken off the cable pinch nut, using two spanners.

Engage first gear and wedge the lever in this position. Grip the inner cable with pliers and pull upwards as far as possible.

Make a mark on the cable at the exact point where it protrudes through the trunnion.

Push the inner cable downwards as far as possible and make a similar mark on the cable.

Pull up the cable to the first position and make a mark halfway between the other two. Push the cable back downwards until this halfway mark is in line with the top of the trunnion. Tighten the pinch nut.

Rapier Series I. Chassis No. A3602318 and later:

This adjustment is made at the gearbox (see **FIG 6:10**).

With the steering column changespeed lever in the neutral position press is downwards to the first/second speed stop and wedge it in this position, taking care not to pull out the reverse knob on the lever.

Slacken the cable pinch nut at the selector lever on the gearbox. Move the selector lever sideways in each direction and find its midway position.

Insert a $\frac{3}{16}$ inch diameter pin through the hole in the gearbox as shown in the diagram and move the lever to and fro until the pin also passes through the hole in the selector lever shaft.

Tighten the cable pinch nut, using two spanners to avoid kinking the cable. The selector cable is now located in the first/second speed neutral position. Remove the wedge and check the lever for normal operation.

Adjusting the steering column gearshift lever:

If necessary this may be done by placing the lever in the neutral position and then disconnecting the ball joint from the end of the gearchange actuating lever at the bottom of the control shaft.

Rotate the ball joint as necessary to adjust the length of the control rod so that the knob on the end of the gearshift lever is one inch above the horizontal. With this setting the gearshift lever should not foul the column cowl when moved to the reverse position.

Check the oil level. Check that the clutch is adjusted correctly. Bleed the hydraulic system and check for correct operation.

6:8 Overdrive

The Laycock de-Normanville overdrive unit which is fitted at the factory as an optional extra has a ratio of .802:1 or in other words gives the propeller shaft an increase in speed over the gearbox output shaft speed

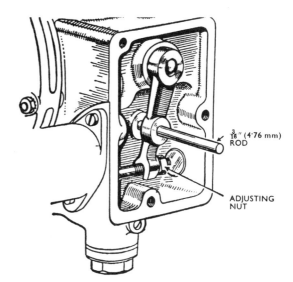

$\frac{3}{16}$" (4·76 mm) ROD

ADJUSTING NUT

FIG 6:14 Control adjustment

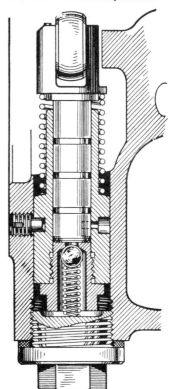

FIG 6:15 Oil pump and valve

of 24.67 per cent to enable high cruising speeds to be maintained at reduced engine revolutions. The sectional view of the unit given in **FIG 6:11** in conjunction with the two diagrams in **FIG 6:12**, will show the operator how the system functions and help him use the following maintenance instructions.

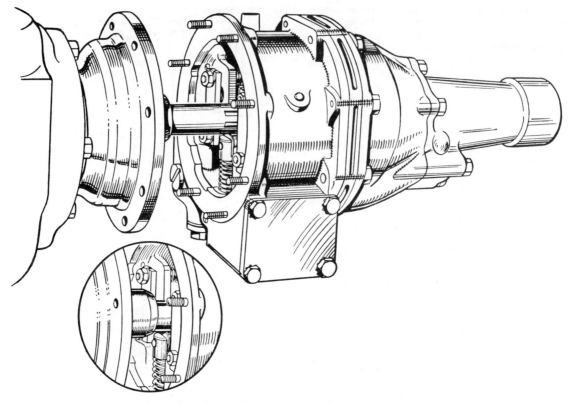

FIG 6:16   Fitting overdrive unit to gearbox

FIG 6:12A shows the unit in direct drive where it will be seen that the cone clutch, fixed to an extension of the sunwheel, is held to the rear by spring pressure causing the inner friction band to contact the outside of the annulus. This locks the gear train and the drive is transmitted directly through the uni-directional clutch. Any over-run or reverse torque is taken by the cone clutch.

FIG 6:12B shows the unit in overdrive, when the cone clutch is held forward by hydraulic pressure so that its outer friction band is locked to the stationary brake ring. The sun wheel is also held stationary being splined to the cone clutch. The planet carrier is splined to the input shaft and so the planet wheels are driven round the stationary sun wheel and thus rotate the annulus and the output shaft at a speed greater than that of the input shaft.

The hydraulic pressure required is generated by a pump of which the plunger is driven by a cam connected to the gearbox mainshaft. A constant pressure is maintained by means of a relief valve. The oil under pressure from the pump is passed to the operating cylinders by way of the operating valve which is shown diagrammatically in **FIG 6:13**. When the overdrive control is operated the valve is lifted, as in the lefthand drawing, against the pressure of the plunger spring and allows the oil to flow to the cylinders forcing the pistons forward as already mentioned.

When the overdrive control is returned to the disengaged position the spring pushes the ball down on to its seat and so prevents any oil from the pump from reaching the cylinders and at the same time the oil in the cylinders is permitted to return to the sump through the hole drilled in the centre of the valve. See the right-hand drawing in **FIG 6:13**.

The overdrive control is actuated by a solenoid controlled by a switch on the steering column. An isolator switch in the gearbox top cover ensures that overdrive can be obtained only in third and top gears. A self-cancelling switch is incorporated which returns the overdrive switch to the disengaged position when the gearlever is moved out of the third and top plane, thus making it necessary to reselect overdrive when changing up again from second gear.

Maintenance

The oil in the overdrive unit is common with that in the gearbox and the level is checked and the filling-up done at the gearbox. To drain, however, it is necessary to remove both gearbox and overdrive drain plugs. The overdrive drain plug is that the nearest the left (near) side of the unit. The pump valve plug in the centre and the relief valve plug on the right are wired together and are not removed unless attention to the valves is required.

The combined capacity of the two units is 4 pints (2.3 litres) and with this type of transmission it is more than ever important that clean oil of the correct grade should be used. When the units are refilled after draining for any reason the oil level should be checked after running for a short while since a certain amount of oil will be taken up in the hydraulic system.

The operation of the controls can be checked as shown in **FIG 6:14**. For the correct setting it is necessary to be able to pass a $\frac{3}{16}$ inch diameter rod through the hole in the solenoid lever into the hole in the overdrive casing with the ignition switched on, top gear engaged and the steering column switch in the overdrive position.

If the solenoid operates but does not move the setting lever far enough to permit the rod to be inserted the plunger must be adjusted. This is effected by screwing the self-locking nut on the plunger in or out, while the plunger is pushed into the solenoid as far as it will go. Flats are milled on the plunger to hold it with a spanner against rotation. With the $\frac{3}{16}$ inch rod in position the fork should just contact the adjusting nut.

If the solenoid does not operate the help of a service agent should be obtained.

Faults:

In this section an attempt will be made to list the faults which are most likely to occur in the operation of the overdrive and some hints as to possible causes. It must be emphasized, however, that in view of the number of special tools required for the complete servicing of these units some of the faults listed will be outside the scope of this manual.

Overdrive does not engage:

1 Insufficient oil in the gearbox
2 Solenoid not operating. Fault in the electrical system
3 Control mechanism out of adjustment
4 Insufficient hydraulic pressure due to leaks or faulty relief valve
5 Leaking operating valve due to dirt or faulty spring
6 Leaking non-return valve due to dirt or faulty spring
7 Choke oil pump filter
8 Damaged or broken gears etc. within the unit

Overdrive does not release:

This calls for prompt attention. Do not engage reverse gear.
1 Control mechanism out of adjustment
2 Fault in the electrical system
3 Blocked restrictor jet in operating valve
4 Sticking clutch
5 Damaged internal parts

Clutch slip in overdrive

1 Insufficient oil in gearbox
2 Control mechanism out of adjustment
3 Low hydraulic pressure due to leaks or dirt in valves
4 Worn or polished clutch lining

Hydraulic knock:

This knocking sound occurs once per mainshaft revolution in direct drive and can usually be eliminated by relieving the hydraulic pressure at the operating ball valve seat. All that is necessary is to remove the valve

described later and either score with a sharp point or lightly tap with a ground screwdriver blade to make two small grooves in the seating.

This method does not apply after Laycock Nos. 3082, 3083.

Before attempting to remove either of the valves it is necessary to release the hydraulic pressure by switching on the ignition, engaging top gear and operating the overdrive switch about a dozen times.

Operating valve:

Remove the coverplate (see **FIG 6:1**), in the centre of the floor and, after releasing the hydraulic pressure, remove the valve plug, plunger and spring and take out the ball with a magnet. The valve may be removed by levering gently with a tapered piece of wood.

The small hole near the bottom of the valve is the restrictor jet through which the oil returns to the sump from the operating cylinders. This drilling must be kept clear.

If the overdrive unit fails to operate after this valve has been found to be in order the functioning of the pump must be checked.

Jack up the rear wheels of the car and, with the engine ticking over in top gear, remove the valve plug and watch for oil being pumped into the valve chamber. If none appears check the relief valve and the pump valve.

Relief valve:

Remove the valve plug. (The righthand plug of the three beneath the main casing.) This will release the valve spring and plunger (and ball on early units). Remove the valve body. Inspect the O-ring, spring, plunger and body for wear or damage. The plunger should be a good sliding fit in the body.

Pump valve:

Remove the centre plug (see **FIG 6:15**), underneath the casing and drain off the oil. Unscrew the valve cap and take out the spring and ball. After cleaning, or replacing any faulty parts, the valve may be reassembled making sure that the soft copper washer is held tightly in its place to prevent leakage.

To remove unit from gearbox:

The unit is split at the front coverplate which is bolted to the gearbox and the front casing and is secured by eight $\frac{5}{16}$ inch studs. Remove the eight nuts and withdraw the unit leaving the front coverplate in position (see **FIG 6:16**).

To refit:

It is first necessary to align the splines of the planet carrier and the uni-directional clutch with a dummy mainshaft. This is a special tool from V. L. Churchill & Co. Ltd. Insert the tool and engage the internal splines of the planet carrier. Turn the dummy shaft and press inwards until it engages the internal splines of the clutch.

Turn the gearbox mainshaft until the highest point of the cam is facing upwards. The lowest point will then coincide with the overdrive pump plunger (see **FIG 6:16**).

The splines in the overdrive unit and the gearbox mainshaft are now correctly lined up and must be fitted together without any further turning on either side. The edge of the cam facing the overdrive unit is chamfered to enable the pump plunger to ride up on to the cam.

6:9 Fault diagnosis

(a) Jumping out of gear

1 Broken spring behind locating ball for selector rod
2 Excessively worn groove in selector rod
3 Worn coupling dogs
4 Fork to selector rod securing screw loose

(b) Noisy gearbox

1 Insufficient oil
2 Excessive end play in lay gear

3 Worn or damaged bearings
4 Worn or damaged gearteeth

(c) Difficulty in engaging gear

1 Incorrect clutch pedal adjustment
2 Worn synchromesh cones

(d) Oil leaks

1 Damaged joint washers
2 Worn or damaged oil seals
3 Front, rear or top covers loose or faces damaged

CHAPTER 7

PROPELLER SHAFT, REAR AXLE, REAR SUSPENSION

7:1 Universal joints. Description

The propeller shaft used on these cars is illustrated in **FIG 7:1** together with the original and two later types of universal joint.

The sliding spline portion on all models is enclosed within the rear end of the gearbox and receives its lubrication from the gearbox system.

The original type of front universal joint has a greasing nipple as shown, and the same type is also used at the rear.

On the two later types of shaft the front universal joint has sealed needle roller bearings (Inset A) and no further lubrication is provided for.

At the rear end the original type of joint is superseded on later cars by either a rubber to metal coupling as shown in the inset B, or a needle roller bearing joint incorporating a bonded rubber vibration damper as shown in C. It will be seen, therefore, that no maintenance is required on these later joints.

7:2 Servicing

Four bolts and nuts with shakeproof washers are used to secure and must be removed, noting that the heads of the bolts should face the differential unit. Always use new washers when refitting.

The metal to rubber type of joint has two nuts to connect the shaft to the rear axle coupling, and on replacement these should be tightened to a torque of 48 to 53 lb ft. There are four nuts and shakeproof washers securing the vibration damper type of joint.

After removing the nuts and bolts the propeller shaft may be lowered and removed towards the rear. The component parts should be marked to ensure replacement in the same positions.

Refitting is the reverse of the above. Ensure that after cleaning the splines and the sleeve are slightly lubricated before assembly.

To dismantle:

Remove the snap ring or circlip by pinching with a pair of pliers, then, holding the joint in one hand, tap gently on the ear of the yoke as shown in **FIG 7:2**. The needle bearings will emerge and may be removed with the fingers. Hold the bearing in a vertical position and remove the race from the bottom so as to avoid dropping the needles. (see **FIG 7:3**).

Repeat for the other bearings and wash all parts in petrol or paraffin.

A rear universal joint of the type seen in the inset C of **FIG 7:1** is dismantled in the same way as the front joint after removing the coupling.

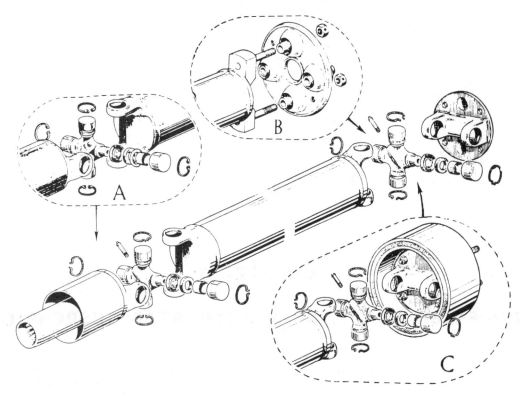

FIG 7:1 Types of universal joints

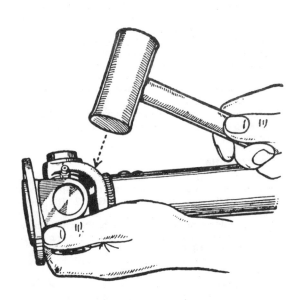

FIG 7:2 Tapping the yoke to extract bearings

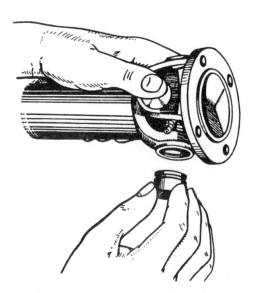

FIG 7:3 Withdrawing bearings

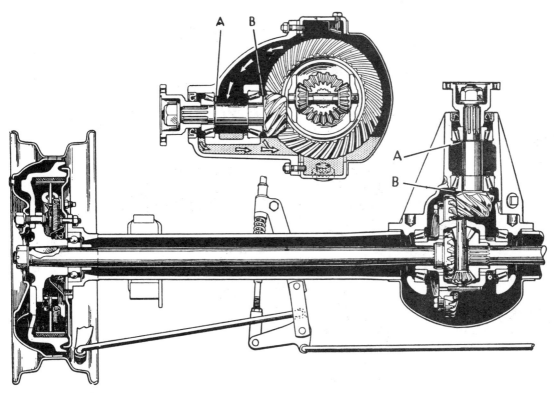

FIG 7:4 Sectional view of rear axle. Hypoid bevel drive

No attention is necessary on the rubber to metal type, and it cannot be overhauled in service. In the event of wear or damage a new joint must be fitted.

Individual parts of the bearing assemblies should not be renewed singly, and if any replacements are found to be necessary a complete set of parts comprising journal, gaskets and retainers, needle bearing assemblies and snap rings should be fitted.

To reassemble:

When refitting the original parts pack the bearings with the recommended grade of oil or grease including the oil channels where applicable. Any difficulty in assembling the rollers in the housing may be assisted by smearing the walls with vaseline. The journal shoulders may be coated with shellac prior to fitting the retainers in order to make a good oil seal.

Insert the journal into the yoke holes, and using a soft drift slightly smaller than the hole tap the bearing into position. Repeat for the other three bearings. Fit new snap rings and ensure that they fit firmly in their grooves.

There should be no play between the roller races and the bores of the yokes. If the yoke holes have worn the yoke must be renewed. In the case of the inner yokes, as they are welded to and balanced with the propeller shaft, a new shaft must be fitted.

7:3 Rear axle. Description

The rear axle fitted to most of the cars covered by this manual is of the semi-floating type with hypoid bevel drive and is shown in section in **FIG 7:4** and exploded in **FIG 7:5**.

A few Rapier cars are fitted with spiral bevel drive axles and these will be described later in this chapter.

Adjustment for the crownwheel and pinion engagement is provided by means of shims, but in view of the high degree of accuracy required and the special tools involved the home operator is strongly advised to have this work carried out by a qualified service station.

Certain service operations which may become necessary in the course of normal use may well be done by the owner-driver, most of them without requiring the removal of the axle from the car.

7:4 Servicing

Bevel pinion oil seal:

This seal 27 in **FIG 7:5.** can be seen fitted just to the rear of the propeller shaft coupling. 33, and is easily removed for renewal by unbolting the coupling. When the replacement seal is fitted the lip and spring should face the rear axle and the outside of the cage should be coated with a jointing compound before pressing into position.

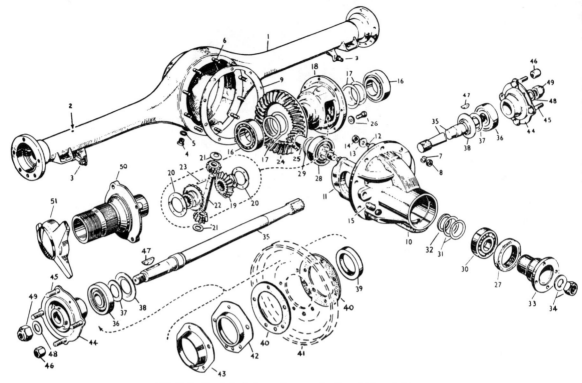

FIG 7:5 Exploded view of rear axle. Hypoid bevel drive

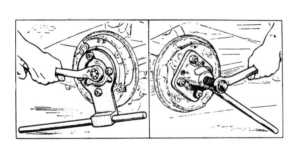

FIG 7:6 Removing hub for oil seal renewal

Hub oil retainer:

This is made up of an oil splash guard outer ring 38, overlapping an inner ring 37, supplemented by an oil seal 39. The oil seal is replaceable after the removal of the rear hub, as described later in this section, and the three plain bolts and two dowel bolts passing through the dust shield, seal housing 42, brake backplate 41, and the axle casing flange. Care should be taken to see that these bolts are refitted in the correct holes.

The hub may be removed for oil seal replacement without removing the axle shaft using Special Tool RG.188B as shown in **FIG 7:6.**

Axle shaft:

Note. Rapier cars have axle shafts of unequal length. The longer shaft is fitted to the righthand side and the shorter to the left. Alpine cars have shafts of equal length.

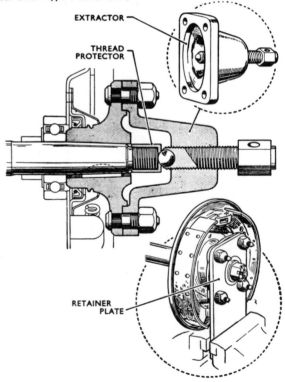

FIG 7:7 Hub retainer plate and extractor in use

To remove:

Jack-up the car, remove the road wheel and clean off the brake backplate to prevent the entry of dirt into the axle tube. Remove the setscrews securing the brake drum and remove the drum.

Uncouple the hydraulic pipes from the brake backplate and protect them against the entry of foreign matter. Remove the nuts and bolts securing the backplate to the flange on the axle casing.

Disc wheels. Fit the axle shaft removing tool (VLC.RG.16A) and the adaptor (RG.16A-4 or 188-B) over the four wheel studs and secure with the nuts.

Centre lock wire wheels. First screw the four extension legs (RG.16A-5) into the brake drum securing holes, then fit the axle shaft removing tool and secure.

Move the sliding weight sharply along the shaft of the tool to withdraw the axle shaft from its casing and remove complete with brake backplate 41, oil seal 39, dust excluder and hub 44. Remove the outer ring of the splash guard 38, from the bearing recess.

To refit:

First ensure that all parts are clean.

Using a little grease to hold it fit the splash guard 39, with the recess inwards.

If it has been removed press the bearing 36, on to the axle shaft with the inner ring 37, between the bearing and the shoulder on the shaft. (Information on the removal and fitting of the bearing is given later in this Section).

Insert the axle shaft into the casing and ease the splines into engagement with the differential wheels 19. Press the bearing into the recess in the casing and drive the assembly into position with the bearing outer face flush with the casing.

Fit a new joint washer, 40. (.006 inch. Brown), then fit the brake backplate, and then new joint washers 40, according to those removed. Either one brown washer on early cars, or two on later models. Very late cars in this series were fitted with one grey (.010 inch) washer.

Place the oil seal 39, in the retainer 42, and fit the retainer and the oil catcher 43, to the backplate. Fit the five bolts, nuts and spring washers and tighten the bolts diagonally. Check that the bearing is fully home in the casing.

Fit the key 47, to the shaft and replace the hub. Tighten the hub nut to 180 lb ft and fit the splitpin.

Replace the brake gear, drum and hydraulic pipes in the reverse order to their removal. Bleed and adjust the brakes.

To remove differential unit:

Drain the oil from the axle case and remove both axle shafts as described.

Disconnect the propeller shaft from the rear axle coupling.

Remove the nuts 8, and washers 7, securing the differential housing to the axle casing. Lift out the assembly.

To refit:

Reverse the above instructions, taking care that the joint faces are clean and undamaged. Always use a new joint washer and coat both sides with jointing compound.

Remember to bleed the brakes.

No instructions are offered for the dismantling and assembly of the differential unit as this is an operation for a service station with specialist equipment.

The maintenance required on the rear axle is none apart from periodic checking of the oil level and topping up if necessary. This should be done every 3000 miles (5000 km.).

At 6000 miles the axle should be drained and refilled with fresh oil. At this time also the axle breather hole should be cleared. On Alpine cars this is a small hole in a setscrew mounted on top in the centre of the casing. On Rapier cars this hole is drilled in the top of the axle casing on the righthand side towards the hub.

7:5 Axle removal and replacement

Remove the rebound straps. (Alpine I and II only).

Jack-up the rear of the car and support the underframe on stands or suitable blocks of wood.

Remove the road wheels. Disconnect the propeller shaft at the rear coupling. Remove the rear dampers.

Disconnect the cable from the handbrake linkage and the brake hydraulic hose from the 3-way union on the axle casing. The end of the hose should be raised to prevent the loss of fluid and covered to protect against the entry of any foreign matter.

Remove all the spring U-bolts. Withdraw the axle from between the springs.

To refit:

The rear axle is refitted by reversing the procedure for removal.

To ensure that there is no distortion of the bonded rubber eye bushes when in the static laden condition it is important that the final tightening of the U-bolts, shackle assemblies and pivot pins should be carried out after the jacks and stands have been removed and the car is standing normally on the road wheels. The requisite torque figures for the U-bolts are:—Alpine. All models 42 lb ft. Rapier. All models 16 lb ft.

Bleed the brake hydraulic system.

7:6 Servicing rear hubs

To remove hub from axle shaft (see FIG 7:7):

Disc wheels. Attach the retaining plate (part of hub removing kit RG.188A or 188B) to the four wheel studs. Clamp the plate in a vice, withdraw the splitpin and remove the hub retaining nut 49, and washer 48.

Release the vice. Remove the retaining plate and fit the short protector over the shaft, and the extractor tool (part of kit 188A or A88B) over the wheel studs and secure with the four wheel nuts.

Centre lock wire wheels. Attach the retaining plate to the hub by means of the setscrews supplied. Clamp the plate holding the shaft in a vice and remove the splitpin (see the holes in the side of the hub). Remove the hub retaining nut and washer.

Release the vice, remove the retaining plate and fit the four extension pieces (special tool RG.16A-5) to the hub by screwing the threaded end into the brake drum securing holes. Place the longer type protector over the

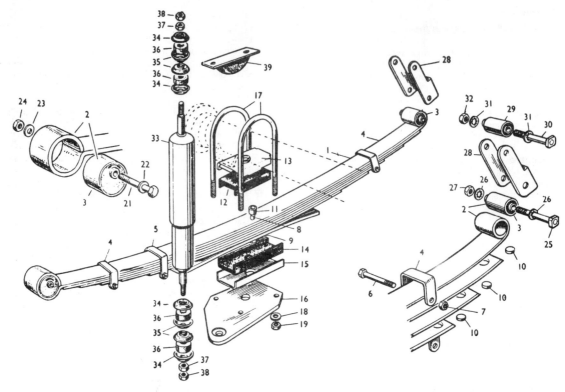

FIG 7:8 Rapier rear suspension. Component parts

Key to FIG 7:8   1 Rear spring   2 Main leaf   3 Spring eye bush   4 Bundle clip   5 Bundle clip
6 Bolt and nut securing bundle clip to spring   7 Rubber lining   8 Dowel bolt   9 Dowel bolt securing nut
10 Thrust button   11 Dowel bolt sleeve   12 Top clamp rubber (securing spring to axle casing)   13 Rubber
retainer (securing spring to axle casing)   14 Bottom clamp rubber (securing spring to axle casing)   15 Rubber retainer
(securing spring to axle casing)   16 Clamp plate (securing spring to axle casing)   17 'U'-bolt (securing spring to axle
casing)   18 Washer (securing spring to axle casing)   19 Nyloc nut (securing spring to axle casing)   21 Pivot pin
(front spring eye to frame)   22 Washer (front spring eye to frame)   23 Washer (front spring eye to frame)   24 Nut
(front spring eye to frame)   25 Shackle pin (rear spring eye to frame)   26 Washer (rear spring eye to frame)
27 Nut (rear spring eye to frame)   28 Shackle   29 Shackle bush   30 Shackle pin (shackle to frame)
31 Washer (shackle to frame)   32 Nut (shackle to frame)   33 Shock absorber   34 Retaining washer (securing
chock absorber to frame and axle)   35 Separating washer (securing chock absorber to frame)   36 Rubber washer
(securing shock absorber to frame and axle)   37 Nut (securing shock absorber to frame and axle)   38 Locknut
(securing shock absorber to frame and axle)   39 Rubber abutment (bump stop)

shaft thread and secure the extractor to the extension pieces with the four wheel nuts.

Both types. Secure the assembly in a vice by the flats on the extractor, screw in the centre bolt of the tool to take the load and smartly tap the end of the extractor bolt. Remove the hub and the extractor. Remove the dust shield, oil seal, carrier and brake backplate. Remove the key from the tapered end of the axle shaft.

To remove hub bearing:

Having removed the hub, brake gear etc., as described, slide the solid ring (part of kit RG.188A-1) over the splined end of the axle shaft until it rests on the inner race of the hub bearing. Screw in the four extension legs and fit the extractor and the short protector. Rotating the centre bolt of the extractor will pull the bearing off the shaft.

To refit:

Fit the split bush (part of kit 188A-1) to the solid ring and slide the assembly over the axle shaft, with the flanged side of the bush away from the spline, until it presses against the sleeve on the inner side of the bearing.

Fit the four extension legs, the short protector and the extractor. Turn the centre bolt of the extractor until the sleeve has been pulled $\frac{1}{32}$ inch (.8 mm.) towards the outer end of the shaft. Remove the split bush. Remove the axle shaft from the tool assembly.

Pass the splash guard and bearing, 38 to 36, over the end of the shaft. Press the bearing onto the shaft. Fit the key and the hub, and place the retaining plate over the wheel studs securing it by the nuts. Place the whole assembly in the vice and fit the nut and washer. This should be tightened to a torque of 180 lb ft.

Check that full tightness has been obtained by attempt-

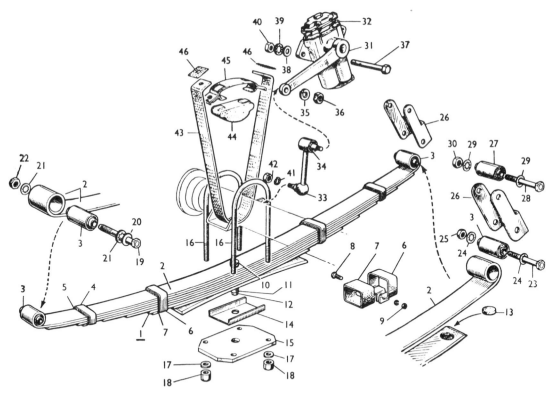

FIG 7 : 9 Alpine rear suspension. Component parts

Key to FIG 7 : 9   1 Rear spring   2 Main leaf   3 Spring eye bush   4 Bundle clip   5 Rubber lining.   6 Bundle clip   7 Rubber lining   8 Bolt (securing bundle slip to spring)   9 Nut (securing bundle clip to spring)   9 Nut (securing bundle clip to spring)   10 Dowel bolt   11 Dowel bolt locating collar 12 Dowel bolt securing nut   13 Rubber thrust button   14 Location plate (securing spring to axle casing) 15 Clamp plate (securing spring to axle casing)   16 'U'-bolt (securing spring to axle casing)   17 Washer (securing spring to axle casing)   18 Nylon nut (securing spring to axle casing)   19 Pivot pin (front spring eye to frame) 20 Washer (front spring eye to frame)   21 Washer (front spring eye to frame)   22 Nut (front spring eye to frame) 23 Shackle pin (rear spring eye to frame)   24 Washer (rear spring eye to frame)   25 Nut (rear spring eye to frame) 26 Shackle   27 Shackle bush   28 Shackle pin (shackle to frame)   29 Washer (shackle to frame) 30 Nut (shackle to frame)   31 Shock absorber   32 Gasket   33 Link   34 Rubber bush—link 35 Washer (link to shock absorber)   36 Nut (link to shock absorber)   37 Bolt (link to shock absorber) 38 Washer (shock absorber to frame)   39 Washer (shock absorber to frame)   40 Nut (shock absorber to frame) 41 Washer (link to rear axle)   42 Nut (link to rear axle)   43 Rebound strap   44 Rubber abutment (bump stop) 45 Abutment bracket   46 Lockwasher

ing to turn the inner splash guard between the sleeve and the bearing inner race. Fit the splitpin. (Later cars have self-locking nuts).

Refit the whole assembly into the axle casing as previously described.

7 : 7 Suspension system. Description

The rear suspension is by means of two semi-elliptic springs secured to the rear axle casing by two inverted U-bolts. Both the spring eyes and the shackle bracket have bonded rubber bushes, and thrust buttons are located between the leaf ends which are held in alignment by rubber lined clips.

Hydraulic dampers are used on all models. Girling telescopic on Rapier cars, and Armstrong lever type on Alpine I and II. Bump and rebound is checked by means

of a rubber block and on early Alpine cars by a rebound strap also. Alpine III cars have telescopic dampers without a rebound strap.

On the later Rapier cars the front spring eye is fitted with an eccentric rubber bush and it is this type of suspension system which is illustrated in **FIG 7 : 8**. The system fitted to early Alpine cars is shown in **FIG 7 : 9** and the same diagram illustrates the Alpine III layout apart from the exclusion of the rebound strap and the fitting of the later telescopic dampers and eccentric bushes in the front eyes.

7 : 8 Rear springs and shackles

To remove :

Jack-up the car and support it on stands placed under the frame just in front of the forward spring anchorage. Remove the road wheels.

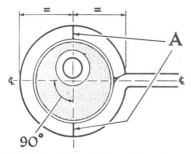

FIG 7:10   Method of marking spring eye

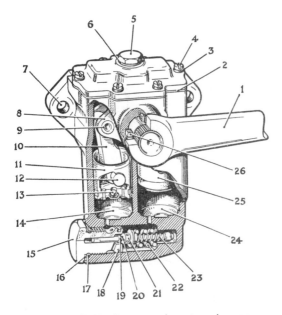

FIG 7:11   Armstrong lever type damper

Clean the threads of the U-bolts, dampers and mounting bolts. Remove the dampers.

Unscrew the Nyloc nuts and washers from the U-bolts and jack-up the rear axle until it is clear of the spring and support it on suitable stands. Remove the U-bolts.

Remove the nut and washer 27 and 26 from the lower shackle pin, tap out the pin and lower the rear end of the spring.

Similarly remove the front pivot pin and the spring is free.

To refit:

The replacement of the springs is the reverse of the above procedure.

It is important to note that the final tightening of the U-bolts, shackle pins and pivot pins should be carried out after the removal of the jacks and stands and with the car standing normally on its road wheels. This is to ensure

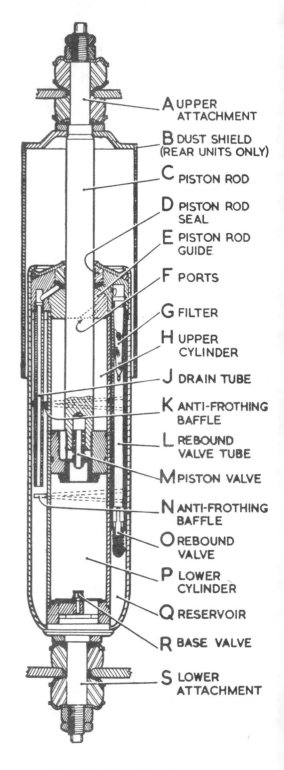

A UPPER ATTACHMENT

B DUST SHIELD (REAR UNITS ONLY)

C PISTON ROD

D PISTON ROD SEAL

E PISTON ROD GUIDE

F PORTS

G FILTER

H UPPER CYLINDER

J DRAIN TUBE

K ANTI-FROTHING BAFFLE

L REBOUND VALVE TUBE

M PISTON VALVE

N ANTI-FROTHING BAFFLE

O REBOUND VALVE

P LOWER CYLINDER

Q RESERVOIR

R BASE VALVE

S LOWER ATTACHMENT

FIG 7:12   Girling telescopic damper

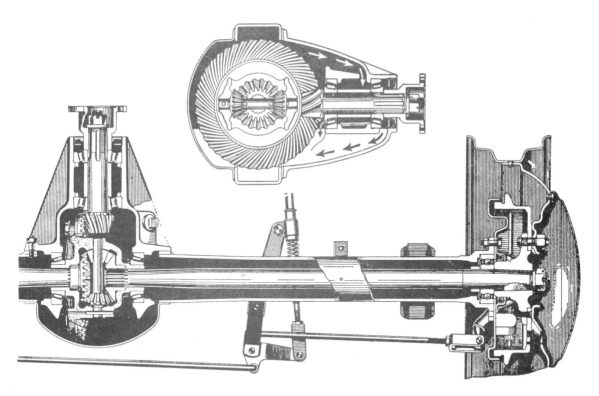

FIG 7:13 Sectional view of rear axle. Spiral bevel drive

that the rubber in the spring eyes is not subjected to abnormal twisting loads in use. The correct torque loading figures for the U-bolt nuts are: Alpine 42 lb ft.

Rapier 16 lb ft.

To dismantle a spring is quite straightforward, but the operator is strongly advized against renewing individual leaves in the event of damage. It is recommended that a complete new spring should be fitted.

The rubber bushes should be examined for damage or deterioration and, if necessary, renewed. They may be pressed out of the spring eyes or frame for replacement.

If a new front eccentric front eye bush is to be fitted it is essential that when in position the pivot pin location is at the top of the eye. A tolerance of $\pm \frac{1}{32}$ inch (.8 mm) must not be exceeded. In order to ensure this setting the spring should be marked as shown at A in FIG 7:10 before fitting.

7:9 Dampers. Description and maintenance
Alpine I and II

The suspension on these cars is controlled by Armstrong lever type hydraulic units which require no adjustment and normally no fluid replenishment. However, if for any reason it appears that topping up may be necessary, the instructions for this operation are given below. The unit must be removed from the car.

To test the operation of the damper secure it in a vice, holding it by the fixing lugs, and work the arm up and

down seven or eight times to expel any air which may be present.

Move the arm up and down through one complete stroke and note the resistance. It should be moderate throughout. If it is erratic or any free movement is felt it may indicate a lack of fluid. If the addition of fluid makes no improvement a new damper should be fitted.

Too much resistance suggests a broken internal part or a siezed piston which also indicates a replacement unit. No attempt should be made to dismantle the damper.

When topping up first clean the casing, particularly in the vicinity of the filler orifice which is sealed by the hexagon headed plug in the centre of the top cover. Use only Armstrong Shock Absorber fluid No. 624. Fill the body up to the bottom of the filling orifice at the same time working the arm up and down to expel any air.

The Armstrong damper is shown in section in FIG 7:11.

After refitting the damper and before connecting the link the unit should be finally primed to ensure that no air remains.

Rapier:

Girling telescopic Dampers are fitted to these cars and they are completely sealed. Apart from periodically inspecting the mountings and the rubber bushes no servicing of any kind is required and none is provided for. In the evnt of a damper requiring attention the faulty unit should be removed and a replacement fitted.

If a damper does not appear to be functioning correctly an indication of its resistance can be obtained from the

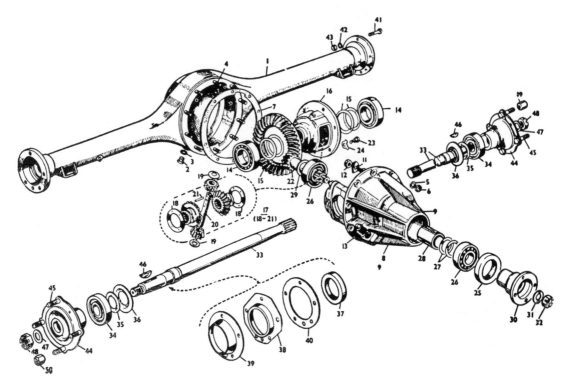

FIG 7:14 Exploded view of rear axle. Spiral bevel drive

following test:

Remove the damper from its mounting and clamp it vertically in a vice, gripping the lower spindle between two pieces of wood. Holding the top half of the casing with the hands work it up and down several times to expel the air, then move it slowly through one complete cycle and not the resistance. It should be moderate and even throughout both strokes. If the resistance is only light or erratic the unit is faulty and should be exchanged.

This type of damper is shown diagrammatically in **FIG 7:12**.

Alpine III:

The dampers are very similar to the type fitted to Rapier cars and the information given above applies also to these.

7:10 Rear axle. Spiral bevel drive

Some Rapier cars are fitted with a rear axle incorporating a spiral bevel final drive, which is illustrated in section in **FIG 7:13** and in exploded view in **FIG 7:14**.

It will be seen that the differences from the hypoid drive axle are few and are in that portion of the assembly which the owner-driver has been advised not to attempt to dismantle himself.

7:1 Fault diagnosis

(a) Noisy axle

1 Insufficient or incorrect lubricant
2 Worn bearings
3 Worn gears

(b) Excessive backlash

1 Worn gears, bearings or bearing housings
2 Worn axle shaft splines
3 Worn universal joints
4 Loose or broken wheel studs
5 Worn hub splines on wire wheels

(c) Oil leakage

1 Defective seals in hub
2 Defective pinion shaft seal
3 Defective seals on universal joint spiders

(d) Vibration

1 Propeller shaft out of balance
2 Worn universal joint bearings

(e) Rattles

1 Rubber bushes in damper links worn
2 Dampers loose
3 Spring U-bolts loose
4 Loose spring clips or damaged rubber liners
5 Worn bushes in spring eyes and shackles
6 Broken spring leaves

(f) 'Settling'

1 Weak or broken spring leaves
2 Badly worn shackle pins and bushes
3 Loose spring anchorages

CHAPTER 8

FRONT SUSPENSION AND HUBS

8:1 Description

The front suspension on both Rapier and Alpine cars is of the unequal length wishbone type, with coil springs and telescopic hydraulic damper control and is shown in the sectioned illustration (see FIG 8:1).

Long inner fulcrum pins are employed which are threaded at each end to carry the bushes of the upper and lower links. It is by the insertion of shims between the upper fulcrum pin and its bracket on the crossmember that the camber angle is adjusted.

The stub axle is located by means of a ball and socket on to the outer end of the upper link, and by a short swivel pin into a trunnion which is connected to the lower link by an eyebolt. Thrust is taken by way of a nut and thrust washer to the lower face of the grub axle swivel.

On early models a grease nipple is provided for the lubrication of such parts as the swivel pins and the trunnion and fulcrum pin joints, but these are discontinued on later models when self-lubricated bearings or bonded rubber bushes are used.

Maintenance consists or regular greasing of these few nipples on the earlier models and the periodic removal of the hubs for packing with grease and checking of the bearing end float.

8:2 Front hubs

Removal and dismantling:

Slacken the road wheel nuts (see FIG 8:2), jack-up the front end of the car and support it with suitable stands under the front crossmember. Remove the road wheel.

When removing centre lock wheels note the condition of the rubber sealing ring just inside the spline. This ring is to prevent lubricant from reaching the brake disc.

Remove the disc caliper as described in **Chapter 10.** Remove the hub cap 2 the splitpin and the hub retaining nut 3 and the large plain washer 4.

Withdraw the hub from the stub axle 6 at the same time catching the bearing cage of the outer taper bearing 7. Remove the cage of the inner taper bearing 8 and the seal 10. The outer shells of the hub bearings may now be tapped out of the hub using a suitable drift for the purpose.

Note that on Alpine cars the hub distance piece 11 is a press fit on the stub axle. On Rapier cars it is loose and may be removed.

To reassemble and refit:

Press the outer shells of each of the two taper bearings into the hub—in each case the larger internal diameter is towards the outside of its respective end of the hub.

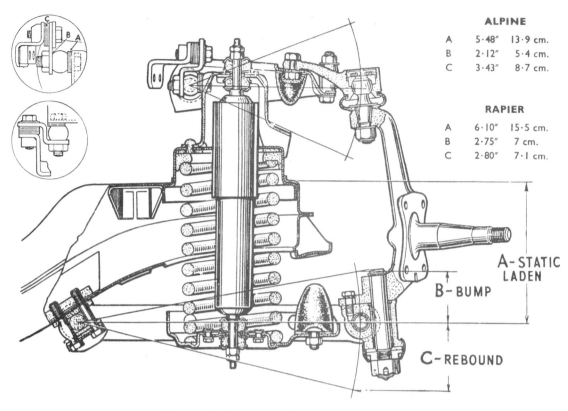

A - STATIC LADEN

B - BUMP

C - REBOUND

FIG 8:1 Sectional view of front suspension. Near side

Pack the hub and bearings with the correct grade of grease. The amount required is one capful distributed as shown in **FIG 8 : 3**. Note that the hub cap when fitted should not contain grease.

Refit the hub to the stub axle. Replace the hub outer bearing roller race, washer and retaining nut. Adjust the bearings as follows:

Tighten the hub to a torque reading of 15 to 20 lb ft then release the nut by one and a half flats in order to provide the necessary end float and to line up one of the splitpin holes in the stub axle with the slots in the nut.

Check the hub end float with a dial test indicator and if it is outside the permitted figures of .002 to .007 inch (.05 to .018 mm) the nut must be further adjusted until correct. Lock the nut with a new splitpin of the correct diameter.

Tap the hub cap firmly into position.

Refit the disc brake caliper and bleed the system.

Refit the road wheel.

8 : 3 Stub axle assembly

To remove :

It is first necessary to remove the damper 12 (see **FIG 8 : 2**), as follows: Load the vehicle to compress the springs and to avoid strain on the damper and its mountings. Remove the two nuts 13 on the upper spindle mounting and remove the rubber bush and cup washers 14. Slacken off the two nuts at the lower mounting.

Remove the nuts around the lower plate 16 and lift it to clear the studs, rotate it through 90 deg. and withdraw downwards complete with the damper, rubber bush and cup washers 17.

Jack-up the car and remove the road wheel.

Undo the bolts securing the steering arm, brake caliper and dust shield, noting the position of any shims. Remove the hub assembly from the stub axle. Using the spring compressor (special tool No. RG.50.D) inserted inside the coil spring, compress the spring sufficiently to release the upper and lower links. Remove the splitpin and nut 18 the adjusting nut 19 and thrust washers 20 from the lower swivel pin. Remove the nut and washer 22 securing the upper swivel assembly. Remove the upper swivel assembly 21 from the stub axle.

Lift out the stub axle and the swivel pin from the lower link. The upper swivel pin is left on the link, but may be removed if desired by removing the rebound rubber and unscrewing the three nuts and bolts which secure it to the upper link.

Dismantling. Swivel pin bush :

Remove the lower link eye bolt 25 from nuts 18 and 19 and the thrust washers 20 from the bottom of the swivel pin 47. Remove the trunnion 26 from the stub axle. Press out the bush 27 from the trunnion.

The new bush should be pressed into position, using the necessary parts of tool kit RG.194 if desired, until the bottom edge is .38 inch (9.65 mm) from the thrust face on

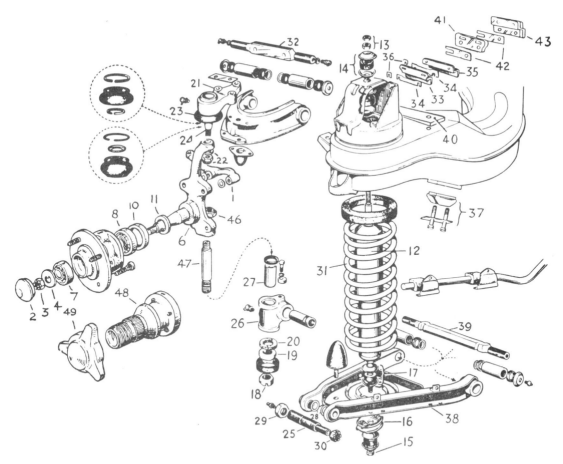

FIG 8:2 Exploded view showing components

the trunnion and the hole in line with the grease nipple tapping.

Lower eye bolt and bush:

If it is required to renew the bush the old bush must be pressed out towards the front of the car and the new bush inserted from the rear with the knurled portion to the rear.

Before fitting the lower eye bolt the two sealing rings 28 (renewed if necessary) should be placed on the bosses of the trunnion and slid into position later. The eye bolt is screwed in from the rear until its shoulder butts firmly against the front inner face of the link. Securely fit the locknut 29 and then the castellated nut 30 and tighten to 85 and 40 lb ft respectively. When the slots do not line up with the splitpin hole **tighten up** to the next mating position.

Swivel pin:

Should it become desirable to renew the swivel pin it is recommended that the work be taken to a service station where the special equipment required will be available.

Top link:

Remove the damper as already described. Jack-up the car and support it on stands placed under each side member of the frame. Remove the road wheel.

Compress the spring 31 and remove the upper swivel 21 from the axle carrier 6. Remove four bolts and washers to free the top link together with the fulcrum pin bracket and shims 41 and 42 from between the crossmember, fulcrum pin and under frame. Note carefully the position of the shims.

On Series IV cars the fulcrum pin bracket is not used and only two bolts, those securing the fulcrum pin to the crossmember, need to be removed.

Refitting is the reverse of the above procedure and must be followed by checking the various angles of the steering geometry.

Bottom link:

Remove the damper, jack-up the front of the car and place stands under the sidemembers. Remove the road wheel.

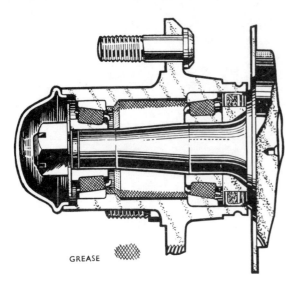

FIG 8:3   Section of hub showing packing of grease

GREASE

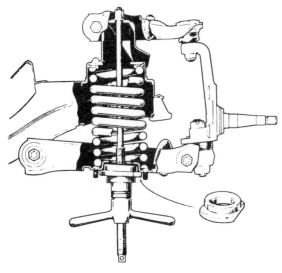

FIG 8:4   Spring compressor in use

Compress the spring and remove the lower link eye bolt 25. Disconnect the anti-roll or stabilizer bar and remove the four bolts securing the bottom link fulcrum pin 39 to the crossmember.

Carefully release the spring compressor until both the road spring and the bottom link 38 can be removed.

Refitting the bottom link is the reverse of the above, but note: Ensure that the rubber insulating ring is correctly located at the top of the road spring when refitting.

Compress the spring until the fulcrum pin can be bolted to the crossmember and tighten the bolts to a torque of 32 lb ft and using new lock washers.

Check that the sealing rings 28 are correctly located when the eye bolt is fitted.

It is advisable to use a smear of graphite to the bushes when fitting the anti-roll bar.

Refitting the stub axle :

Fit the sealing ring to the swivel pin 47 and insert the swivel pin into the trunnion 26. Refit the upper swivel assembly 21 into the upper end of the stub axle 6 and secure with the nut and washer 22.

On to the lower protruding portion of the swivel pin fit the thrust washer 20 and the adjusting nut 19 followed by the locking nut 18. By means of the adjusting nut set the end float to .015 to .018 inch (.38 to .46 mm) and lock it with the locking nut and fit a new splitpin. Fit the rubber seal over the adjusting nut and washer.

The spring compressor may now be removed. Refit the front hub assembly and set the hub end float as described earlier in **Section 8 : 2**. Fit the steering arm, the brake disc shield and the brake caliper, checking that the disc is running centrally within the caliper. Bleed the brake hydraulic system.

Fit the front wheel and remove the stands and jacks. Fit the damper.

8:4 Servicing the springs

To remove :

Remove the front damper as described in **Section 8 : 3** above.

Jack-up the front of the car and support it on stands placed under the side frame members. Remove the road wheel.

Using the spring compressor (Tool No. RG.50.D) or any other suitable tool compress the spring 31 and remove the lower link eye bolt 25. Disconnect the anti-roll bar and remove the four bolts securing the bottom link fulcrum pin 39 to the crossmember.

Release the spring compressor gradually until the spring and the bottom link can be withdrawn.

Testing :

Road springs are normally tested either by comparing them side by side with a new spring and noting by the relative lengths if the old spring has weakened, or by measuring the length of the spring and comparing it with the standard dimension. The free length of the springs fitted to the various models under review will be found in Technical Data at the end of this manual.

A rough check on the condition of the front springs may be made in the following manner without removing them from the car:

Place a load of 300 lb (136 kg) evenly across the front compartment of the car and measure the height between the top fixing face of the crossmember and the centre of the grease nipple at the front end of the lower link eye bolt 25. This distance should be: **Alpine** 5.48 inch ± .125 inch (13.9 cm ± .32 cm) **Rapier** 6.10 inch ± .125 inch (15.5 cm ± .32 cm).

To refit :

The road springs are refitted by reversing the procedure for their removal from the car, but note the following points:

Ensure that the rubber insulating ring seen in **FIG 8 : 2** is correctly positioned when fitting the spring.

Compress the spring steadily until the fulcrum pin securing bolts can be fitted to the crossmember. Using new lock washers they should be tightened to a torque of 32 lb ft.

Make sure that the sealing rings 28 are correctly fitted when replacing the eye bolt.

8:5 Dampers

The front dampers employed in all cases are Armstrong Direct-acting hydraulic telescopic units, and they are similar to those fitted at the rear end of all cars except the early Alpine models.

Instructions for the removal of these dampers have already been given in the earlier **Section 8:3** and details of the testing procedure in **Chapter 7** will apply to these front dampers also. As already mentioned the dampers are not adjustable, nor is there any provision for topping up with the hydraulic fluid, and in the event of a damper developing a fault it will be necessary to remove it and fit a new one.

8:6 Suspension geometry

For the values of the angles included in the suspension geometry the operator is referred to Technical Data at the end of this book, and in the event of accidental damage to the front end of the car, or uneven or excessively rapid tyre wear these settings should be checked. Special equipment is necessary to carry out these checks and unless the operator is competent to use such equipment when available he is strongly advised to take the car to a service station.

Caster angle:

This is the backward tilt of the axle carrier pivot and is not adjustable, since it is built into the car and is likely to be affected only in the event of heavy accidental damage.

Caster angle will change with the loading of the vehicle and is greatest when the rear end is heavily loaded.

Camber angle:

This is the inclination of the road wheel from the vertical when viewed from the front and is adjustable by the addition or removal of shims at the positions shown in the insets to **FIG 8:1**.

On Rapier Series I cars having the cranked bracket the camber angle may be increased by removing shims from the road wheel side of the upper fulcrum pin 32 in **FIG 8:2** or decreased by adding shims as necessary to obtain the correct angle. Note that if shims are removed from the first position they should be refitted between the frame bracket 35 and the frame, and vice versa.

On Series II cars and later the camber angle is increased by moving shims from the position A to B. To decrease the camber angle remove the required number of shims from C and add to A. If shims are already fitted at B remove them as required and fit at A.

Swivel pin inclination:

This is the angle at which the swivel pin, kingpin or axle carrier centre line is inclined from the vertical when seen from the front of the car.

This angle is not separately adjustable and, unless the stub axle assembly is damaged, will be correct when the camber is correctly set.

Front wheel toe-in:

When viewed from vertically above it will be seen that the two front wheels are not parallel, but that the distance between them is less at the front than at the rear. This is known as toe-in and maintenance of the correct setting is most important to good steering and tyre wear.

Wheel lock angles:

The limits to which the front wheels may be turned from side to side in steering the car are set by small levers welded to the upper face of each bottom link near its outer end and a lug cast in the base of each stub axle.

8:7 Modifications

There are some alterations to the front suspension unit as fitted to Series IV models which are designed to reduce the maintenance requirements of the system and to cut down the transmission of road noises to the interior of the car.

By using metal and rubber bonded bushes on the top and bottom links and pre-packed bearings on the swivels and track rods all lubrication nipples have been eliminated and the only components requiring lubrication are the front hubs, which should be removed, cleaned and re-packed with grease and the end float as previously described, and at the intervals stated in the Owners Handbook.

(a) Wheel wobble

1 Worn hub bearings
2 Broken or weak front springs
3 Unevenly worn tyres
4 Worn suspension linkage
5 Loose wheel fixings

(b) 'Bottoming' of suspension

1 Check 2 in (a)
2 Rebound rubbers worn or missing
3 Dampers not working

(c) Heavy Steering

1 Neglected swivel pin inclination
2 Wrong suspension geometry

(b) Excessive tyre wear

1 Check 4 in (a); 3 in (b) and 2 in (c)

(e) Rattles

1 Check 2 in (a)
2 Neglected pivot lubrication. Worn rubber bushes
3 Loose damper mountings
4 Anti-roll bar mountings loose or worn

(f) Excessive rolling

1 Check 2 in (a) and 3 in (b)
2 Anti-roll bar broken or loose

CHAPTER 9

THE STEERING GEAR

9:1 Burman P type. Rapier Series I. Description

This early type of steering unit operates on the worm and nut principle and is shown in section in **FIG 9:1**. It will be seen that the nut is part of a long tube having a socket assembly incorporated at the lower end, and supported at the upper end by a brass bush and seal. The ball peg of the socket assembly is a tapering fit in the rocker arm.

The axial movement of the tubular sleeve is converted to a rotary movement of the rocker shaft, which is splined to the swing lever at its lower end, and thence by way of the track rods to the road wheels.

Two grease nipples are provided for the periodic lubrication of the rocker shaft bearings and of the worm and ball peg.

9:2 Removing gearbox

Jack up the car and remove the road wheel adjacent to the steering unit. Disconnect the track rods from the swing lever.

Disconnect the battery. Withdraw the horn ring after loosening the three screws round the hub of the steering wheel. Remove the steering wheel.

Take out the screw on the right of the steering column cowling and remove the warning light panel. Disconnect the electric connectors behind the panel.

The lefthand side of the cowling is removed after taking out two screws, and the righthand portion may then be eased away from the trafficator switch which is then removed.

Release the parcel tray adjacent to the hanger clip on the steering column. Disconnect the gearchange linkage at the lower end of the column and move the lever and shaft up into the car.

Remove the reverse light switch and bracket. Take the clip from the hanger on the dash panel.

Remove the bolts holding the steering column to the underframe sidemember. Remove the drivers seat. Raise the lower end of the steering column and pull out the assembly forwards and upwards.

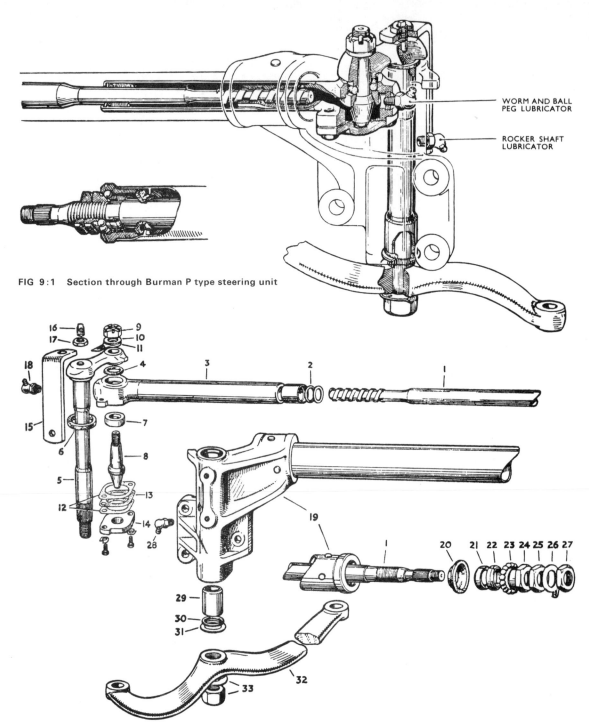

FIG 9:1   Section through Burman P type steering unit

WORM AND BALL PEG LUBRICATOR

ROCKER SHAFT LUBRICATOR

FIG 9:2   Exploded view of Burman P type steering unit

Key to Fig 9:2   1 Inner column   2 Seal   3 Sleeve assembly   4 Seal   5 Rocker shaft   6 Felt seal
7 Ball peg bush   8 Ball peg   9 Nut   10 Washer   11 'Oil only' tab   12 Joint   13 Shim   14 Baseplate
15 Adjustment bracket   16 Adjusting screw   17 Locknut   18 Greaser   19 Main casing   20 Seal
21 Collar   22 Lower track   23 Balls   24 Adjusting nut   25 Locknut   26 Trafficator cancelling ring
27 Locknut   28 Greaser   29 Bush   30 Seal   31 Backing washer   32 Swing lever   33 Nut and washer

Refitting is the reverse of the above with particular attention to the following points:

Do not tighten the facia bracket bolts until the lower fixing bolts are secure. This will ensure that there is no strain on the assembly.

The rocker shaft and swing lever are marked for correct reassembly.

Turn the steering into the straight-ahead position before refitting the rubber-bushed joints on the track rods.

9:3 Dismantling (see FIG 9:2)

Release the lockwasher and nut 33 securing the swing lever 32 to the rocker shaft 5 and remove. Remove the rocker shaft adjustment bracket 15 from the steering box.

Remove the splitpin and nut 9 from the ball peg assembly. Remove the baseplate 14, shims 13 and paper washers 12, noting carefully the quantity of each.

Using a suitable tool press out the ball peg 8 as shown in FIG 9:3. Withdraw the rocker shaft 5. Unscrew the sleeve 3 from the inner column 1. Remove the locknut 25 and the adjusting nut 24 from the inner column and take out the sixteen balls 23. Pull out the inner column from the outer casing.

9:4 Reassembling

Insert the inner column into the outer casing ensuring that the collar 21 and the inner cone 22 are fitted with the steeper side of the inner cone facing down the column. Apply a small quantity of grease and insert the sixteen balls and screw in the adjusting nut by hand. Refit the lower sleeve over the inner column worm. Fit the rocker shaft into the socket assembly. Fit the baseplate, shims and washers.

The cone bearing at the upper end of the inner column is adjusted by slackening the locknut and turning the adjusting nut until end float is removed and the column can just be turned by hand.

Using a new felt washer 7 fit the rocker shaft arm on to the peg. Refit the washer, nut and splitpin.

Refit the swing lever together with nut and washer.

The rocker shaft end float is adjusted by the screw 16 and locknut 17 on top of the adjustment bracket 15. Slacken the locknut and turn the screw clockwise to give a slight preload to compress fully the felt washer then retighten the locknut.

The remainder of the reassembly follows the dismantling procedure in reverse.

9:5 Burman F type. Rapier Series II and later. Alpine

Description and maintenance:

The type of steering gear fitted to all these models is the recirculating ball system which is illustrated in the exploded view given in FIG 9:4 and by the sectional drawings in FIG 9:5.

The steering gearbox is connected to the steering wheel through either a fixed or a telescopic column in a plastic cowling. The horn is operated by a horn ring in the centre of the steering wheel.

Reference to FIG 9:4 will assist in following the description of the operation of the system. The rotation of the steering wheel and with it the inner column and worm 23 moves the nut 14 through the recirculating balls

16. located within the nut. As the nut moves from side to side it causes the rocker shaft 13 to rotate and to turn the drop arm 19 which is splined to it, and so actuate the movement of the road wheels by way of the track rods.

Should it be necessary to do so, the end float of the inner column may be adjusted by means of the shims 4 and the end float of the rocker shaft by means of the shims shown at 5. This will be mentioned in Section 9:8. The double coil springs 10 and the damper 11 are fitted to reduce the transmission of road shocks to the rocker shaft and thence to the steering wheel.

Maintenance consists of regular attention to the level of the oil in the gearbox which should be examined every 3000 miles (5000 km) and, if necessary, topped up to the bottom of the filler orifice, taking care that the rubber filler plug is firmly replaced. At the same time the steering joints and the swivel bearings should be examined for wear and for damage to the seals.

At 6000 miles (10,000 km) the system should be checked for any looseness in the nuts and bolts.

9:6 Removing the steering gearbox

Before the gearbox can be removed it is necessary to remove certain other components and it will be convenient to deal with these first and in order.

Steering column cowling:

This is made of plastic and is in two halves clipped or screwed together and located on the steering column by dowels.

Alpine. The cowling is removed by a sharp pull on the offside of the cowling to release the securing clips and then on the near side half and manipulating it clear of the indicator switch.

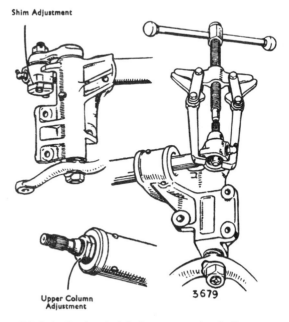

Shim Adjustment

Upper Column Adjustment

3679

FIG 9:3 Rocker shaft ball peg removal and adjustment points

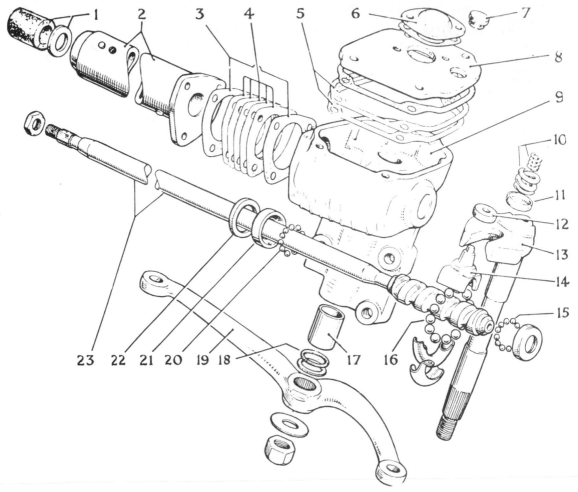

FIG 9:4   Exploded view of the steering gearbox

Key to Fig 9:4   1 Felt bush and washer   2 Outer column   3 Paper gaskets   4 Shims   5 Shims
6 Spring cap   7 Filler plug   8 Top cover   9 Steering box   10 Double coil spring   11 Damper button
12 Guide roller   13 Rocker shaft   14 Nut   15 Steel balls (lower track)   16 Steel balls (nut)
17 Rocker shaft bush   18 Oil seal   19 Drop arm   20 Steel balls (upper track)   21 Upper track
22 Distance piece   23 Inner column and worm

Rapier. Remove the two clamping screws, split the two halves of the cowling, and withdraw it clear of the indicator switch.

Refitting in each case is the reverse of the removal procedure, taking care that the halves fit together accurately and that the direction indicator lever is not obstructed.

Direction indicator switch:

This is removed after disconnecting the battery and removing the cowling as described above. Mark the position of the switch on the steering column for correct reassembly and withdraw the clamping screws from the securing clip. Disconnect the wiring at the snap connectors under the facia panel.

To refit:

Locate the switch on the raised keyway on the column and position it so that the panel of the striker ring engages fully with the trip mechanism without fouling the cowling when fitted. Replace the snap connectors. Reconnect the battery.

Overdrive switch:

Alpine. The overdrive switch is mounted on the offside half of the steering column cowling and will be removed with it.

Rapier. The switch is mounted on the offside of the steering column by means of a clip and is removed similarly to the direction indicator switch.

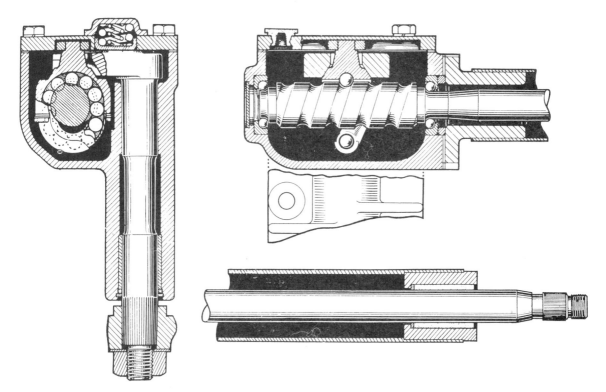

FIG 9:5 Sectional view of steering gearbox

Horn ring assembly:

This is removed after disconnecting the battery by unscrewing the three grub screws recessed into the steering wheel boss. Lift up the horn ring assembly, withdraw the snap connector from the socket inside the boss and remove.

Refitting is the reverse of the above, taking care to ensure that the lower contact plate of the horn ring assembly is correctly located over the key inside the steering wheel boss.

Steering wheel:

After removing the horn ring assembly, release the centre securing nut. Mark the position of the steering wheel boss for correct refitting and lift it off.

Reverse this procedure for refitting. With the road wheels in the straight-ahead position the steering wheel spokes should be horizontal.

Steering gearbox:

To remove:

Alpine. Remove the bonnet which is attached to its hinges by eight bolts. Disconnect the battery. Remove the column cowling, the direction indicator switch and the striker ring from the inner column. Remove the overdrive switch if fitted, the horn ring assembly and the steering wheel.

Remove the bolts securing the righthand side scuttle bracing tube to the bulkhead and the forward mounting.

Take out the dipstick. Remove the distributor from the engine (see **Chapter 3, Section 3:3**). Disconnect the tachometer drive from the engine. Remove the fuel pump (see **Chapter 2, Section 2:3**). Drain off the oil and remove the oil filter element and casing.

Disconnect the steering column hanger clip from the hanger on the bulkhead.

Jack-up the front of the car and remove the nut and washer securing the drop arm 19 to the rocker shaft 13 which should be marked to ensure correct reassembly. Slacken off the three bolts which secure the steering unit to the front sidemember and remove the drop arm from its splines on the rocker shaft. (Tool No. RG.198 is available if required). Lower the jack.

Remove the facia crash padding which is bolted to the underside of the facia and to the steering column bracket. Remove the bolts securing the steering column to the upper bracket under the facia. Remove the facia reinforcement which is held by two spire fixings and two nuts at each end.

Withdraw now the three bolts securing the gearbox to the front sidemember and lower the upper end of the steering column clear of the facia panel. Remove the grommet from the hole in the bulkhead. Ease the steering gearbox forward until it is just behind the header tank then turn it through 180 deg tilt upwards and withdraw it through the bonnet aperture.

Rapier. Disconnect the battery. Remove the steering column cowling, the direction indicator switch and the striker ring, the overdrive switch when fitted, and the steering wheel and horn ring.

Loosen the parcel tray on the driver's side and drop it clear of the steering column.

Jack-up the front of the car and remove the nut and washer securing the drop arm to the rocker shaft. Loosen the three bolts securing the steering gearbox to the front sidemember, and, with special tool RG.198 if required, remove the drop arm. Lower the jack.

Disconnect the steering column support clip from the upper column bracket. Move the front seat as far back as possible and loosen the bolts securing the clutch and brake master cylinders to the bulkhead. Withdraw the three bolts securing the gearbox to the sidemember.

Lower the upper end of the steering column and remove the grommet from the bulkhead. Raise the gearbox, twist it sideways and draw it out through the bonnet aperture.

9:7 Dismantling the gearbox

Having removed the assembly from the car, refer to **FIG 9:4**, clean the outside of the unit and remove the spring 6 springs 10 and the damper 11.

Unscrew the bolts securing the top cover 8 and remove it together with the joints and shims 5. Drain off the oil from the box.

Remove the guide roller 12 from the nut 14. Withdraw the rocker shaft 13. Unscrew the three bolts securing the outer column 2 to the steering box 9 and lift off together with the paper gaskets 3 shims 4 and the distance piece 22.

Unscrew the inner column 23 from the nut 14 and withdraw, catching the twelve balls 20 from the upper track 21 which will now be released. Lift out the nut assembly and remove the balls 16. Remove the twelve balls 15 from the lower track.

If necessary the top bush 1 and the rocker shaft bush 17 may be removed and renewed.

9:8 To reassemble the gearbox

Insert the balls 15 into the lower bearing track, and the balls 16 into the channel of the nut 14. This will be greatly assisted by first smearing the surfaces with grease.

Insert the nut assembly through the cover plate aperture and hold it in position while the inner steering column is passed through the top hole of the box and screwed into the nut. Gently lower the shaft onto the lower bearing in its location.

After smearing the upper bearing track 21 with grease, slide it over the inner column, insert the twelve balls 20 and position it in the top aperture of the box. Slide down the distance piece 22 and the outer column 2 which should be loosely bolted to the steering box.

Refit the rocker shaft 13 locating the arm over the spigot of the nut assembly and place the guide roller 12 in position.

Measure the gap between the bottom face of the outer column and the upper face of the steering box with a feeler gauge. Remove the three bolts and carefully withdraw the outer column and refit it together with a quantity of shims 4 equal in thickness to the gap just measured less .0015 inch (.038 mm) and the thickness of the paper gaskets 3 which are as follows:
K.29826 .002 inch (.051 mm).
K.21724 .005 inch (.127 mm).

This operation applies the pre-loading to the inner column bearings.

The following procedure sets and is used to adjust the rocker shaft end float:

Fit the top cover 8 together with a small number of shims 5 and the two paper gaskets. With the spring cap 6 removed measure the gap between the rocker shaft and the top cover with either a feeler gauge or a dial test indicator. With the steering in the straight ahead position the clearance should be .004 to .008 inch (.10 to .20 mm). Remove the top cover and by the removal or addition of extra shims adjust until the required clearance is obtained.

Fit the damper button 11 the coil springs 10 and secure the spring cap with the two bolts and washers.

Fill the gearbox with the recommended grade of oil and replace the filler plug 7. The steering unit is now ready to be refitted to the car.

9:9 Refitting

Alpine:

Holding the whole assembly in a horizontal attitude place the splined end of the steering column in the hole in the bulkhead and twist the assembly until it is upside down i.e. the rocker shaft is pointing upwards. Push the column through the hole until the gearbox is clear of the radiator header tank then rotate it through 180 deg into its normal position. Refit the grommet into the hole in the bulkhead.

Attach the steering column loosely to the dash and bulkhead brackets and bolt the gearbox to the front sidemember. Check the alignment of the steering column clip relative to the upper column bracket. Should there be any misalignment it will be necessary to unbolt the steering box from the sidemember and refit it with packing washers to the extent required to bring the clip into alignment with the bracket. It is most important that there should be no strain or tension in the assembly when the nuts and bolts are finally tightened which may now be done.

Jack-up the car while refitting the drop arm onto the correct splines on the rocker shaft. Use a new locking washer when fitting the nut.

Reft the facia reinforcement and the column securing bracket under the facia. The steering wheel, electrical switch gear and the steering column cowling should be refitted in the reverse order to which they were removed.

Replace the oil filter, the fuel pump and the distributor, etc. Reconnect the battery. Refit the tachometer drive. Test.

Rapier:

With the steering box held in the inverted position insert the splined end of the steering column into the hole in the bulkhead and push inwards until the steering box is clear of the bonnet aperture. Twist the assembly until the gearbox is in its correct attitude when it should be lowered and the bolts which secure it to the sidemember inserted.

Check the alignment of the support clip with the upper steering column bracket, and if there is any misalignment which would cause any strain when the two are bolted together the box must be unbolted from the sidemember and packing washers inserted to the required thickness to bring the parts correctly together. Replace the grommet in the hole in the bulkhead.

Jack-up the front of the car and fit the drop arm to the splines on the rocker shaft. Secure it with the nut and a new washer.

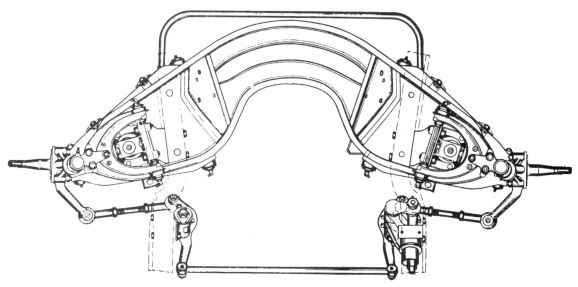

FIG 9:6 Plan view of steering linkage

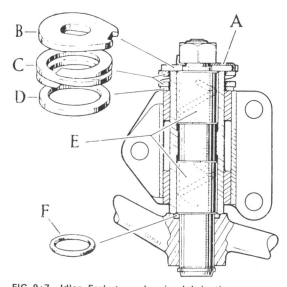

FIG 9:7 Idler. Early type showing lubrication grooves

Key to Fig 9:7   **A** Tab washer   **B** Thrust washer
C Spring   **D** Washer   **E** Bush bearings   **F** Sealing ring

Tighten the bolts securing the brake and the clutch master cylinders to the bulkhead.

Refit the steering wheel, the steering column cowling, the horn ring, etc. in the reverse order to their removal.

Reconnect the battery and test.

9:10 Servicing the idler

The idler, or steering relay, is fitted on the opposite side of the car to the steering gearbox and transmits the steering motion to the wheel farthest from the steering box i.e. the lefthand wheel in the case of righthand drive cars (see **FIG 9:6**).

The rear end of the idler lever is connected across the car to the rear end of the drop arm on the steering box, while the front end of the lever arm couples up with the lefthand front wheel through a short track rod. It will be seen that this track rod is directly comparable to that on the righthand side and that both rods are adjustable for length. It is by the adjustment of these rods that the track or toe-in of the front wheels is set.

FIG 9:7 shows a cross-section through the idler assembly used on Series I to IIIA models and fitted with a grease nipple for periodic lubrication. This type of idler was followed by the type shown in **FIG 9:8** for Series IV models and onwards .It will be seen that by the use of self-lubricating washers the need for maintenance has been removed.

The idler assembly is attached to the front sidemember of the frame by three bolts and nuts. Undo these to remove the idler after removing the outer and centre track rods from the front and rear ends of the idler lever.

To dismantle:

Early type (see **FIG 9:7**):

Before dismantling, the lever should be suitably marked to facilitate reassembly. Remove the nut, washers, and spring items A B C and D and withdraw the idler lever and shaft from the support bracket.

Remove the sealing ring F from the upper face of the lever and renew it if it is worn. Do not remove the lever from the shaft.

Later type (see **FIG 9:8**):

Remove the splitpin and nut at the top of the assembly and lift off the thrust washer A the sealing ring B the distance piece C the P.T.F.E. washer D and the bearing washer E.

Withdraw the idler lever and shaft from the support bracket and remove the bearing washer E the P.T.F.E. washer D the Belleville washer pack F and the sealing ring G from the upper face of the lever. Do not attempt to separate the lever from the shaft.

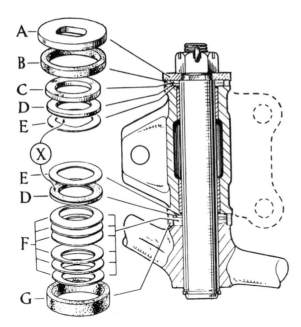

FIG 9:8 Idler. Later type showing method of assembling washers

Key to Fig 9:8   **A** Thrust washer   **B** Narrow sealing ring   **C** Distance piece   **D** P.T.F.E. washers   **E** Bearing washers   **F** Belleville washer pack   **G** Sealing ring   **X** shows P.T.F.E. surface

To reassemble. Early type:

This is the reverse of the dismantling procedure, but note: Ensure that the sealing ring F is in good condition and is correctly placed in the groove on the lever. When inserting the idler shaft into the bracket see that the shorter arm of the idler lever is nearer to the lower front securing bolt hole.

When finally assembled there should be .007 inch (.18 mm) end float when the nut is correctly fitted and locked.

Lubricate well before refitting.

Later type:

Reassembly is the reverse of the dismantling procedure, but attention must be paid to the following points:

Grease all parts well before refitting.

A new pack of Belleville washers should be fitted, and they are assembled into two packs of three each with the raised outside edges in contact as shown at F in **FIG 9:8**.

Note the direction of the P.T.F.E. surfaces on the washers D and the order of assembly of the other washers and rings.

The shaft is inserted into the support bracket so that the shorter arm of the lever is nearer to the front lower securing bolt hole.

Finally tighten the castellated nut to a torque of 60 lb ft and slacken off one and a half flats. If the splitpin hole is not in alignment with a slot slacken off to the first position for its insertion.

Idler bush bearings:

These are pressed into the support bracket and after the old bush have been removed a new bush is fitted as follows:

Early type. Insert the bush so that the ends having the start and finish of the lubrication groove are towards the grease nipple in the centre of the bracket and press until the outer ends of the bush are flush with the two end faces of the support bracket.

Later type. These are of the P.T.F.E. type needing no lubrication and should be carefully pressed into the support bracket until the outer ends are just below the end faces of the bracket.

Refitting the idler:

This is the reverse of the removal procedure. In order to avoid any unnecessary strain on the rubber bushes set the steering and relay levers in the straight-ahead position when fitting the centre track rod to the rear ends of both levers. Fit the new splitpins where applicable.

Check the front wheel alignment (see **Section 9:11**).

9:11 Adjusting track

As has already been stated in Chapter 8. Front suspension, the setting of the front end geometry should be carried out by a service station with the necessary equipment for accurate measurement according to the values given in Technical Data.

A fairly accurate check may be made by the following method:

Stand the car on level ground with the front wheels in the straight-ahead position and measure the distance between the wheel rims at the front and at wheel centre height. Roll the car forward for one half of a road wheel revolution, after marking the rim at the point of measurement, and measure the distance between the two rim markings which will now be on the back of the wheel.

The toe-in i.e. the distance by which the first measurement is less than the second, should be $\frac{1}{8}$ inch and it is necessary to adjust the two outer track rods equally to obtain this figure. Slacken off the lock nuts at each end of each track rod and rotate each rod as necessary. Tighten the locknuts and re-check the setting as before (see **FIG 9:6**).

9:12 Telescopic steering unit

Some later models are fitted with a Burman telescopic steering unit which is similar to the standard unit apart from the necessary changes at the steering wheel location. This steering wheel assembly is shown sectionally in **FIG 9:9** which illustrates the internal construction and the operation of the unit.

Cowling:

The steering column cowling is made in two halves. An upper section secured to the steering column by a clip and four screws and a lower section attached to the upper with three screws.

Removal is effected by withdrawing the three screws from the lower portion of the cowling and then the four screws and the clip from the upper half.

When refitting note that the upper section is located by a dowel inserted into a hole in the outer steering column,

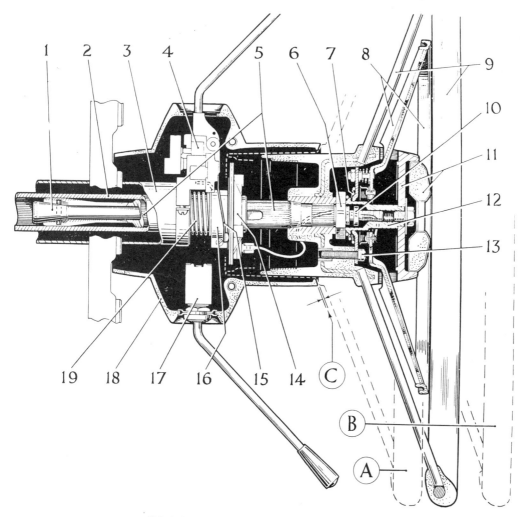

FIG 9:9 Sectional view of telescopic steering column

Key to Fig 9:9   1 Expander bolt   2 Inner column   3 Outer column   4 Direction indicator switch
5 Splined extension piece   6 Steering wheel nut   7 Conical spring   8 Horn ring
9 Steering wheel   10 Split nylon bush   11 Steering wheel adjusting nut and motif
12 Expander bolt extension   13 Screw, horn ring assembly to steering wheel   14 Slip ring   15 Leaf spring
16 Striker ring   17 Overdrive switch   18 Steering column cowling   19 Column bearing spring
A Lower position of steering wheel   **B** Upper position of steering wheel   **C** .050 inch (1 mm) clearance

and that the clip is fitted with the spire nut towards the front of the car.

The overdrive switch, or in its absence a blank, should be located between the two cowling halves before the lower half is fitted.

Note the gap of .050 inch at C between the top edge of the cowling and the steering wheel centre when in its lowest position.

The location of the overdrive and the direction indicator switches may be seen in **FIG 9:9** and before removing the latter its position should be marked to ensure correct replacement.

Horn ring assembly:

This differs from the earlier type and is removed for servicing as follows:

Disconnect the battery and lift the steering wheel to its limit position. Remove the lower cowling and pull off the electrical connector from the slipring 14. Prise off the motif from the adjusting nut 11 which may be withdrawn after removing the retaining nut and washer. The horn ring 8 may now be withdrawn after removing the three screws 13 and washers.

When refitting make sure that the split nylon bush 10 is at the bottom of the thread on the expander bolt 1.

Remove the expander bolt extension 12 and withdraw the conical spring 7. Unscrew the nut 6 and after marking the position of the wheel centre 9 on the splined extension the wheel may be lifted off.

The steering wheel is refitted by reversing the above. Set the front wheels in the straight-ahead position and fit the steering wheel so that the two spokes are horizontal.

The conical spring 7 is fitted small end downward on top of the steering wheel nut 6 before the expander bolt extension is fitted. Smear lightly with grease.

9:13 Fault diagnosis

(a) Wheel wobble

1 Unbalanced wheels and tyres
2 Slack steering connections
3 Incorrect steering geometry
4 Excessive play in steering gear
5 Broken or weak front springs
6 Worn hub bearings

(b) Wander

1 Check 2, 3 and 4 in (a)

2 Front suspension and rear axle mounting points out of line
3 Uneven tyre pressures
4 Uneven tyre wear
5 Weak springs or dampers

(c) Heavy steering

1 Check 3 in (a)
2 Very low tyre pressures
3 Neglected lubrication
4 Wheels out of track
5 Steering gear mal-adjusted
6 Steering column bent or misaligned
7 Steering column bushes tight

(d) Lost motion

1 End play in steering column
2 Loose steering wheel or worn splines
3 Worn steering box and idler
4 Worn ball joints
5 Worn suspension system and swivel axle

CHAPTER 10

THE BRAKING SYSTEM

10:1 Description

Hydraulically operated braking systems are employed on all cars covered by this manual, with all four wheels being served by the foot pedal and the rear wheels only by an independent mechanical system operated by the handbrake lever.

All the models in the Alpine range are fitted with braking systems manufactured by Girling, in which disc-type brakes are used on the front wheels and drum brakes with one leading and one trailing shoe on the rear wheels. In all cases the foot pedal pressure is augmented by a vacuum servo unit coupled to the inlet manifold. Servo assistance, therefore, is available only when the engine is running.

Lockheed equipment is fitted to all the Rapier models, of which Series III, IIIA and IV have an arrangement similar to that used on the Alpine models described above, and it will be convenient to deal with these types in full before describing the simpler system employed on Rapier Series I and II.

Alpine Girling brakes:

10:2 Maintenance and adjustment

The only hydraulic fluid that may be used in this system is Girling Brake Fluid SAE.70.R.3 and the level in the master cylinder reservoir should be checked periodically and the level maintained to within $\frac{1}{2}$ inch of the filler cap orifice.

At all times when working on any part of the braking system strict cleanliness is most important, and before removing the filler cap to top up the reservoir the area around the cap should be cleaned to avoid the possibility of any foreign matter finding its way into the fluid.

The front brakes are entirely self-adjusting and require no maintenance other than an occasional check on the thickness of the friction pads. These must be renewed when worn to a thickness of $\frac{1}{16}$ inch (1.6 mm).

Rear brakes are adjusted as follows: With chocks under the front wheels and the handbrake off jack-up one rear wheel.

Turn the adjuster at the rear of the brake backplate (See **FIG 10:1**) in a clockwise direction until solid resistance is felt, then slacken it back until the wheel may be rotated by hand. There may be a slight drag from the trailing shoe which can be ignored.

Spin the wheels and apply the brakes hard to centralize the shoes and recheck the setting. Repeat for the other rear wheel.

This adjustment of the rear brakes will automatically adjust the handbrake.

On series I and II cars there is a lubricator on the handbrake cable. An occasional drop of oil should be applied to any moving joints in the system.

The hydraulic hoses should be inspected from time to time and examined for leaks, chaffing or deterioration and any faulty piece should be renewed.

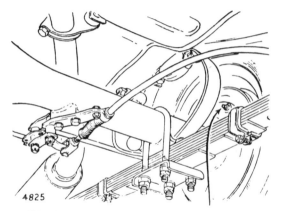

FIG 10:1   Rear brake adjuster and compensator

10:3 Master cylinder, removal

The master cylinder is situated on the forward side of the bulkhead immediately in front of the brake pedal to which it is attached by means of a clevis pin through the fork on the pushrod 13 in **FIG 10:2**. On righthand drive cars the fluid reservoir and the cylinder body are cast in one unit as shown and are connected by a drilling into the end of the pressure cylinder. On lefthand drive cars the fluid reservoir is mounted on the wing valance and connected to the cylinder by means of a pipe. See inset to **FIG 10:2**.

Remove the pressure pipe union—and the feed pipe on lefthand drive cars—collecting any spillage of fluid in a suitable container. Remove the clevis pin connecting the brake pedal to the pushrod. Release the two securing bolts and pull-out the master cylinder towards the front, noting any packing washers.

Refitting is the reverse of the above procedure, after which the hydraulic system must be bled as described later.

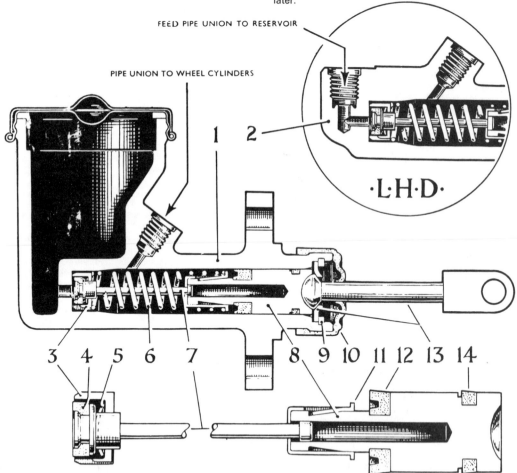

FIG 10:2   Sectional view of Girling master cylinder

Key to Fig 10:2   1 Cylinder body and reservoir (righthand drive)   2 Cylinder body (lefthand drive)   3 Valve spacer
4 Valve seal   5 Spring washer   6 Plunger return spring   7 Valve stem   8 Plunger   9 Circlip   10 Rubber dust cover
11 Thimble   12 Plunger seal   13 Pushrod and dished washer   14 Plunger seal

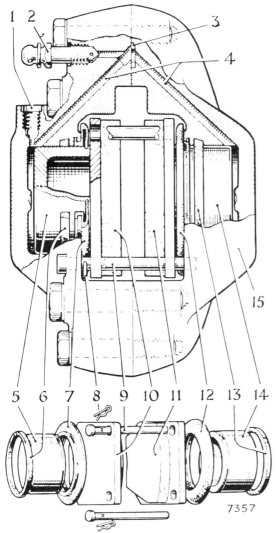

FIG 10:3 Exploded view of caliper assembly

Key to Fig 10:3   1 Flexible connection   2 Bleed screw
3 Fluid channel seal 4 Internal fluid channels 5 & 14 Pistons
6 & 13 Piston sealing rings 7 & 12 Dust covers 8 Retaining
clips   9 Retaining pins   10 & 11 Brake pads
15 Caliper body

10:4 Servicing the brakes, front

Pads, to remove and refit (see FIGS 10:3 and 10:4):

Apply the handbrake, jack-up the front of the car and
remove the road wheel.

Remove the two retaining pins 9 and withdraw the
brake pads and, if fitted, the anti-rattle springs and the
antisqueal shims.

When refitting, which is the reverse of the above, it
may first be necessary to siphon-off a small quantity of
brake fluid to prevent overflowing as the pistons are
pushed into their bores. If anti-squeal shims or anti-rattle
springs are to be fitted **FIG 10:4** illustrates the method

of their installation. The pad retaining pins 9 pass through
the slotted ends of the springs and the tongues bear
against the pad backing plates.

When shims and springs are both fitted to the same
caliper the outward end of the shim is cut off to accom-
modate the spring as shown in the inset.

Bleeding is not necessary, but give the brake pedal a
few pumps until solid resistance is felt.

Calipers, to remove and refit:

Apply the handbrake, jack-up the car and remove the
road wheel. Remove the hydraulic pressure pipe. Remove
the two securing bolts noting the position of any washers
or splash guard when fitted, and ensure that they are
replaced in the same positions.

When fitting replacement calipers to Series I and II
models the disc must be centred within the caliper to
within .025 inch (.64 mm). Any off centre must be
corrected by fitting shims between the caliper and the
stub axle carrier with an equivalent thickness of packing
washers between the front steering arm lug and the stub
axle carrier. On Series III models and onwards no washers
are necessary.

Bleed the system as described later.

To dismantle:

Having removed the caliper from the car clean the
exterior and remove the brake pads. Withdraw the pistons
5 and 14 and remove the dust covers 7 and 12. The
piston sealing rings 6 and 13 are removed by prizing them
out with a screwdriver taking great care not to damage the
grooves. If at all worn the rings should be renewed.

**Do not attempt to split the two halves of the
caliper.**

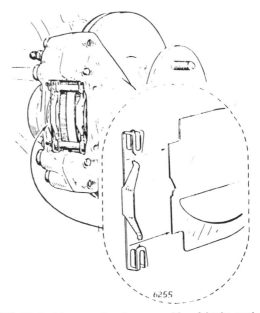

**FIG 10:4 Diagram showing assembly of brake anti-
rattle springs and anti-squeal shims**

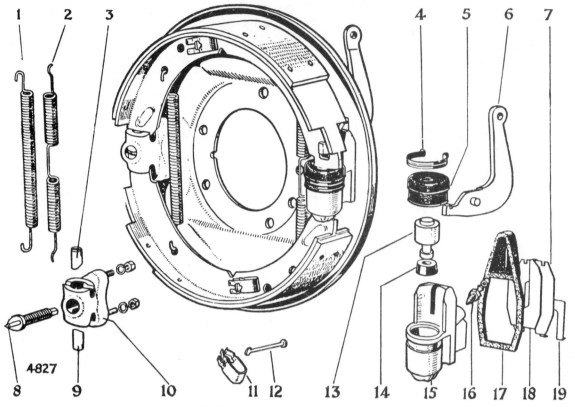

FIG 10:5   Exploded view of rear brake

Key to Fig 10:5
6 Handbrake lever   1 Return spring   2 Return spring   3 Adjuster link   4 Dust cover clip   5 Dust cover
12 Peg   13 Piston   7 Retaining plate   8 Wedge   9 Adjuster link   10 Adjuster housing   11 Leaf spring
19 Distance piece   14 Seal   15 Cylinder body   16 Bleed screw   17 Dust cover   18 Spring plate

To reassemble:

Clean all parts in brake fluid before assembly and note that petrol or any similar cleaning agent should never be used on the internal parts of hydraulic systems.

Refit the sealing rings in the larger grooves in the caliper bores. Fit the dust covers with the projecting lips inserted into the smaller grooves.

Insert the pistons, closed ends first, into the bores and fit the outer lips of the dust covers into the grooves in the pistons. Push the pistons to the ends of the bores and insert the brake pads.

Splash guards

These are fitted to protect the inner faces of the discs from foreign matter thrown up from the road.

Early Series I cars. After raising the car and removing the road wheel, withdraw the two bolts and remove the splashguard from the stub axle carrier.

Later Series I and II cars. First remove the caliper from the stub axle carrier and the hub assembly from the stub axle as already described. Split the distance piece with a cold chisel, remove the three nuts and washers and withdraw the splashguard.

Series III cars and onwards. After removing the caliper and the hub the splashguard is removed after unscrewing three nuts from the mounting brackets.

Refitting is the reverse of the above. In the case of the Series II cars it is necessary to heat the distance piece before pressing it on to the stub axle.

Reset the hub end float. Ensure that the guard does not foul the brake disc.

Discs, to remove and refit:

Remove the caliper and the hub assembly as previously described. Withdraw four securing bolts and remove the disc from the hub.

Before refitting clean the disc and inspect for damage or scoring and renew if not in good condition. The protective coat on a new disc should be removed before use.

Tighten the bolts to a torque of 38 lb ft but do not lock the tab washers, when used, until the disc runout has been checked. This should be measured about 1 inch from the outer edge of the disc and should not exceed .004 inch (.10 mm). Provided that the disc is not distorted it is normally possible to reposition it on the hub to obtain an acceptable figure.

Fit the hub and adjust the end float. Bleed the system.

Rear brakes (see FIG 10:5):

It will be seen that there is a single hydraulic cylinder operating the leading and trailing shoes from the foot pedal and which also includes the lever operated by rod and cable from the handbrake lever. The adjustment of the rear brakes has already been described in **Section 10:2**.

Brake shoes, to remove and refit:

Chock up the front wheels, jack-up the rear end of the car, remove the wheel and release the handbrake. Remove the countersunk screw and pull off the brake drum. It may here be necessary to warn the operator that on no account should any pressure be applied to the brake pedal after the drum has been removed, as to do so would cause ejection of the internal parts of the cylinder and considerable spilling of hydraulic fluid. The use of rubber bands or wire around the cylinder will prevent these unhappy results in the event of accidental use of the pedal.

Remove the leaf springs 11 and the pegs 12. Pull out the leading (rearmost) shoe from the slot in the adjuster link 3 and lift the other end of the shoe clear of the piston 13 and handbrake lever 6. Disconnect the return springs 1 and 2 and remove the two shoes.

Repeat for the other wheel.

It is recommended that advantage should be taken of factory reconditioned shoes rather than reline them at home, also that the return springs be renewed when renewing the shoes.

Carefully clean and dry all the parts and apply a smear of grease to the ends of the shoes. Fit the return springs in the order shown. Position the toe, the end of the shoe showing the larger area of unlined metal platform, of the leading (rearmost) shoe in the slot of the cylinder piston and the handbrake lever in the slot in the flange of the shoe. Fit the heel end of the shoe in the slot in the adjuster link. Lever the heel and toe of the other shoe into their respective slots, noting that the heel of one shoe is adjacent to the toe of the other.

Insert the pegs 12 through their holes in the brake backplate and replace the leaf springs 11 smeared with a small quantity of grease. Refit the brake drum and the road wheel.

Repeat for the other wheel and make several applications of the brakes before adjusting them as described.

Wheel cylinders, to remove and refit:

Having removed the brake shoes disconnect the handbrake operating rod from the lever 6 by withdrawing the clevis pin. Disconnect the hydraulic pipe from the cylinder union. Remove the dust cover 17 from the rear of the backplate. Prize the retaining plate 7 and the spring plate 18 apart and pull the retaining plate from beneath the cylinder. Withdraw the handbrake lever. Remove the spring plate and the distance piece 19 and take off the wheel cylinder 15 from the backplate.

Refit the neck of the cylinder through its slot in the brake backplate. Fit the distance piece 19 between the cylinder neck and the backplate with the open end away from the backplate.

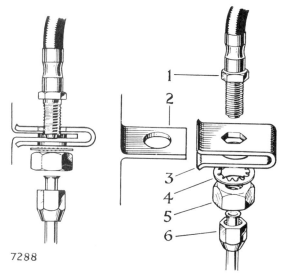

FIG 10:6 Flexible hose connection

Key to Fig 10:6   1 Sleeve hexagon   2 Support bracket
3 Locating plate   4 Washer   5 Nut   6 Feed pipe union nut

Fit the spring plate 18 between the distance piece and the backplate also with the open end away from the handbrake lever location and the cranked tips away from the handbrake lever location and the cranked tips away from the backplate.

Replace the handbrake lever 6. Locate the retaining plate 7 between the distance piece and the spring plate with its open end facing towards the handbrake lever and tap it into the position where the two cranked tips of the spring plate locate in the retaining plate. Refit the rubber dust cover 17 and reconnect the handbrake linkage. Refit the hydraulic pipe. Replace the brake shoes. Bleed the system.

Flexible hoses:

If, on examination, a flexible hose appears to be damaged or is choked it should not be cleared with a wire or similar device nor should it be put back into use. A new hose should be obtained.

The correct method for the removal of a flexible hose is as follows. Refer to **FIG 10:6**. The metal pipe is first removed by holding the nut 5 with one spanner and unscrewing the union nut 6 with another. The flexible hose may then be removed by holding the sleeve hexagon 1 while unscrewing the locking nut 5. The other end of the hose may now be removed by unscrewing it and at the same time allowing it to rotate.

Reverse the above for refitting.

10:5 Servicing the master cylinder and wheel cylinders

Instructions for the removal of the master cylinder were given in **Section 10:3**, but before dismantling is commenced it must be again emphasized that strict cleanliness is essential when handling any components of the hydraulic system. It is stressed that petrol must be avoided nor must paraffin or other cleaning compounds

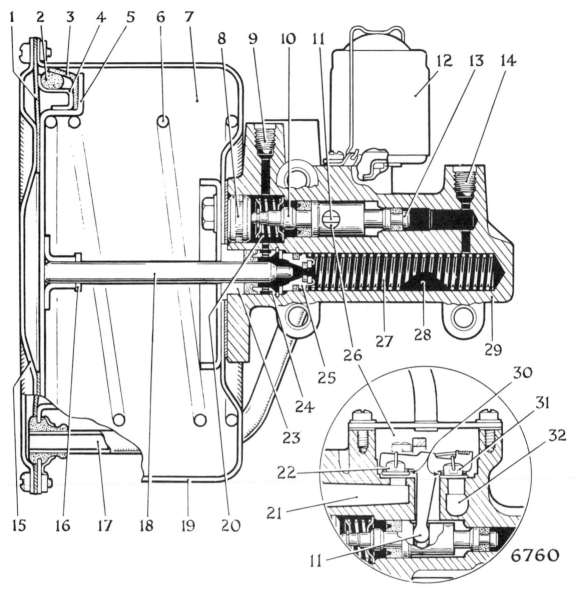

FIG 10:7 Girling vacuum servo unit

Key to Fig 10:7   1 End cover gasket   2 Piston backing ring   3 Piston seal   4 Piston seal retainer   5 Piston
6 Piston return spring   7 Constant vacuum   8 End plug   9 Hydraulic inlet port   10 Valve control piston, low
pressure end   11 T-shaped lever   12 Air filter assembly   13 Valve control piston, high-pressure end   14 Hydraulic
outlet port   15 End cover   16 Piston buffer   17 Transfer tube   18 Piston rod   19 Vacuum cylinder
20 Control piston spring   21 Vacuum inlet   22 Vacuum valve   23 Bearing bush   24 Nylon spacer   25 Output piston
26 Valve chest   27 Output piston spring   28 Output cylinder   29 Cast body   30 Valve springs   31 Air valve   32 Air inlet

be used. Brake fluid, of the recommended grade, should always be used for cleaning and lubricating the parts before assembly. Great care is also required when dealing with rubber seals, and any doubtful seals should be renewed.

Having removed the master cylinder from the car the outside should be cleaned and any fluid drained off into a suitable container.

Depress and withdraw the return spring cap to release the return spring. See **FIG 10:2**. Pull back the rubber dust cover 16 and remove the circlip 9 to release the dished washer 13. Withdraw the pushrod and washer. Remove the plunger 8 (this will be simplified by using air pressure applied to the outlet port) and take off the thimble 11 and the return spring 6.

Compress the spring and withdraw the valve stem 7

through the elongated hole in the thimble. Remove the valve spacer 3 and the spring washer 5. Remove the seals 4, 12 and 14 (seal 14 is omitted from later models).

To reassemble:

Having cleaned all parts in brake fluid and renewed any, particularly rubber seals, which are worn they may be left lying in fluid until needed.

Replace the valve seal 4 in its seating on the valve head with the lip facing outwards. Position the spring washer 5 with the dome against the valve head and fit the spacer 3 with the legs towards the valve seal. Replace the spring 6 on the spacer.

Insert the thimble 11 into the spring and press until the valve stem 7 passes through the elongated hole in the thimble and locates correctly in the centre of the thimble. Check that the spring also is centrally located on the spacer. Refit the seals 12 and 14 on the plunger 8 with the lips facing towards the thimble as shown. Press the small end of the plunger into the thimble until the thimble engages under the shoulder of the plunger. Press the leaf well home.

Insert the assembly into the bore of the cylinder 1 taking care that the lips of the seal 12 are not turned back. Refit the pushrod assembly 13 into the cylinder securing it with the circlip 9 which engages in the groove in the bore and replace the rubber dust cover 10 as shown. Refit the return spring and cap.

The master cylinder is refitted to the car in the reverse order to its removal described in **Section 10:3**.

Wheel cylinders (see FIG 10:5):

Having removed the cylinder from the brake backplate as described above, release the clip 4 and remove the rubber dust cover 5. Withdraw the piston 13 and the rubber seal 14. On some models there is a return spring between the piston and the end of the bore.

Reverse the above to reassemble. Note that the rubber seal is fitted with its widest end towards the closed end of the cylinder. The smaller end of the piston return spring is towards the piston.

10:6 Girling vacuum servo unit:

The servo unit is fitted in the brake hydraulic system between the master cylinder and the road wheels, and its function is to increase the braking pressure exerted by the driver. This added pressure is obtained by admitting atmospheric pressure to one side of a piston located in a cylinder in which a high degree of vacuum is maintained by means of a pipe connecting with the inlet manifold.

In order to assist in following the operation of the Girling unit it is shown in section in **FIG 10:7** but the operator is strongly advised to return it to the manufacturers in the event of failure.

When the unit is at rest there is an equal vacuum on each side of the piston 5 but when the brake pedal is applied the air valve 31 is opened and the vacuum valve 22 is closed. Air is then admitted via the transfer tube 17 to the outer side of the piston and drives it forward together with the piston rod 18 and the output piston 25. Continued movement applies additional pressure in the hydraulic pipes to the wheel cylinders through the outlet port 14.

When the brake pedal is released the valve control piston 10 moves back towards its rest position causing the 'T' lever 11 to open the vacuum valve 22 and so extracting the air from the outer side of the piston which returns to its original position and with it the outlet piston, thus relieving the pressure in the brake assemblies. At the same time the hole in the output piston is cleared and fluid flows back to the reservoir.

The air filter element should be taken out and renewed as instructed in the Owners Handbook. On some models the cover is released by pushing the spring clip aside, and after cleaning the baseplate the new filter is placed in position and the cover refitted. On other models the centre screw is withdrawn to release the cover and expose the elements. Clean the rubber washer before replacing it. Fit the new filter element. Replace the cover and the centre screw.

Testing:

The following simple tests of the unit's operation may be carried out without removing it from the car and may be used to determine possible causes of failure. It is assumed that other possible faults in the braking system have been located and rectified.

1 With the unit correctly connected, run the engine and apply the brake. It should be possible to hear the hiss of the air inlet and with the hand to feel the movement of the piston inside the vacuum cylinder. Failure to do so indicates an internal breakdown.

2 Run the engine for half a minute, switch off and leave 2 minutes. On applying the brake the unit should be detected operating as just described. Failure indicates a leak in a gasket, air valve or the rubber grommet at the outer end of the transfer tube.

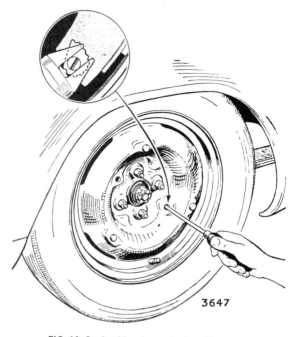

FIG 10:8 Lockheed rear brake adjustment

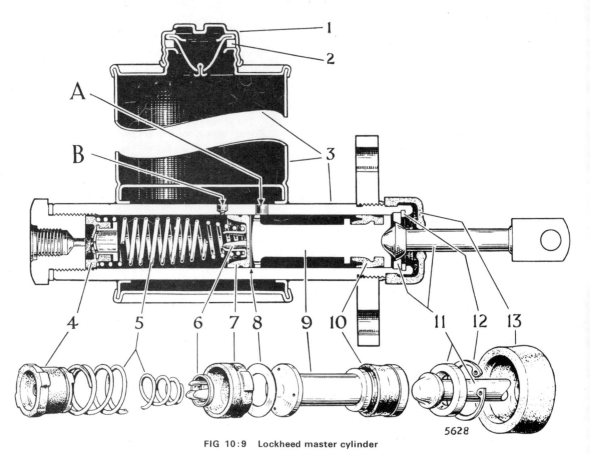

FIG 10:9   Lockheed master cylinder

Key to Fig 10:9   1 Filler cap   2 Washer   3 Master cylinder body   4 Check valve (On earlier models the shape of this item differs from that shown)   5 Return spring   6 Spring retainer   7 Main cup   8 Washer   9 Piston   10 Secondary cup   11 Pushrod assembly   12 Circlip   13 Rubber boot   A Main port   B By-pass port

3   Run the engine and apply the brake hard for twenty seconds. There should be no creep in the brake pedal. Any creep would indicate a leak somewhere which can be found by elimination if no signs are visible. Clamp each hose in turn and repeat the test. If the creeping is still evident with the hoses clamped and the master cylinder outlet plugged the servo unit is faulty.

4   Jack-up the front of the car, run the engine, apply the brake and release. The front wheels should be free to turn half a second after releasing the pedal. If the brakes remain on disconnect the vacuum pipe, operate the brakes and test again. If the brakes do not release the fault is not in the servo unit.

10:7   Bleeding the system

This is not an item of routine maintenance, but is required whenever a part of the hydraulic system has been disconnected or air has been allowed to enter the master cylinder, usually through the level in the reservoir falling too low. It is important that the level in the reservoir be maintained throughout this operation and that the wheels are treated in the correct order.

Remove the rubber cap from the nearside rear wheel bleed screw and fit the bleed tube the free end of which should be immersed in a glass jar containing a small quantity of brake fluid.

Unscrew the bleed nipple $\frac{3}{4}$ of a turn and operate the brake pedal. An assistant should tighten the screw at the end of the stroke and the pedal allowed to return normally. Slacken the bleed screw and repeat the pedal applications, tightening the screw at the end of each stroke, until the fluid entering the jar is free of air bubbles. Tighten the bleed screw during the last pedal application.

Repeat this procedure for the other three wheels finishing at the wheel nearest to the master cylinder. Tighten the bleed screws to a torque of 6 lb ft. Top up the reservoir to $\frac{1}{4}$ inch below the bottom of the filler orifice with Girling Fluid SAE.70.R.3

10:8   Handbrake adjustment

As mentioned previously the adjustment of the rear brakes will automatically adjust the handbrake, but if with the rear brakes correctly set there is more than four to six notches of handbrake movement before the wheels are locked proceed as follows:—

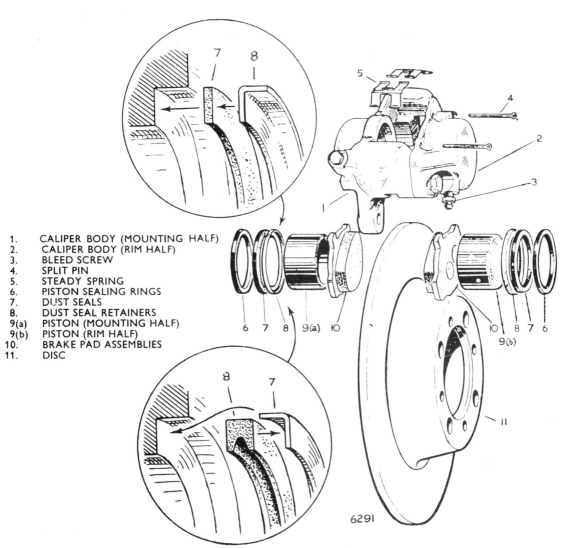

1. CALIPER BODY (MOUNTING HALF)
2. CALIPER BODY (RIM HALF)
3. BLEED SCREW
4. SPLIT PIN
5. STEADY SPRING
6. PISTON SEALING RINGS
7. DUST SEALS
8. DUST SEAL RETAINERS
9(a). PISTON (MOUNTING HALF)
9(b). PISTON (RIM HALF)
10. BRAKE PAD ASSEMBLIES
11. DISC

FIG 10:10 Exploded view of caliper

Chock up the front road wheels, release the handbrake and jack-up the rear of the car. Lock the wheels by means of the adjuster—arrowed in **FIG 10:1**. Take up any slack by means of the compensator by slackening off the locking nut, removing the jaw pin and screwing in the jaw as necessary. Readjust the brakes as described in **Section 10:2**.

10:9 Rapier Series III, IIIA and IV. Lockheed brakes

Maintenance and adjustment:

The front brakes on these models are self-adjusting and the only attention necessary is to examine for wear at regular intervals and renew the friction pads when they have worn to a minimum thickness of $\frac{1}{16}$ inch. See **Section 10:11**.

The level of the fluid in the reservoir should be checked periodically and maintained to within $\frac{1}{2}$ inch of the filling orifice. Before removing the filler cap clean the area around it to prevent the entry of any dirt. Check also that the hole in the filler cap is not obstructed. The only fluid to be used in this system is Lockheed Super Heavy Duty Brake Fluid SAE.70.R.3.

An occasional check should also be made on the condition of the flexible hoses and the tightness of the brake mounting bolts and the hydraulic unions.

The rear brakes are adjusted as follows: Chock up the front wheels, release the handbrake and jack-up one rear wheel. Turn this wheel until the slotted head of the "micram" adjuster can be seen through the hole in the wheel. (See **FIG 10:8**). Using a screwdriver turn the adjuster in a clockwise direction until solid resistance is felt. Slacken the adjuster back—usually two clicks— until the wheel may be turned by hand, disregarding the slight drag from the trailing shoe.

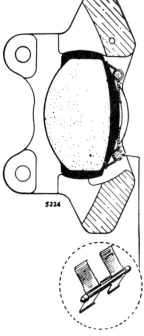

FIG 10:11 Section through caliper showing early type retaining pin

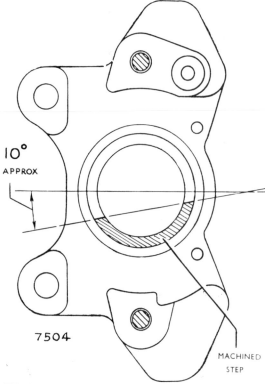

FIG 10:12 Diagram showing location of anti-squeal steps

Spin the wheel and apply the brakes hard to centralize the shoes and recheck the setting. Repeat for the other wheel. When correctly set there should be $\frac{1}{4}$ inch free movement of the brake pedal. This adjustment of the rear brakes will automatically adjust the handbrake.

On early models there is a lubricator for the handbrake cable, and an occasional drop of engine oil should be applied to the exposed moving joints.

10:10 Master cylinder, removal and refitting

The Lockheed master cylinder is shown exploded and in section in **FIG 10:9**. It is mounted on the engine side of the bulkhead and is coupled directly to the brake pedal by means of a clevis pin through the fork at the outer end of the pushrod.

Disconnect the pressure pipe from the union at the front of the cylinder, collecting any fluid in a clean container. Remove the clevis pin and the two bolts securing the master cylinder to the bulkhead. The assembly may now be withdrawn.

After refitting, which is the reverse of the above, the brakes must be bled as described in **Section 10:14**.

10:11 Servicing the brakes, front

Pads, to remove and refit (see FIG 10:10):

The friction linings are bonded to their pressure plates and can only be renewed by fitting complete new assemblies which are supplied in kits including steady springs and splitpins.

Jack-up the front of the car and remove the road wheel. Remove the two steady springs 5 by withdrawing the two splitpins 4. On earlier cars retaining pins of the type shown in **FIG 10:11** were used. The brake pad assemblies 10 may now be removed after rotating them within the caliper and withdrawing.

Clean all parts before refitting. Push the pistons to the bottom of their bores. This will cause the fluid level in the reservoir to rise and it may be necessary to siphon off a quantity to prevent overflowing.

The brake pad assemblies are inserted into the caliper with the outside edges facing away from the caliper. On later models this edge is recognised by the rectangular boss on the pressure plate. On earlier models there is no boss but it will be seen that the pressure plate extends beyond the friction lining along that edge (see **FIG 10:11**). Having inserted the pads, lower ends first, rotate them until they are correctly located.

Fit the new springs and splitpins or the retaining pins as shown in the diagram. It will be noted that the longer legs of the two springs face each other. Pump the brake pedal until solid resistance is felt. Refit the road wheel. Lower the jack.

Servicing the calipers:

Jack-up the front of the car and remove the wheel. Disconnect the hydraulic pressure hose and remove the two bolts securing the caliper to the adaptor plate and swing it clear of the disc. Clean the outside of the assembly and remove the brake pads. It may be necessary to apply air pressure to force out the pistons and a pan should be placed to catch the fluid which will spill out.

Carefully prize out the sealing ring 6 in **FIG 10:10** and also the dust seal and retainer 7 and 8. The rubber

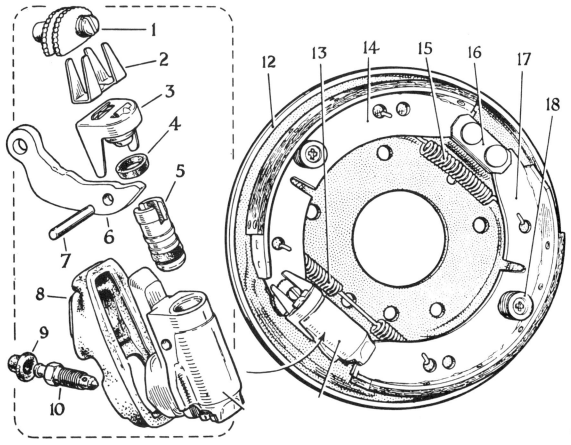

FIG 10:13   Exploded view of rear brake

Key to Fig 10:13 1 Micram adjuster 2 Mask 3 Outer piston 4 Seal (outer piston) 5 Inner piston
6 Handbrake lever 7 Pivot pin 8 Rubber boot 9 Dust cap 10 Bleed screw 11 Cylinder body
12 Backplate 13 Pull-off spring 14 Brake shoe assembly 15 Pull-off spring 16 Abutment 17 Brake
shoe assembly 18 Damper spring assembly

sealing rings should be renewed if they are worn or damaged and if a new dust seal is to be fitted a new retainer should also be used.

Clean all parts in brake fluid and assemble while still wet.

Refit the sealing ring 6 into the groove in the caliper bore. Open the bleed screw 3. Insert the pistons 9a and 9b squarely into the bores with the anti-squeal steps machined on the outer ends of the pistons towards the bottom of the aperture in the rear of the caliper (see **FIG 10:12**).

Two types of dust seal and retainer are used as shown in the two insets to **FIG 10:10** and it is essential that they are assembled as shown. The earlier seal is of rectangular section as shown in the upper diagram, while the drawing in the lower circle shows the later U-shaped seal with the retainer reversed as compared with the earlier type.

Tighten the bleed screw. Refit the brake pads. Replace the two bolts securing the caliper and bleed the system.

Do not attempt to split the two halves of the caliper.

Discs, to remove and refit:

After removing the caliper as described above, remove the hub assembly as described in **Section 8:2**. The disc is then removed by withdrawing the four securing bolts.

Refitting is the reverse of the removal procedure, but note:—Before locking the tab washers on the bolts securing the disc it is necessary to check the disc runout. This must be done after tightening the hub retaining nut to eliminate hub end float. The runout is measured about 1 inch from the outer edge of the disc and should not exceed .004 inch (.10 mm). Repositioning the disc on the hub will usually make it possible to correct any excess. Tighten the four bolts to a torque of 38 lb ft and lock the washers. Reset the hub end float as described in **Section 8:2** and bleed the system.

Servicing the rear brakes (see FIG 10:13):

Brake shoes. Chock up the front wheels, jack-up the rear of the car and remove the road wheel. Release the

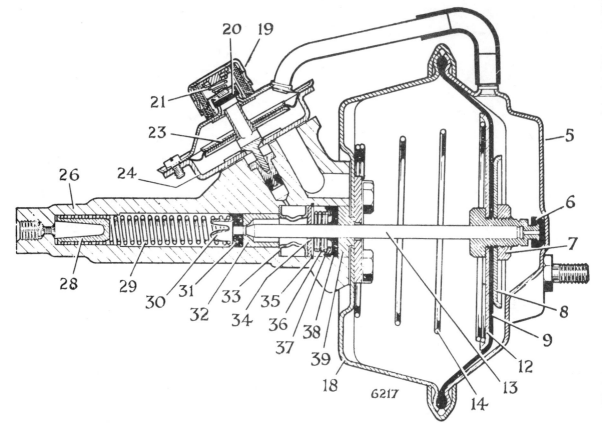

FIG 10:14   Sectional view of Lockheed vacuum servo unit

Key to Fig 10:14   1 Rubber elbow   2 Clamping ring   3 Clamping screw   4 Nut   5 End cover   6 Rubber buffer
7 Nut   8 Small plate   9 Booster diaphram   10 Seal   11 Valve piston   12 Large plate   13 Pushrod
14 Return spring   15 Bolt   16 Locking plate   17 Abutment plate   18 Vacuum shell   19 Air valve cover
assembly   20 Air valve   21 Air valve spring   22 Screw   23 Control valve diaphragm assembly   24 Valve housing
25 Gasket   26 Slave cylinder body   27 Gasket   28 Spring retainer   29 Spring   30 Spring guide
31 Main cup   32 Hydraulic piston   33 Distance piece   34 Washer   35 Circlip   36 Spring   37 Cup
spreader   38 Secondary cup   39 Guide piece

handbrake. Remove the brake drum from the axle flange by withdrawing the countersunk screw.

Release the damper spring assemblies 18 by pressing in the cups and turning through 90 degs. Withdraw the pegs from the rear. Disengage the leading shoe 14 from the slots in the piston 3 and the abutment 16 by pulling against the pull-off springs 13 and 15. The trailing shoe 17 will also be released. Remove the "micram" adjuster and mask 1 and 2 from the toe end of the leading shoe.

Rather than reline the old shoes it is recommended that a replacement set be obtained.

Lay the two shoes on a bench and fit the pull-off springs in the manner shown in the diagram. Fit the micram adjuster and mask into the slot on the toe of the leading shoe and place the ends of the shoe in the slots in the piston and the abutment. Lever the ends of the trailing shoe into their respective slots. Refit the damper springs. Replace and secure the brake drum. Adjust the brakes and lower the jack.

Wheel cylinders:

These are removed after removing the brake shoes. Unscrew the hydraulic pipe from the wheel cylinder. Disconnect the handbrake cable from the lever 6. Remove the rubber boot 8 and the bleed screw 10 from the cylinder and withdraw.

Reference to the exploded view in **FIG 10:13** will facilitate dismantling and reassembly of the cylinder. Note that the tapered rubber seal fits into the groove in the inner piston 5 with the lip facing away from the slotted end. The seal 4 fits into the groove in the outer piston 3. The inner piston fits into the cylinder body closed end first and with the longest slot next to the slot in the body. Care needs to be taken not to turn back the lip of the seal.

Place the handbrake lever 6 in position and refit the pivot pin 7. Refit the outer piston into the bore. Refit the cylinder to the brake backplate by reversing the removal procedure. Bleed the system.

10:12 Servicing the master cylinder

The master cylinder fitted to the Rapier range is shown in section and exploded in **FIG 10:9**, and instructions for its removal from the car were given in **Section 10:10**.

Remove the filler cap and drain off the fluid into a clean container. Press in and withdraw the return spring cap and the return spring. Remove the rubber boot 13. Press in the pushrod 11 and take out the circlip 12. Remove the piston 9, the washer 8, main cup 7, retainer 6, return spring 5, and the check valve 4. The secondary cup 10 is removed by stretching it over the end flange of the piston.

Reverse this procedure for reassembly having first cleaned all parts in brake fluid.

The secondary cup is fitted with its lip towards the drilled end of the piston. Fit the spring retainer 6 and the check valve 4, on to the spring 5, as shown and insert into the bore large end first. Insert the main cup 7, lip first and the washer 8, with the curved edge towards the main cup. Insert the piston and pushrod and secure with the circlip. Refit the return spring and cap and replace the rubber boot over the end of the cylinder and into its groove.

Fill the reservoir and test by pumping the pushrod a few times and observing the flow of fluid through the outlet.

10:13 Lockheed vacuum servo unit (see FIG 10:14)

The functions of a vacuum servo unit have already been described in **Section 10:6** and the operator is again reminded that in the event of a failure it is recommended that the unit be sent to a qualified service station for attention. The design is such that normal unassisted braking is still available if the servo unit should fail to operate.

To remove the unit disconnect the vacuum pipe and the hydraulic inlet and outlet pipes. Plug the ends of the pipes to prevent loss of fluid or entry of dirt. Remove two nuts and bolts then remove the unit.

Reverse this procedure to refit and bleed the system.

Maintenance consists of a regular inspection of the air filter in the air valve cover 19 as follows:—With the ignition off, pump the foot brake a few times to eliminate any vacuum, withdraw the five securing screws and remove the air valve cover assembly. Lift the air valve 20 off its seat and blow out any foreign matter from the filter chamber. Do not oil the filter or remove it from the cover, but if necessary fit a complete air valve cover.

The vacuum non-return valve fitted in the inlet manifold cannot be serviced and in the event of trouble it should be renewed.

10:14 Rapier Series I and II. Description

On these cars the rear brakes are similar to those already described, but the front are drum brakes having two leading shoes as shown in **FIG 10:15**.

There is no vacuum servo unit and the hydraulic pressure generated in the master cylinder on application of the brake pedal is transmitted directly to the wheel cylinders.

10:15 Adjustment

There should be $\frac{1}{4}$ inch free movement of the brake pedal before the piston in the master cylinder starts to move.

Front brakes. Apply the handbrake and jack up the front of the car. Remove the nave plate and turn the wheel to be adjusted until the hole in the wheel and brake drum is opposite the slotted head of one of the 'micram' adjusters as shown in **FIG 10:16**.

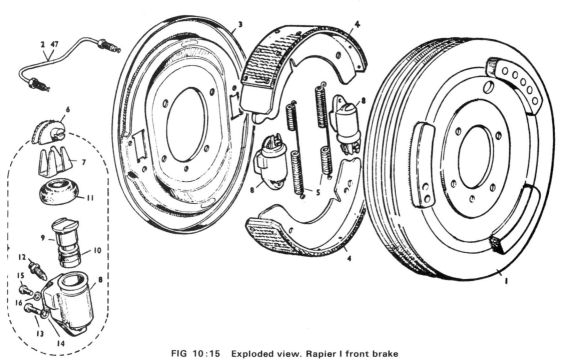

FIG 10:15   Exploded view. Rapier I front brake

Turn the adjuster in a clockwise direction until the brake shoe comes into contact with the drum, then turn it back one notch. Spin the wheel and apply the brake hard to position the shoe correctly. Check and readjust if necessary.

Rotate the road wheel for one half turn and repeat the above operation on the second micram adjuster.

Repeat the above procedure on the other front wheel.

Rear brakes. These are adjusted as described in **Section 10:9**.

10:16 Servicing the front brakes

Apply the handbrake, jack up the front end of the car and remove the appropriate road wheel. Turn the micram adjusters as far as possible in an anticlockwise direction.

Remove the countersunk screws securing the brake drum and lift off. Remove the pull-off springs by levering with a screwdriver and remove the brake shoes.

Disconnect the flexible pipe from the underframe bracket. Unscrew the two nuts securing the bridge pipe to the wheel cylinders and remove.

The wheel cylinders are secured to the backplate by nuts and spring washers after whose removal the cylinder may be lifted off.

The servicing instructions given in **Section 10:11** apply also to these brakes.

Refitting:

This is the reverse of the foregoing procedure, but the following should be noted:

First assemble the top pull-off spring to the shoes as shown in **FIG 10:17** and position the top ends of the shoes against the ends of the wheel cylinder.

Assemble the bottom pull-off spring as shown, pull the lower ends of the shoes apart and locate them on the lower wheel cylinder. Pull the shoes back against the springs and insert the micram adjusters and masks.

10:17 Bleeding the system

The instructions given in **Section 10:7** apply to the Lockheed system also but it should be noted that on Rapier IV cars there is no bleed screw on the offside rear wheel.

10:18 Handbrake adjustment

The adjustment of the rear brakes will normally adjust the handbrake also, but if excessive travel should develop on the brake lever adjust as follows:

With the rear of the car jacked-up and the handbrake off turn each micram adjuster clockwise until both brakes are locked on. Take up any slack in the cable by loosening the locking nut on the compensator linkage underneath the rear axle, remove the jaw pin and unscrew in the jaw as necessary. Release each adjuster until the wheels are free to rotate.

On later Rapier IV cars with self-adjusting rear brakes any slackness in the cable may easily be taken up by means of the adjuster shown in **FIG 10:18**.

10:19 Fault diagnosis

(a) Spongy pedal

1 Leak in the system
2 Worn master cylinder
3 Leaking wheel cylinders
4 Air in the system
5 Gaps between shoes and underside of linings

FIG 10:16   Front drum brake adjustment

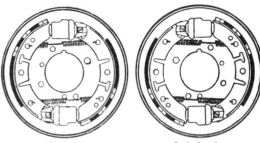

Left hand   *Right hand*

FIG 10:17   Fitting pull-off springs to front brake

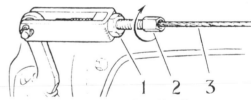

FIG 10:18   Handbrake cable adjuster
The arrow indicates the direction of rotation to shorten the cable

(b) Excessive pedal movement

1 Check 1 and 4 in (a)
2 Excessive lining wear
3 Very low fluid level in reservoir
4 Too much free movement of pedal

(c) Brakes grab or pull to one side

1 Brake backplate loose
2 Scored, cracked or distorted drum
3 High spots on drum
4 Unbalanced shoe adjustment
5 Wet or oily linings
6 Worn or loose rear spring fixings
7 Front suspension or rear axle anchorages loose
8 Worn steering connections
9 Mixed linings of different grades
10 Uneven tyre pressures
11 Broken shoe return springs
12 Siezed handbrake cable

CHAPTER 11

THE ELECTRICAL EQUIPMENT

11:1 Description

The electrical system fitted to all models is a 12-volt earth return type in which the positive terminal is earthed, and consists of the following units:—

1 Battery; 2 Generator, control box and fuse unit; 3 Starter and starter switch; 4 Ignition coil, distributor and plugs; 5 Lamps, flashers, wipers and switches, etc.

Wiring diagrams will be found in Technical Data at the end of this manual which, in conjunction with the information given in this chapter, will enable the operator to locate and test any faulty components. It must be stressed, however, that specialist equipment may be necessary and that the fullest use should be made of the extensive Lucas Service System for the exchange of faulty equipment.

11:2 The battery

On Alpine models the battery is located under the floor behind the righthand seat. On Rapier models it is mounted in the engine compartment.

Maintenance consists of regular inspection and servicing. Keep the battery and its surroundings clean and dry, particularly on the top surface between the terminals. Check that the holes in the filling plugs are clear. Maintain the level of the electrolyte up to the perforated splashguard. Occasionally remove the battery connectors and after removing any corrosion smear the terminals lightly with petroleum jelly before replacing the connector and again after tightening the screw.

Check the specific gravity of the electrolyte in each cell with a hydrometer. The indications are as follows:—

Cell fully charged   Specific gravity 1.270—1.290
Cell half charged   Specific gravity 1.190—1.210
Cell discharged   Specific gravity 1.110—1.130

These values are for an electrolyte temperature of 60°F (15.6°C). To obtain the true specific gravity at other temperatures add or subtract 0.002 to the hydrometer reading for each 5°F (2.8°C) over or below 60°F.

It at any time it is required to use Sulphuric Acid for filling a battery cell always mix the electrolyte to the correct gravity by slowly adding the acid to the water and never water to the acid.

11:3 The generator

The generator is driven from the crankshaft by a belt which also drives the water pump and fan. The tension of the belt should be checked regularly and if necessary adjusted to give $\frac{5}{8}$ inch movement in the centre of the longest run.

To adjust the tension slacken the nuts and bolts at the bottom of the generator front and rear, the link locating bolt and the screw through the slot in the strap. Rotate the body of the generator until the correct tension is obtained and retighten all bolts.

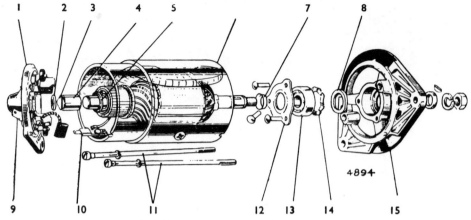

FIG 11:1   Exploded view of generator

Key to Fig 11:1   1 Commutator end bracket   2 Felt ring   3 Felt ring retainer   4 Bronze bush   5 Fibre washer
6 Yoke   7 Retaining cup   8 Felt ring   9 Terminal 'D'   10 Terminal 'F'   11 Through bolts   12 Bearing
retainer   13 Driving end bearing   14 Corrugated washer   15 Driving end bracket

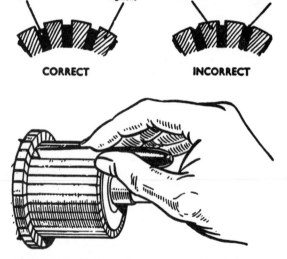

FIG 11:2   Undercutting commutator insulation

Lubrication consists of an occasional drop of engine oil into the hole marked OIL in the commutator end bracket. An internal felt washer acts as a reservoir.

Testing:

Check that the driving belt is correctly adjusted.

Check that the wiring to the terminals 'D' and 'F' is correctly connected to the control box 9 and 10 in FIG 11:1.

Switch off all lights and accessories, pull off these two connectors and short circuit the terminals with a length of wire. Start the engine and run at idling speed.

Attach the negative lead of a moving coil voltmeter—0–20 volts—to one terminal, and the positive lead to a good earthing point on the yoke. Increasing the engine speed to about 1.500 rev/min should cause the meter reading to rise rapidly and steadily. Do not race the engine to increase the voltage nor allow the reading to reach 20 volts. If there is no fast and steady rise in the voltage there is a fault in the generator. If there is much sparking at the commutator the armature is faulty and must be renewed. Note that if a radio suppression capacitor is fitted it should be disconnected and the above test repeated. If the test is now satisfactory the capacitor is at fault.

If the generator passes this test the link between the two terminals may be removed and the original connections restored.

11:4   Removal and dismantling, see FIG 11:1

Disconnect the leads. Slacken all attachment bolts and remove the belt. Withdraw the bolts and remove the generator.

Take off the driving pulley and the Woodruff key. Unscrew and withdraw the two through bolts 11. Remove the commutator end bracket 1 from the yoke 6. Remove the driving end bracket 15 from the yoke together with the armature assembly noting the fibre washer 5. It is not necessary to separate the armature and its bearing from the driving end bracket unless the bearing is suspected or the armature is to be replaced.

11:5   Servicing, the brush gear

Lift up and secure the brushes in their boxes by pressing the springs on the sides of the brushes.

Fit the commutator end bracket over the commutator and release the brushes.

Ensure that the brushes move freely in their boxes by polishing lightly with a smooth file. If the brushes are badly worn or are shorter than the minimum length of $\frac{1}{4}$ inch they must be renewed.

The commutator in good condition will be smooth and free from pitting or burning. It may be cleaned with a petrol wetted cloth or, if this is not effective, very fine glasspaper

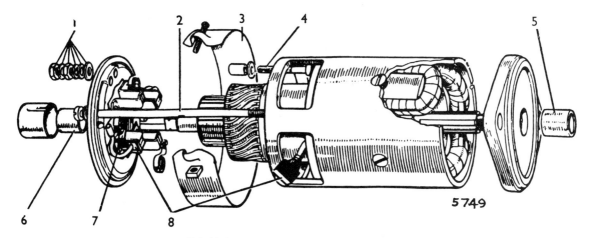

FIG 11:3   Exploded view of starter motor

Key to Fig 11:3   1 Terminal nuts and washers   2 Through bolt   3 Cover band   4 Terminal post   5 Bearing
bush (drive end)   6 Bearing bush (commutator end)   7 Brush spring   8 Brushes

—never emerypaper—while rotating the armature. The minimum finished diameter is 1.450 inches (36.8 mm) and if the armature cannot be satisfactorily cleaned without going below this measurement it must be renewed. It may also be necessary to undercut the insulation between the segments (see **FIG 11:2**). A hacksaw blade ground down to the correct thickness is a suitable tool. The width of the undercut slots must not exceed 0.040 inch (1 mm) with a depth of 0.020—0.035 inch (.5—.9 mm).

The field coils should be tested with an ohmmeter and a reading obtained of 5.9 ohms. If an ohmmeter is not available connect a 12-volt supply in series with an ammeter between the field terminal 10 and the yoke. The reading should be about 2 amps. A zero reading on the ammeter or an infinity on the ohmmeter indicates a break in the field winding.

A reading of much more than 2 amperes or less than 5.9 ohms indicates faulty insulation in the field coils. In either case the field coils must be renewed or a replacement generator fitted.

11:6   Reassembling

Fit the drive end bracket to the armature shaft. The inner journal of the bearing should be supported by a tube about 4 inches long, $\frac{1}{8}$ inch thick and with an internal diameter of $\frac{5}{8}$ inch. Do **not** use the drive end bracket as a support for the bearing while fitting the armature.

Fit the yoke to the drive end bracket. Raise and hold the brushes in their boxes by pressing the springs on the sides.

Fit the fibre thrust washer 5. Taking care not to trap the brush connectors fit the commutator end bracket to the yoke with the dowel on the bracket locating in the groove in the yoke. A thin screwdriver inserted through a ventilation hole may be used to release the brush springs and locate the brushes.

Refit the two through bolts. Lubricate the commutator end bearing. Refit the generator to the engine.

11:7   Starter motor

Testing:

If the starter does not operate check first that the battery is well charged and that the wiring is in good condition. Switch on the lights and operate the starter control. If the lights go dim but the starter does not turn either the starter is faulty or, more frequently, is jammed in mesh. If the lights do not dim check the starter control and its associated wiring.

A starter which has jammed can usually be released by using a spanner on the squared end of the starter shaft or by rocking the car to and fro with a gear engaged.

If the starter is free and is receiving the current and still will not function it will be necessary to remove it.

First disconnect the positive battery terminal and then the heavy cable from the starter motor before removing the fixing bolts.

See **FIG 11:3**. Remove the coverband 3. Hold back the brush springs 7 and ensure that the brushes move freely in their holders, polishing them if required and marking them for replacing in the original positions. If the brushes are worn to the extent that they no longer bear on the commutator, or the connector has become exposed on the running face they must be renewed. Check the tension of the springs. This should be between 15 and 25 oz.

If the commutator has become blackened it should be cleaned with a cloth soaked in petrol. If further cleaning is required it may be done with a fine glasspaper. Never use emerypaper nor try to undercut the insulation between the segments.

Hold the motor in a vice and connect it to a 12-volt battery with two heavy-duty cables of which one should go to the starter terminal 4 and the other to the starter body. The motor should now run at a very high speed—10,000 rev/min. Failure to do so indicates a need for further dismantling and testing.

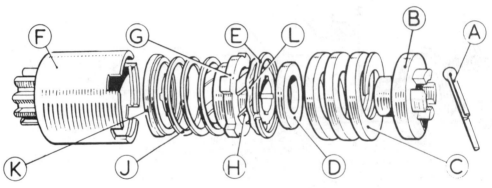

FIG 11:4 Exploded view of starter drive

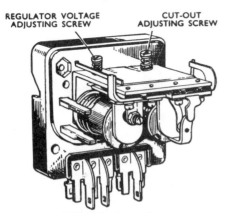

REGULATOR VOLTAGE ADJUSTING SCREW   CUT-OUT ADJUSTING SCREW

FIG 11:5 Control box

Dismantling:

Remove the brushes 8. Remove the terminal nuts and washers 1. Withdraw the through bolts 2 and lift off the commutator end bracket from the yoke. Remove the drive end bracket complete with armature and drive. Inspect the two brushes connected to the tappings on the field coils and, if necessary, remove them by unsoldering. New brushes should be carefully soldered in position. As they are already preformed they do not need bedding-in.

The field coils are tested by connecting a 12-volt battery and bulb in series between the points on the field coils to which the brushes are connected. If the bulb fails to light there is a break in the coil windings.

Check next for earthing of the coil by connecting one of the test leads to one of the field coil tapping points and the other to a clean point on the yoke. If the lamp lights it shows that the field coils are earthed to the yoke. In either case the starter should be taken to a service station.

Starter drive (see FIG 11:4):

The most frequent causes of trouble with the starter drive are dirt on the moving parts or a broken spring. By removing the splitpin 'A' and unscrewing the shaft nut 'B' the remaining parts may be lifted off in the order shown for cleaning or replacement.

Reassemble in the reverse order, but note that if either the control nut 'G' or the screwed sleeve 'H' are damaged a new assembly of **both** nut and sleeve must be fitted.

The starter is reassembled and refitted by reversing the above procedure.

11:8 The control box

This is the Avo Model 12 and comprises a generator voltage regulator and a cutout. It is shown in **FIG 11:5.**

In the event of trouble in the charging circuit and having checked that the generator driving belt is not slipping and that the battery is in good condition check the wiring by disconnecting the wire from terminal 'A' on the control box and connecting it to the negative terminal of a voltmeter and the positive voltmeter terminal to an earthing point on the chassis. If a voltmeter reading is given the wiring is in order and the regulator must be examined.

Remove the wires from terminals 'A' and 'A1' and join them together. Connect the negative of a moving coil voltmeter to terminal 'D' and the positive lead to 'E'. Increase the engine speed until the needle flicks and then steadies. This should occur with a voltmeter reading according to the ambient temperature as shown:—

Ambient temperature	Voltage
10°C or 50°F	16.1 to 16.7
20°C or 68°F	16.0 to 16.6
30°C or 86°F	15.9 to 16.5

If the voltage at which the reading becomes steady is outside these limits the regulator should be adjusted.

Stop the engine and remove the control box cover. Turn the voltage adjusting screw clockwise to raise the setting, or vice versa, a fraction of a turn at a time and repeat the test until the correct setting is obtained.

If, after setting the regulator, the battery is still not being charged the setting of the cutout should be tested. Connect the voltmeter between terminals 'D' and 'E'. Start the engine and increase the speed until the cutout contacts are seen to close. This should occur at a reading of between 12.7 and 13.3 volts and if a reading outside these limits is obtained the cutout should be reset. The adjusting screw should be turned a fraction at a time, clockwise to raise the voltage setting, and the test repeated until correct.

If the cut-out does not operate there may be a break in the internal wiring and the unit should be removed for examination or renewal.

Fuse unit:

There are two 35 amp fuses, one of which, between terminal blocks 1 and 2, protects auxiliary circuits independent of the ignition switch, the other, between 3 and 4, protects those circuits controlled by the ignition switch. Two spare fuses are also provided.

11:9 The headlamps

On early cars Lucas combined reflector and lens assemblies are fitted in which prefocus bulbs are used. This type of headlamp is shown in **FIG 11:6**. To dismantle, it is first necessary to remove the screw from the bottom of the lamp front and pull the rim off. Press in the lens and reflector assembly 1 and turn it slightly in an anticlockwise direction to free it from the three springloaded screws 4 and 5 which are also the beam setting adjusting screws. If the bulb adaptor 3 is now pressed inwards and turned to line up the two arrows on the adaptor and the reflector it may be withdrawn and the bulb removed. Reassembly is the reverse of this procedure.

It is recommended that the beams be set at a service station with an optical type beam setter but the operator can carry out the task by pointing the car at a wall on which two aiming marks have been painted at the same height as the lamps and the same distance apart. Using one lamp at a time turn the adjusting screws until the correct setting is obtained.

On later cars Sealed-beam units are fitted as shown in **FIG 11:7**. This unit, which includes bulb, reflector and lens in one sealed assembly, is removed by releasing the front rim 1, the sealing ring 2, and the three screws holding the retaining rim 3. The unit may then be withdrawn and detached from the slotted connector plug 10.

The beam setting is adjusted by turning the two screws 7 and 9 for lateral and vertical setting respectively.

11:10 Direction indicators

The flashing lights of the direction indicators are supplied on the early cars in this range by a second and more powerful filament in the front side lamps and at the rear by the bright stop lamp filament of the tail lamps. The installation at the rear was later modified to incorporate a separate flasher bulb at the same time continuing with the dual filament bulb in the front.

For Rapier Series IV cars a separate front flasher lamp is fitted in the side lamp assembly.

A correctly operating direction signal is indicated in all cases by the simultaneous flashing of the green pilot light on the instrument panel.

The flasher unit is plugged into a socket under the panel and operates by the expansion and contraction of a length of wire heating up as current is passed through it and cooling when the current ceases to flow. This action opens and closes a pair of contacts inside the unit and so passes an intermittent current to the indicators. It is not possible to adjust the unit and in the event of failure it must be renewed.

If a direction indicator is switched on and the green light does not flash, switch the control to the opposite direction and observe the green light. If it now flashes the first indicator is faulty. If it still does not light up both indicator bulbs may be faulty, but check on the pilot bulb, the fuse (A4 in the fuse box) and the flasher unit itself in that order.

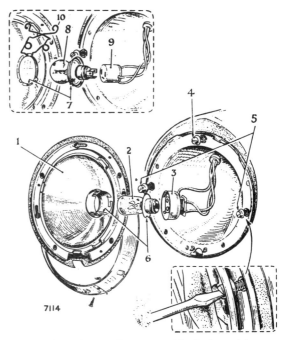

FIG 11:6   Headlamp assembly. Early models

Key to Fig 11:6   1 Reflector   2 Bulb   3 Bulb adapter
4 Vertical adjustment screw   5 Lateral adjustment screw
6 Bulb location   7 Bulb location (European type)
8 Bulb (European type)   9 Bulb adapter (European type)
10 Bulb retainer (European type)

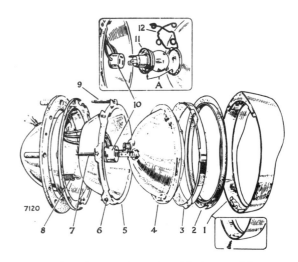

FIG 11:7   Headlamp assembly. Late models

Key to Fig 11:7   1 Front rim   2 Sealing ring
3 Retaining rim   4 Sealed-beam light unit   5 Seating rim
6 Retaining rim screw   7 Lateral adjusting screw
8 Tensioning spring   9 Vertical adjusting screw
10 Slotted connector-plug   11 Bulb (European type)
12 Bulb retainer (European type)   A Location for bulb

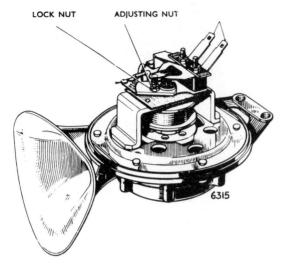

FIG 11:8   Horn adjustment. Model WT.618

Type WT.618:

Remove the screw and take off the domed cover and the cover retaining strap. Rotate the adjusting nut clockwise until the horn just fails to sound, then turn it back one half turn and lock.

Type 9.H:

Turn the screw adjacent to the horn terminals in an anticlockwise direction until the horn just fails to sound then turn it back for one quarter turn.

Clear hooter horn:

Clear hooter horns are fitted to some later cars and adjustment for loss of volume is effected by rotating the adjusting screw slowly clockwise until the volume of sound is restored then back to a point where the volume is just maintained. In some cases it may be necessary to turn the screw in the reverse direction to restore the correct volume. In either case this should occur within 180 degs. of the original setting.

11:12   Windscreen wipers

These require no periodic maintenance as the motor gear box, rack and wheel boxes are packed with grease during original assembly. Worn or perished blades should be renewed and an occasional drop of glycerine applied to the spindle where it passes through the rubber grommet.

Poor performance may be due to a variety of causes and the following points should be checked:—

Remove the wiper arms and disconnect the rack from the motor. Check that there is no binding between the rack and tube caused by sharp bends or kinks. Check that there is no looseness or overtightness in the wheel boxes. Rectify or renew as required.

Check the voltage at the motor while running and if a reading below 11.5 volts is given check further on the battery, switch wiring and connections.

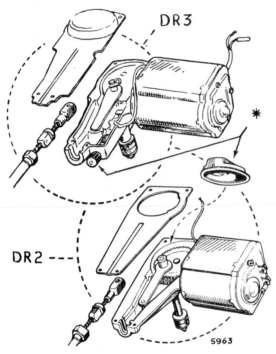

FIG 11:9   Limit switch adjustment. Models DR.2 and DR.3

11:11   Horn adjustment (see FIG 11:8)

The horns are set for tone by the makers and any adjustment provided is only for taking up wear in the moving parts. It is assumed before attempting to adjust the horns that the battery and the wiring have been checked and that the mounting bolts are secure. Always disconnect one horn when making adjustments to the other.

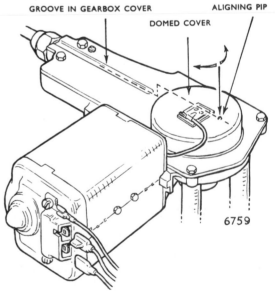

FIG 11:10   DR.3A wiper motor

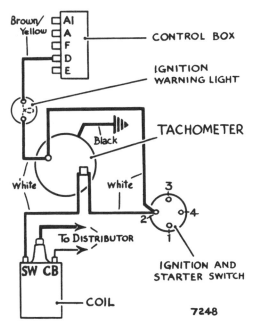

FIG 11:11 Tachometer circuit diagram

Connect a moving coil ammeter in series with the motor supply and observe the reading. This should be 2.7–3.4 amps. If the current is low remove the cover at the commutator end and ensure that the commutator is clean and that the brushes are bearing firmly on it. If the current is too high excessive friction is usually the cause. Check the points given above and also the armature end float. This should be adjusted to between .008 and .012 inch.

The types of limit switch by which the parking position of the blades is set are shown in **FIG 11:9** and should be adjusted with the arms correctly positioned on the splined spindles to place the arms at the lower edge of the windscreen. In the case of the DR.3 motor this is done by turning the knurled nut. On the type DR.2 the arrowed switch portion of the cover is rotated to set the parking position. The DR.3A motor is fitted to late model cars and the correct parking position is obtained by slackening the four screws securing the gearbox cover and turning the domed cover until the setting pip is in line with the groove in the gearbox cover (see **FIG 11:10**).

The wiper arms are removed by lifting the spring retaining clip and sliding the arm off the splined spindle. Each serration on the spindle provides a 5 deg. step in adjusting the area swept by the blade.

11:13 Impulse tachometer

This is an engine speed indicator which operates by "counting" the electrical impulses given by the ignition coil. There is no mechanical drive and no maintenance is required.

The electrical connections are shown in **FIG 11:11** and should be examined in the event of failure. If the wiring is in order the tachometer must be renewed.

11:14 Fuel and temperature indicators

The electrical circuit of the bi-metal resistance equipment is given in **FIG 11:12**. For both fuel contents and temperature indication there is a transmitter unit and an indicator head connected to a common voltage regulator which provides a steady supply of 10 volts.

If the action of the gauges is faulty, check the wiring, connections and the battery. If these are in order it will be necessary to fit a new unit.

11:15 Fault diagnosis

(a) Battery discharged

1 Terminals loose or dirty
2 Lighting circuit shorted
3 Generator not charging
4 Regulator or cutout not working correctly
5 Battery internally defective

(b) Insufficient charging current

1 Loose or corroded battery terminals
2 Generator driving belt slipping

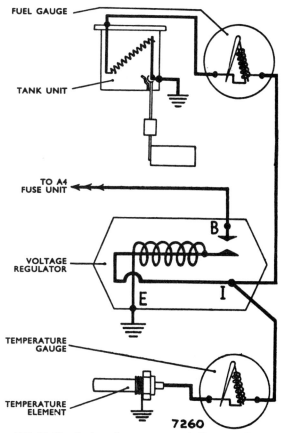

FIG 11:12 Fuel and temperature indicators. Circuit diagram

(c) Battery will not hold charge

1 Low electrolyte level
3 Battery plates sulphated
3 Electrolyte leakage from cracked casing or top sealing compound
4 Plate separators ineffective

(d) Battery overcharged

1 Voltage regulator needs adjusting

(e) Generator output low or nil

1 Belt broken or slipping
2 Regulator unit out of adjustment
3 Worn bearings, loose pole pieces
4 Commutator worn, burned or shorted
5 Armature shaft bent or worn
6 Insulation proud between commutator segments
7 Brushes sticking, springs weak or broken
8 Field coil wires shorted, broken or burned

(f) Starter motor lacks power or will not operate

1 Battery discharged, loose cable connections
2 Starter pinion jammed in mesh
3 Starter switch faulty
4 Brushes worn or sticking, leads detached or shorting
5 Commutator dirty or worn
6 Starter shaft bent
7 Engine abnormally stiff

(g) Starter runs but does not turn engine

1 Pinion sticking on screwed sleeve
2 Broken teeth on pinion or flywheel gears

(h) Noisy starter pinion when engine is running

1 Restraining spring weak or broken

(j) Starter motor inoperative

1 Check 1 and 4 in (f)
2 Armature or field coils faulty

(k) Starter motor rough or noisy

1 Mounting bolts loose
2 Damaged pinion or flywheel teeth
3 Main pinion spring broken

(l) Lamps inoperative or erratic

1 Battery low, bulbs burned out
2 Faulty earthing of lamps or battery
3 Lighting switch faulty, loose or broken wiring connections

(m) Wiper motor sluggish, taking high current

1 Faulty armature
2 Bearings out of alig:.,nent
3 Commutator dirty or short circuited
4 Wheelbox spindle binding, cable rack tight in housing tube

(n) Wiper motor operates but does not drive arms

1 Wheelbox gear and spindle worn
2 Cable rack faulty
3 Gearbox components worn

(o) Fuel gauge does not register

1 No battery supply to gauge
2 Gauge casing not earthed
3 Cable between gauge and tank unit earthed

(p) Fuel gauge registers FULL

1 Cable between gauge and tank unit broken or disconnected

CHAPTER 12

THE BODYWORK

12:1 Removing door trim

It is first necessary to remove the interior handles as follows:—

Rapier (see FIG 12:1)

Turn the escutcheon until the radial groove in its face is parallel with the dowel hole in the handle. Press inwards to expose the retaining pin which may be tapped out to release the handle and the escutcheon.

Alpine (see FIG 12:2)

Push in the cup 4 or 10 until the retaining pin is exposed. Tap out the pin 2 or 8 and take off the handle, cup and spring and the escutcheon.

Refitting is the reverse of the removal procedure.

The trim pads are attached to the doors by concealed spring clips which may be levered out by inserting a screwdriver and working it around the door edge until all clips are free. Pull the trim pad downwards to free the upper edge from the retaining flange on the door.

When refitting push the upper edge of the trim under the retaining flange and press the spring clips onto their holes around the door panel. Refit the interior handles.

12:2 Servicing door locks

To remove:

Remove the interior trim as described above. Remove the screws holding the remote control to the door and swing the assembly vertically downwards as shown in FIG 12:3. In this position it may be detached from the dowel on the operating lever.

Remove the securing screws in the shut face of the door and the screws securing the dovetail on the inner door panel. On Rapier models press the sill control knob downwards into the locked position. Unscrew the knob and swing the control wire down against the lock. Remove the lock unit through the aperture in the shut face of the door.

Refitting is the reverse of the above, but ensure when fitting the remote control unit that there is $\frac{1}{32}$ inch free movement.

On Rapier models check that the safety catch wires do not foul their respective apertures by bending if necessary. Press the control knob downwards into the locked position and screw the knob home leaving a small clearance between the knob head and the door sill.

Exterior door handles (see FIG 12:4)

To remove:

Remove the door trim and from inside the door casing remove the nut in front and the screw at rear. Both are fitted with plain and shakeproof washers.

To adjust:

The correct clearance between the plunger head on the reverse side of the push button and the lock contactor

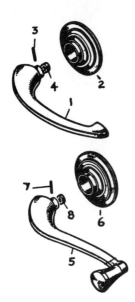

FIG 12:1 Interior door handles. Rapier

Key to Fig 12:1 1 Handle (door lock) 2 Escutcheon
3 Pin   4 Rubber pad   5 Handle (window regulator)
6 Escutcheon   7 Pin   8 Rubber pad

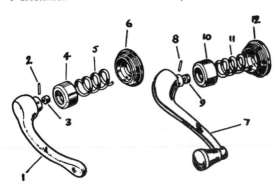

FIG 12:2 Interior door handles. Alpine

Key to Fig 12:2 1 Handle (door lock)   2/8 Pin
3/9 Rubber pad   4/10 Cup   5/11 Spring   6/12 Escutcheon

is $\frac{1}{32}$ inch measured, when the handle is attached to the door, through the large aperture in the inner door. To adjust release the locknut 9 and turn the contact screw 10 in or out as required to obtain the desired clearance.

12:3 Windows and winding mechanism

To remove glass. Rapier (see FIG 12:5)

Remove the interior handles and trim pad. Remove the bottom stop. Temporarily refit the handle and wind the window down to the bottom of the door and clear of its operating arms. Remove the screw, nut and washer from the rear end of the guide channel. Remove the top stop and lift the glass up the channel and out of the top of the door.

Replacement is the reverse of the above.

FIG 12:3 Removing lock remote control

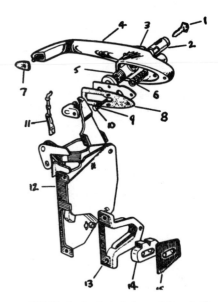

FIG 12:4 Exploded view of door lock

Key to Fig 12:4 1 Key   2 Lock   3 Weathershield
4 Outside handle   5 Spring   6 Spring (push button)
7–8 Washers   9 Nut   10 Contact screw   11 Link
12 Door lock   13 Dovetail   14 Striker   15 Backplate

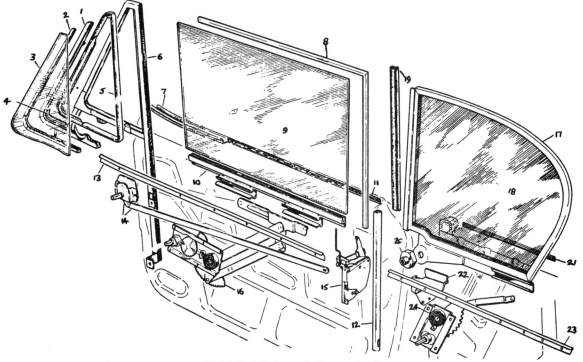

FIG 12:5   Window winding mechanism

Key to Fig 12:5   1 Inner frame   2 Glazing rubber   3 Glass   4 Drain channel   5 Weatherstrip
6 Outer frame   7 Weatherstrip   8 Lifting glass frame   9 Lifting glass   10 Glass channel and camplate   11 Seal
12 Glass run channel   13 Retainer (door trim pad)   14 Remote control   15 Door lock   16 Window regulator
17 Quarterlight frame   18 Glass   19 Weatherstrip   20 Nut   21 Seal   22 Mounting bracket   23 Retainer
(trim pad)   24 Quarterlight regulator

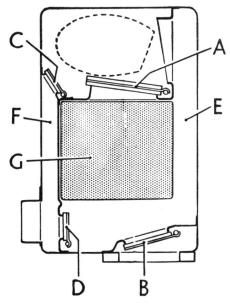

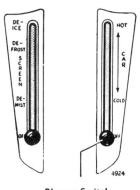

Blower Switch
Pull—"ON"
Push—"OFF"

(Series I-III, IIIA.
Separate blower switch on Series IV.)

FIG 12:6   Internal view of heater and controls

Key to Fig 12:6   **A** Air mixing valve   **B** Air outlet valve
to car   **C** Cold demist valve   **D** Hot demist valve
E Car cold air passage   **F** Demist cold air passage
G Heater matrix

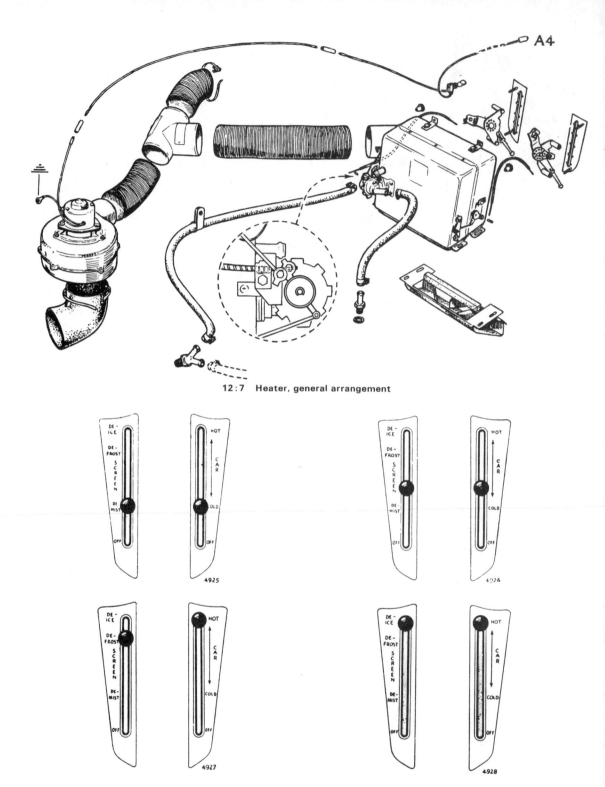

12 : 7   Heater, general arrangement

4925

4926

4927

4928

FIG 12 : 8   Heater control positions

Alpine:

Remove the interior handles and trim pad. Using the handle wind the window down until the camplate is visible through the aperture in the inner door panel. Spring out the operating arms from their location. With a screwdriver lever out the anti-rattle strips. Release the front and rear glass channels. Turn the window and lift it up and out of the top of the door.

When refitting replace the anti-rattle strips first but leave the rear ends free until after the glass has been fitted.

Quarterlight glass:

To remove:

Remove the winding handle. Remove the rear seat cushion and squab, the retaining screws for which are accessible from inside the boot. Remove the trim pad below the window. Remove the cotter pin and large nut from the quarterlight pivot 20 in **FIG 12:5.** Wind the window about halfway down and release the operating arm from its guide channel. Pull the glass, upper forward edge first, clear of the pivot upwards out of the body.

No-draught ventilators:

To remove and dismantle:

Remove the winding windows as previously described. Remove the four screws securing the ventilator and frame to the door. Lift the ventilator slightly and withdraw the complete assembly to the rear.

Ease the weatherstrip 5 from the outer frame 6 and press out the inner frame 1 complete with glass. After removing the weatherstrip from the inner frame the glass may be withdrawn.

When reassembling start by applying a coat of "Seelastic" to the inner channel of the weatherstrip in contact with the glass. Fit the glass and weatherstrip to the inner frame again applying Seelastic to the channel. Complete reassembly by reversing the removal procedure.

12:4 Heating and ventilation

Rapier III and IV:

The 4 kw heater is shown in the schematic view of **FIG 12:6** which gives the internal arrangement of the valves and controls by means of which the driver is able to obtain the desired conditions and the general arrangement of the installation is shown in **FIG 12:7.**

Fresh air enters the heater through the blower-ventilator air hose and is boosted by the blower—if fitted —when required. The Air Mixing valve 'A' controls the heating of the cold air and when in the closed position as shown all the air by-passes the heater matrix 'G' and flows through the cold air passages 'E' and 'F' to the car interior and screen respectively via the valves 'B' and 'C' which will be open when the controls are set as shown at 1 in **FIG 12:8**

Moving the controls a little higher in the slots, Diagram 2, gradually opens the valve 'A' to allow cold air to pass through the heater matrix. The Hot Demist valve 'D' also begins to open and pass a quantity of hot air to the screen.

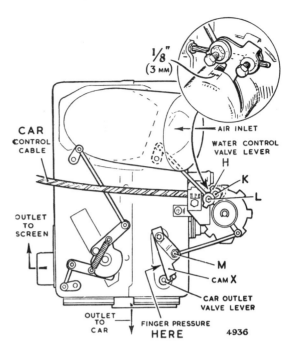

FIG 12:9 'CAR' Control adjustment

Moving the Screen control to Defrost and the Car control to Hot—Diagram 3—closes the Cold Demist valve 'C' and causes the total air flow to be heated and pass equally to the car interior and the screen.

Further movement of the Screen control to De-ice closes the valve 'B' which passes the air to the car, with the result that the whole supply of hot air is directed on to the screen. Diagram 4.

Adjustments:

Should the heater not be working correctly first ensure that all the cables and hoses are in order, then check the following settings:—

Car control (see FIG 12:9):

Move the Car control lever to the Off position and after slackening screw 'K' set the water control valve lever to its fully anticlockwise or closed position. Retighten screw 'K'.

The Air Mixing valve should now be fully closed. Should it not be so, slacken the screw 'L' to allow the valve to drop into the closed position and retighten.

The Air Outlet valve should also be fully closed. If it is not move the Car control up from the Off position until the water lever 'H' is $\frac{1}{8}$ inch from the end of its slot as shown in the inset. Slacken the screw 'M', press on the cam 'X' to close the Air Outlet valve and retighten the screw.

Screen control (see FIG 12:10):

Move the Screen control lever to the De-ice position. Slacken the screw 'N', press on the cam 'Y' to close the Air Outlet valve and retighten the screw.

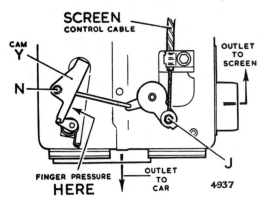

FIG 12:10 'SCREEN' Control adjustment

Ensure that both controls have full movement without slack.

To remove and refit the heater:

Disconnect the battery. Drain the cooling system. Remove the air hose between the branch pipe and the heater. Disconnect each water hose at the heater. Disconnect the Car cable at the water valve and the Screen cable at the heater end. Loosen the rear throttle bracket securing screw and remove the forward one.

Remove the righthand heater securing screw and the two upper screws which hold the heater to the bulkhead. Close the water valve and wire it in this position. Do **not** remove this wire until the heater is completely refitted. The heater may now be removed.

Refitting is the reverse of the above procedure. Check that the controls are correctly adjusted.

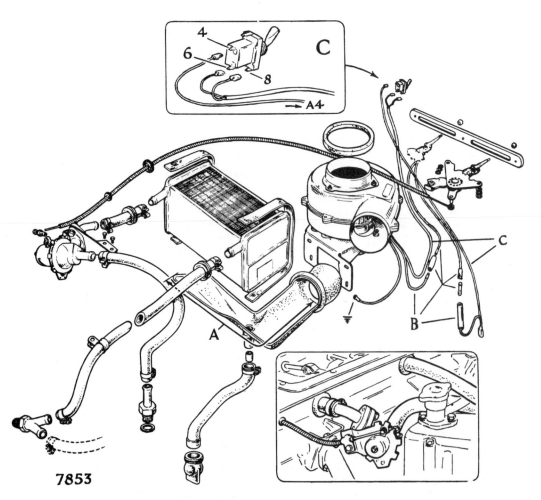

FIG 12:11   Heater. Alpine I-IV

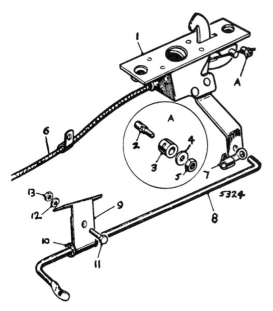

FIG 12:12   Bonnet lock. Rapier

Key to Fig 12:12   1 Catch   2 Pin   3 Bush   4 Washer
5 Nut   6 Control cable   7 Clip   8 Lever   9 Bracket
10 Bush   11 Bolt   12 Washer   13 Nut

Alpine:

The heater and its associated parts are shown in
FIG 12:11. The temperature of the air, directed to either
the car interior or to the screen, is regulated by means
of the Temperature control. Use of the blower increases
the volume of the air.

To remove the heater, set the control to Hot. Drain
the cooling system. Release the bonnet release control at
the air box and remove the air box cover. Disconnect the
inlet and outlet hoses and withdraw them from the
element. In order to withdraw the inlet hose it will be
necessary to remove the water valve by unscrewing the
securing screws and removing the bracket. Lift out the
element.

Reverse this procedure to refit the heater and bleed as
follows:— Release the inlet hose between the water valve
and the element and run the engine to dispel any air in
the system. Replace the hose. Top up the cooling system.

12:5 Bonnet lock

To remove and adjust:

Rapier (see FIG 12:12):

Remove the two bolts and washers and ease the lock
out of its aperture and release the cable from 'A'. Remove
the clip 7 to free the lever 8 and take out the lock.

The striker is removed by loosening the locknut and
turning the striker pin in an anticlockwise direction. The
lock and the striker are replaced in the reverse order.

Adjustment is carried out by screwing the striker pin
in or out as required after slackening the locknut. When
correctly set there is a slight movement in the bonnet top
when in the closed position.

Alpine:

Remove the cotter pin and flat washer retaining the
control rod slide and lift off the slide. Remove the three
setscrews and lift off the lock. The striker is removed by
taking out the two setscrews and their washers.

Adjustment of the striker is carried out by loosening
the locknut and screwing the pin in or out as required.

12:6 Drophead operation

To lower:

Lower the windows in both doors, tilt the seat squabs
fully forward, lower the rear seat backrest and both
side-tray covers. Release the header rail toggle catches.
Release the stud fasteners which retain the hood at each
side of the rear quarter. Tuck in the hood fabric.

Lift the header rail sufficiently to detach the tension
rods and fold them into the nylon recesses at the ends of
the cantrails (see **FIG 12:13**). Hold the header rail about
its centre and carry it rearwards until it covers half of the
rear window. Bring the two tubular hoodsticks together,
tucking the fabric neatly between them.

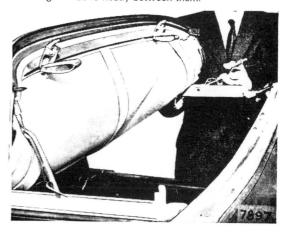

FIG 12:13   Folding the hood (1)

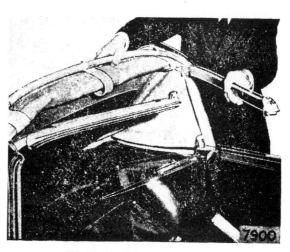

FIG 12:14   Folding the hood (2)

Holding the hoodsticks as shown in **FIG 12:14** fold in the cantrails. Lower the hood fully, tucking in the fabric behind the side-tray covers. Replace the rear seat backrest.

To raise:

Lower the windows in both doors, tilt both seat squabs forward, lower the rear seat backrest and both side-tray covers. Stand at the rear of the passenger's seat, grip the side supports of the hoodsticks with each hand, raise the hood assembly and pull it forward.

From outside the car fold the cantrails outwards and fasten to the tops of the windscreen pillars. Pull the header rail forward and secure with the toggle catches. Fit the stud fasteners and close the side-tray covers. Replace the backrest.

APPENDIX

TECHNICAL DATA

General dimensions   Capacities   Engine   Cooling system
Fuel system   Ignition system   Clutch   Gearbox
Rear axle   Front suspension   Rear suspension   Dampers
Steering gear   Braking system   Electrical equipment
Torque wrench settings

WIRING DIAGRAMS

HINTS ON MAINTENANCE AND OVERHAUL

GLOSSARY OF TERMS

INDEX

TECHNICAL DATA

Dimensions are in inches unless otherwise stated

GENERAL DIMENSIONS

Wheelbase—Alpine	.. ..	7 ft. 2 in.
Rapier..	.. ..	8 ft.
Track: Front—Alpine (disc wheels)	.. ..	4 ft. 3 in.
Alpine (wire wheels)	.. ..	4 ft. 3$\frac{1}{4}$ in.
Alpine IV (disc wheels)	.. ..	4 ft. 3$\frac{3}{4}$ in.
Alpine IV (wire wheels)	.. ..	4 ft. 4 in.
Rapier	.. ..	4 ft. 1$\frac{3}{4}$ in.
Rapier IV	.. ..	4 ft. 3$\frac{3}{4}$ in.
Rear —Alpine (disc wheels)	.. ..	4 ft. 0$\frac{1}{2}$ in.
Alpine (wire wheels)	.. ..	4 ft. 2$\frac{1}{2}$ in.
Rapier	.. ..	4 ft. 0$\frac{7}{8}$ in.
Overall length Alpine	.. ..	12 ft. 11$\frac{1}{4}$ in.
Rapier	.. ..	13 ft. 6$\frac{1}{2}$ in.
Rapier IV	.. ..	13 ft. 7$\frac{1}{4}$ in.
Overall width Alpine	.. ..	5 ft. 0$\frac{1}{2}$ in.
Rapier	.. ..	5 ft. 0$\frac{3}{4}$ in.
Turning circle Alpine	.. ..	34 ft.
Rapier	.. ..	36 ft.

CAPACITIES

Engine—including filter	.. ..	8 pints
Gearbox	.. ..	2$\frac{3}{4}$ pints
Gearbox with overdrive	.. ..	4 pints
Rear axle	.. ..	1$\frac{3}{4}$ pints
Cooling system with heater	Alpine I, II	15 pints
	Alpine III	12$\frac{1}{2}$ pints
	Rapier	13$\frac{1}{4}$ pints
Fuel tank Alpine I, II	.. ..	9 gallons
Alpine III	.. ..	11$\frac{1}{4}$ gallons
Rapier ..	.. ..	10 gallons

ENGINE

Bore:

1390 cc Rapier I	.. ..	3.00 in. (76.2 mm)
1494 cc Alpine I. Rapier II, III ..	.. .. ..	3.11 in. (79 mm)
1592 cc Alpine II, III, IV. Rapier IV	.. .. ..	3.21 in. (81.5 mm)

'A' grade is standard, but subject to grading as indicated below. Individual bores in any engine may conform to any of these grades, i.e. bores in any one cylinder block may not conform to one grade.

Rapier I	A.	3.0000/3.0004 inch	76.200/76.210 mm
	B.	3.0004/3.0008 inch	76.210/76.220 mm
	C.	3.0008/3.0012 inch	76.220/76.230 mm
	D.	3.0012/3.0016 inch	76.230/76.241 mm
Alpine I. Rapier II, III	A.	3.1102/3.1106 inch	78.999/79.009 mm
	B.	3.1106/3.1110 inch	79.009/79.019 mm
	C.	3.1110/3.1114 inch	79.019/79.029 mm
	D.	3.1114/3.1118 inch	79.029/79.040 mm
Alpine II, III, IV and Rapier IIIA, IV ..	A.	3.2102/3.2106 inch	81.539/81.549 mm
	B.	3.2106/3.2110 inch	81.549/81.559 mm
	C.	3.2110/3.2114 inch	81.559/81.569 mm
	D.	3.2114/3.2118 inch	81.569/81.580 mm

Stroke	3.00 inch	76.2 mm

Compression ratio:

Rapier I	8.0:1 (7.0:1 is available for export)
Rapier II	8.5:1 (7.0:1 is available for export)
Alpine I, IV. Rapier III	9.2:1
Alpine II, III. Rapier IIIA, IV ..	9.1:1 (8.4:1 is available for export)

Crankshaft:

Main journal diameter	2.2495/2.2490
Main bearings	Three, steel shell whitemetal lined
Crankpin bearings	Steel shell/copper lead, indium lined
Diameter of crankpin bearings:	
Alpine I. Rapier I, II	1.8760/1.8755
Rapier III	
Alpine II	
Rapier IIIA	2.0010/2.0005
End float	.002/.004
Main bearing running clearance	.0010/.0025
Maximum undersize for regrinding ..	.06

Connecting rods:

Length between centres	5.751/5.749
Big-end bearings	Steel shell/copper lead, indium coated
Big-end bearing diametrical clearance ..	.0015/.002
Big-end end float	.0012/.0075

Pistons:

Type	Aluminium, slotted. Tin plated
Number of rings	Two compression, one scraper
Piston length	3.25
Ring to groove clearance..	.0015/.0035
Fitted gap. Top. Alpine I. Rapier I, II, III	.012/.020
Alpine II, III, IV. Rapier IV ..	.024/.032
Second and third. All models	.009/.014

Grade:

Rapier I	A. 2.9986/2.9982 inch	76.164/76.154 mm
	B. 2.9990/2.9986 inch	76.175/76.164 mm
	C. 2.9994/2.9990 inch	76.185/76.175 mm
	D. 2.9998/2.9994 inch	76.195/76.185 mm
	*E. 3.0002/2.9998 inch	76.205/76.195 mm
	*F. 3.0006/3.0002 inch	76.215/76.205 mm
Alpine I. Rapier II, III	A. 3.1088/3.1092 inch	78.963/78.974 mm
	B. 3.1092/3.1096 inch	78.974/78.984 mm
	C. 3.1096/3.1100 inch	78.984/78.994 mm
	D. 3.1100/3.1104 inch	78.994/79.004 mm
	*E. 3.1104/3.1108 inch	79.004/79.014 mm
	*F. 3.1108/3.1112 inch	79.014/79.024 mm
Alpine II, III and Rapier IIIA, IV ..	A. 3.2088/3.2092 inch	81.503/81.514 mm
	B. 3.2092/3.2096 inch	81.514/81.524 mm
	C. 3.2096/3.2100 inch	81.524/81.534 mm
	D. 3.2100/3.2104 inch	81.534/81.544 mm
	*E. 3.2104/3.2108 inch	81.544/81.554 mm
Alpine IV	A. 3.2092/3.2096 inch	81.514/81.524 mm
	B. 3.2096/3.2100 inch	81.524/81.534 mm
	C. 3.2100/3.2104 inch	81.534/81.544 mm
	D. 3.2104/3.2108 inch	81.544/81.554 mm
	*E. 3.2108/3.2112 inch	81.554/81.564 mm

*For Service use

Gudgeon pin:

Type	Tubular fully floating. Located by circlips
Diameter: Alpine	High grade. Marked white. .8752/.8751

Rapier III				Medium grade. Marked green	.8751/.8750
				Low grade Marked yellow	.8750/.8749
Alpine II–IV				High grade Marked white	.9377/.9376
Rapier IIIA, IV				Medium grade Marked green	.9376/.9375
				Low grade Marked yellow	.9375/.9374
Oversize available					.003

Camshaft:
Bearings	..	Three. Whitemetal steel back
End float	..	.002/.004
Journal diameters	..	1.7477/1.7470
Drive	..	Duplex chain

Valves:
Seat angle. Inlet and exhaust	45 degrees
Head diameter: Inlet. Rapier I	1.374/1.370
Exhaust	1.114/1.110
Inlet. All other models	1.436/1.432
From chassis B.3062665 and B.9117425	1.475/1.471
Exhaust	1.176/1.172
Stem diameter: Inlet	.3110/.3105
Exhaust	.3100/.3095
Stem to guide clearance: Inlet	.0010/.0025
Exhaust	.0020/.0035

Valve guides:
Length: Inlet	2.00
Exhaust	2.15
Interference fit	.0025/.0045

Valve springs:
Free length: Inner	1.93
Outer	2.23
Load at fitted length: Inner	35.9 lbs.
Outer	70.8 lbs.

Valve timing and clearance:
Inlet valve opens. Rapier I		11 deg. BTDC
Inlet valve closes		55 deg. ABDC
Exhaust valve opens		53 deg. BBDC
Exhaust valve closes		13 deg. ATDC
Inlet valve opens	Up to B.33100000 and B.94100000	14 deg. BTDC
Inlet valve closes		52 deg. ABDC
Exhaust valve opens		56 deg. BBDC
Exhaust valve closes		10 deg. ATDC
Inlet valve opens	From B.33100001 and B.94100001	19 deg. BTDC
Inlet valve closes		57 deg. ABDC
Exhaust valve opens		61 deg. BBDC
Exhaust valve closes		15 deg. ATDC
Rocker clearance. Engine hot: Inlet		.012
Exhaust		.014

Lubrication system:
Pump type	Eccentric lobe
Normal pressure	55 lb/sq in
Filter: Type	Fram or Tecalemit full flow renewable element
	(Solex carburetter) Throw away type

COOLING SYSTEM

Thermostat settings:
Bellows type: Alpine	162°F or 72°C
Rapier	176°F or 79°C
Wax type. All models	183°F or 84°C

Relief valve pressures:
Alpine I, II	..	..	..	..	..	..	..	7 lb/sq in
Alpine III, IV	..	..	..	..	..	..	..	9 lb/sq in
Rapier III, IIIA	..	..	..	..	..	..	..	4 lb/sq in
Rapier IV	..	..	..	..	..	..	..	9 lb/sq in

FUEL SYSTEM

Carburetter types:

Rapier I. Early	.. ..	Single Stromberg DIF 36
Late	.. ..	Two Zenith 36WIP
Alpine I. Rapier II	.. ..	Two Zenith 36WIP2
Alpine II ..	.. ..	Two Zenith 36WIP2 or 36WIP3
Alpine III ..	.. ..	Two Zenith 36WIP3
Alpine III GT	.. ..	Two Zenith 36WIA3
Rapier III and IIIA	.. ..	Two Zenith 36WIA2 or 36WIA3
Alpine III, IV. Rapier IV	.. ..	Solex twin choke 32PAIA

Choke diameter:

Rapier I. Stromberg	.. .. ..	$1\frac{1}{32}$ inch
Zenith ..	.. .. ..	26 mm
Rapier II ..	.. ..	26 mm
Rapier III ..	.. ..	28 mm
Alpine I, II	.. ..	28 mm or 30 mm
Alpine III, IIIA	.. ..	29 mm
Rapier IIIA	.. ..	29 mm
Alpine III, IV and Rapier IV. Solex	.. ..	24 mm Primary. 26 mm Secondary

Main jet:

Rapier I. Stromberg	.. .. ..	L.1840
Zenith ..	.. .. ..	107
Rapier II ..	.. .. ..	110
Alpine I	.. ..	130 or 142
Alpine II ..	.. .. ..	112 or 142
Alpine III ..	.. .. ..	127
Alpine III GT	.. .. ..	105
Rapier III ..	.. .. ..	115
Rapier IIIA	.. .. ..	117
Alpine III, IV. Rapier IV. Solex	.. .. ..	120 Primary. 155 Secondary

Bypass jet:

Rapier I. Stromberg	.. ..	.026 inch
Alpine II ..	.. ..	57
Alpine III GT	.. ..	55
Rapier III, IIIA	.. ..	65

Slow-running jet:

Rapier I, II, III. Alpine I	.. .. ..	50
Alpine II, III. Rapier IIIA	.. .. ..	45

Pump jet:

Rapier I, II, III. Alpine I	.. .. ..	50
Alpine II. Rapier IIIA	.. .. ..	70
Alpine III ..	.. .. ..	90
Alpine IV. Rapier IV. Solex	.. ..	70

Pilot jet:

Alpine III, IV. Rapier IV	.. .. ..	60

Fuel pump:

Type	.. ..	AC Mechanical. E/FP.1880B
Pressure ..	.. .. ..	$1\frac{1}{2}$ to $2\frac{1}{2}$ lb/sq. in.

IGNITION SYSTEM

Sparking plugs:

Rapier I ..	.. ..	Champion N.8B
Rapier II ..	.. ..	Champion NA8

Alpine III. Rapier IV KLG.FE75
All other models ..   ..   Champion N.5
Gap: Rapier I, II ..   ..   .028 to .032
     All other models 025

Distributor:
Type   ..   ..   Lucas DM2/P4
Makers number: Rapier I S94
                Rapier II 40490A
                Rapier III. Alpine I 40683B
                Rapier IIIA. Alpine II   ..   ..   ..   40766A or 40799
                Alpine III 40924B
                Alpine IV. Rapier IV 40942A
Contact breaker gap   ..   ..   .015 to .016

Timing:
Full retard: Rapier I   ..   ..   10 to 12 deg. BTDC
           Rapier II   ..   ..   7 to 9 deg. BTDC
           Rapier IV   ..   ..   7 to 11 deg. BTDC
           Alpine IV   ..   ..   9 to 13 deg. BTDC
           All other models, early   ..   ..   ..   5 to 7 deg. BTDC
           From B3062930, B9118359 ..   ..   ..   9 to 11 deg. BTDC

CLUTCH

Type   ..   ..   Borg and Beck single dry plate
Diameter of plate 8.0
Free movement 135
Colour of cover springs and number:
     Alpine I, Rapier III   ..   ..   Light grey (6)
     Alpine II, III and Rapier IIIA   ..   ..   Orange (6), Dark blue/white (3)
Colour of driven plate springs   ..   ..   ..   Light grey/violet
Number of driven plate springs   ..   ..   ..   Six
Fluid: Alpine   ..   ..   Girling Fluid SAE 70 R.3
       Rapier   ..   ..   Lockheed Super Heavy Duty
                                               Brake Fluid SAE 70 R.3

GEARBOX

Type   ..   ..   Four forward speeds and reverse
Synchromesh   ..   ..   Second, third and top gears
Ratios:
     Rapier I II:
         Top 1.00:1
         Third 1.49:1
         Second 2.47:1
         First 3.19:1
         Reverse 4.04:1
     Alpine III:
         Top 1.00:1
         Third 1.39:1
         Second 2.14:1
         First 3.35:1
         Reverse 4.24:1
     All other models:
         Top 1.00:1
         Third 1.23:1
         Second 1.89:1
         First 2.96:1
         Reverse 3.75:1
Layshaft end float 006/.008

REAR AXLE

Type .. .. Semi-floating

Final drive ratio:
- Rapier I 5.22:1
- Alpine I, II .. .. 3.89:1 (4.22:1 with Overdrive)
- Rapier (Spiral bevel axles) .. .. .. 4.55:1 (4.78:1 with Overdrive)
- Rapier (Hypoid bevel axles) .. .. .. 4.22:1 (4.86:1 or from No. B.3062492
  4.44:1 with Overdrive)
- Alpine III 3.89:1
- Rapier IV .. .. 3.89:1 (4.22:1 with Overdrive)

Crownwheel to pinion backlash .. .. .. .005/.009

Adjustment. Bevel pinion .. .. Shims

Differential assembly .. .. Shims

Number of teeth:

Rapier I:	Crownwheel	47			
	Bevel pinion	9			
Rapier II:	Crownwheel	41			
	Bevel pinion	9			
Alpine:	Crownwheel	35 } 3.89	38 } 4.22		
	Bevel pinion	9	9		
Rapier:	Crownwheel	41 } 4.55	43 } 4.78		
	Bevel pinion	9	9		
Rapier:	Crownwheel	38 } 4.22	34 } 4.86	40 } 4.44	
	Bevel pinion	9	7	9	
Rapier:	Crownwheel	35 } 4.89	38 } 4.22		
	Bevel pinion	9	9		

FRONT SUSPENSION

Type .. .. Independent with unequal length

Springs .. .. Wishbones

Alpine I, II:	Outside diameter		3.87
Alpine III:	Outside diameter		4.40
	Free length		11.175 (up to No. B.9106289)
	Free length		11.65 (from No. B.9106290)
Alpine IV:	Outside diameter		4.47
	Free length		12.62
Rapier:	Outside diameter		4.51 (saloon)
	Outside diameter		4.46 (convertible)
	Free length		10.96 (saloon)
	Free length		11.52 (convertible)
Rapier IV:	Outside diameter		4.55
	Free length		11.86

REAR SUSPENSION

Type .. .. Semi-elliptic

Springs:
- Alpine I:
  - Length 44
  - Width 1.75
  - Depth 1.547
  - Number of blades 8
- Alpine II:
  - Length 44
  - Width 2.25
  - Depth 1.172
  - Number of blades 6

Alpine III:

Length	43.5	
Width	2.25	
Depth	1.172	.984 x
Number of blades	6	5 x

x Alpine IV

Rapier:

Length..	47.01/46.89
Width	1.5
Depth	1.72
Number of blades	6 x $\frac{5}{64}$ plus 1 x $\frac{5}{16}$

Rapier IV:

Depth	1.66
Number of blades	5 x $\frac{7}{32}$ plus 1 x $\frac{1}{4}$ plus 1 x $\frac{5}{16}$

DAMPERS

Type: Alpine	Armstrong. Hydraulic lever type
Rapier	Girling. Hydraulic telescopic
Fluid: Alpine	Armstrong S/A Fluid No. 624
Rapier	Not required

STEERING GEAR

Type: Rapier I	Burman 'P' worm and nut
All other models	Burman 'F' recirculating ball

Steering wheel turns, lock to lock:

Rapier I	2.5
All other Rapier models	3.15
All Alpine models	3

Steering angles:

Camber: Rapier I, II	0° 45' ±15'
All other models	0° 30' ±15'
Steering axis inclination	5° 15' ±15'
Castor: Rapier I	3° 40' ±15'
Rapier II	1° 45' ±15'
Rapier III, IV	0° 30' ±15'
Alpine	3° 30'
Toe-in: Rapier I	$\frac{1}{4}$
All other models	$\frac{1}{8}$

BRAKING SYSTEM

Make: Rapier	Lockheed
Alpine	Girling
Type	Hydraulic
Front brakes: Rapier I, II	Two leading shoe
All other models	Disc
Rear brakes	Leading and trailing shoe
Linings: Rapier I	Mintex M11
Rapier II	Ferodo DM53A
Alpine III. Rapier IV: Front	M40
Rear	Don 24
Rapier III, IIIA: Rear	Ferodo DM53A
All other models: Front	Don 55
Disc diameter: Alpine I, II	9.5
Alpine III	9.85
Rapier	10.8
Drum diameter	9
Fluid: Rapier I, II	Lockheed. SAE.70 R.1 or R.2
All other Rapier models	Lockheed. SAE.70 R.3
Alpine	Girling. SAE.70 R.3

ELECTRICAL EQUIPMENT

Battery:
Type and capacity   ..   ..   Lucas. 12 volt, 38 amp/hr
Earthing   ..   ..   Positive
Control box   ..   ..   Lucas RB.106/2
Alpine IV ..   ..   Lucas RB.340

Regulator open circuit setting at 1500 rev/min of generator:

At temperature:		
10°C. 50°F	.. ..	16.1-16.7 volts
20°C. 68°F.	.. ..	16.0-16.6 volts
30°C. 86°F.	.. ..	15.9-16.5 volts
40°C. 104°F.	.. ..	15.8-16.4 volts

Cut-out:
Cut-in voltage   ..   ..   12.7-13.3 volts
Drop-off voltage ..   ..   8.5-11.00 volts

Generator:
Type: Rapier I, II   ..   ..   Lucas C39PV-2
All other models   ..   ..   Lucas C40-1
Maximum output ..   ..   22 amps

Starter motor:
Type   ..   ..   Lucas M.35.G

TORQUE WRENCH SETTINGS

Engine and transmission:

Cylinder head (cold)	48 lb ft
Crankshaft (mains)	55 lb ft
Big-end bolts: Alpine I, Rapier III	20 lb ft
Alpine II, Rapier IIIA on	24 lb ft
Flywheel	40 lb ft
Mainshaft nuts	80 lb ft
Hypoid bevel pinion nut	110 lb ft
Axle shaft	180 lb ft
Universal joint. Metal to rubber	50 lb ft

Suspension and steering:

Fulcrum pin to crossmember (upper)	48 lb ft
Fulcrum pin to crossmember (lower)	32 lb ft
Eye bolt. Trunnion to link (lock)	85 lb ft
(castellated)	40 lb ft
Ball pin. Stub carrier to link	52 lb ft
Ball pin. Housing to link	33 lb ft
Damper to spring pan	6 lb ft
Crossmember to frame	62 lb ft
Road wheel nut	48 lb ft
Rear spring U-bolts: Alpine	42 lb ft
Rapier	16 lb ft
Steering box to frame	30 lb ft
Crosstube ball pin: Centre	30 lb ft
Outer	28 lb ft

Brakes:

Disc to hub	38 lb ft
Caliper to adaptor	52 lb ft
Steering arm to carrier and adaptor	38 and 60 lb ft
Adaptor to carrier	38 lb ft
Bleed screws	6 lb ft
Union nuts: Male	7 lb ft
Female	9 lb ft
Backplate to casing	17 lb ft
Wheel cylinder to backplate	12 lb ft

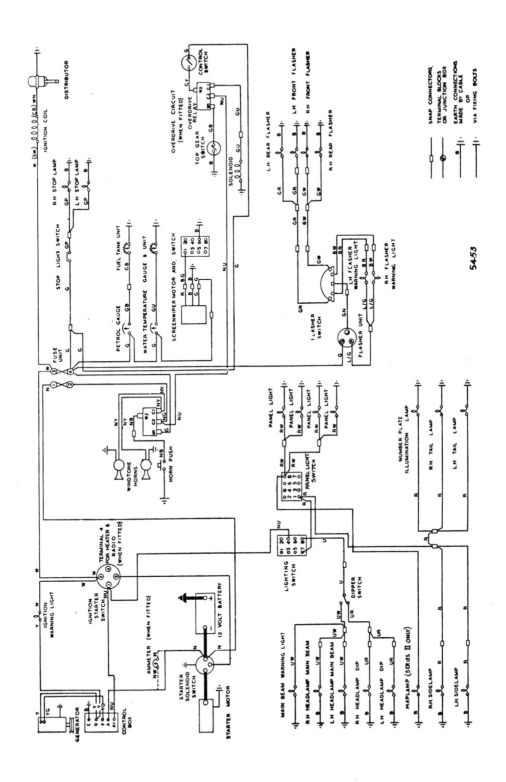

FIG 13:1 Wiring diagram for Alpine Series I

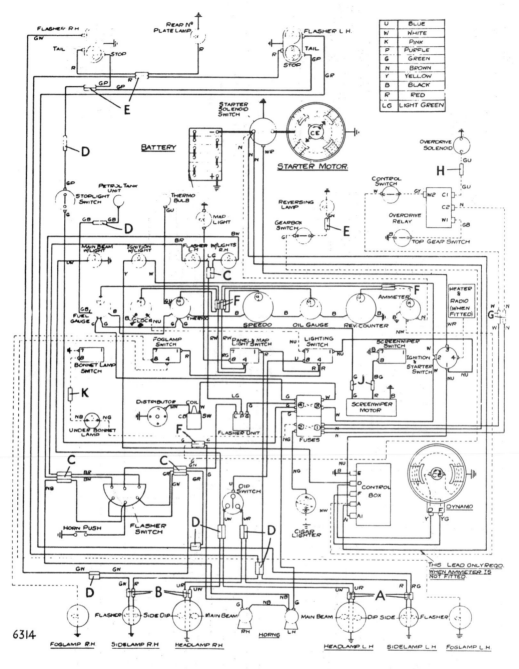

U	BLUE
W	WHITE
K	PINK
P	PURPLE
G	GREEN
N	BROWN
Y	YELLOW
B	BLACK
R	RED
LG	LIGHT GREEN

FIG 13:2   Wiring diagram for Alpine Series II—snap connector locations

6314

Key to Fig 13:2   A Lefthand front wing valance   **B** Righthand front wing valance   **C** Beneath facia adjacent to steering column   **D** On bulkhead below control box
E At extreme rear of car beneath spare wheel compartment   **F** Behind facia at rear of main instruments   **G** Attached to bulkhead on righthand side
H Righthand side of gearbox assembly   **J** Beneath facia adjacent to windscreen wiper motor   **K** Centre of engine bulkhead

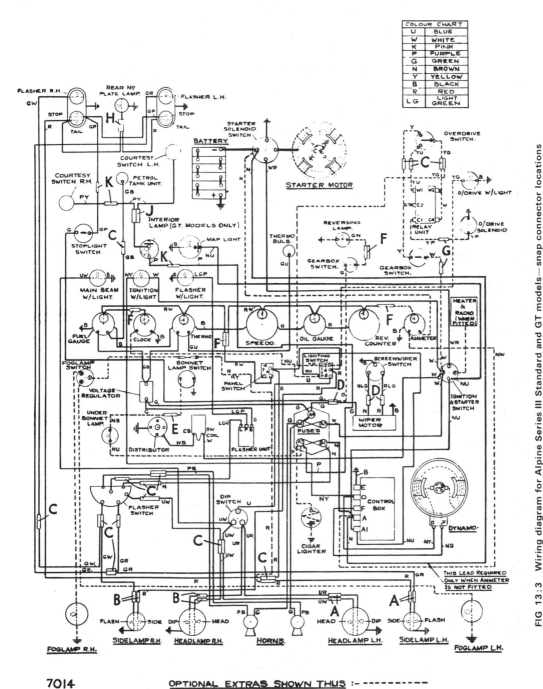

COLOUR CHART

U	BLUE
W	WHITE
K	PINK
P	PURPLE
G	GREEN
N	BROWN
Y	YELLOW
B	BLACK
R	RED
LG	LIGHT GREEN

FIG 13:3   Wiring diagram for Alpine Series III Standard and GT models—snap connector locations

Key to Fig 13:3   A Lefthand front wing valance   B Righthand front wing valance   C Beneath facia adjacent to steering column   D Beneath facia
adjacent to windscreen wiper motor   E Centre of engine bulkhead   F At rear of facia adjacent to instruments   G At lefthand side of gearbox
H At rear of car behind the boot lock   J Beneath facia on lefthand side   K Beneath facia on righthand side

7014   OPTIONAL EXTRAS SHOWN THUS :– – – – – – – –

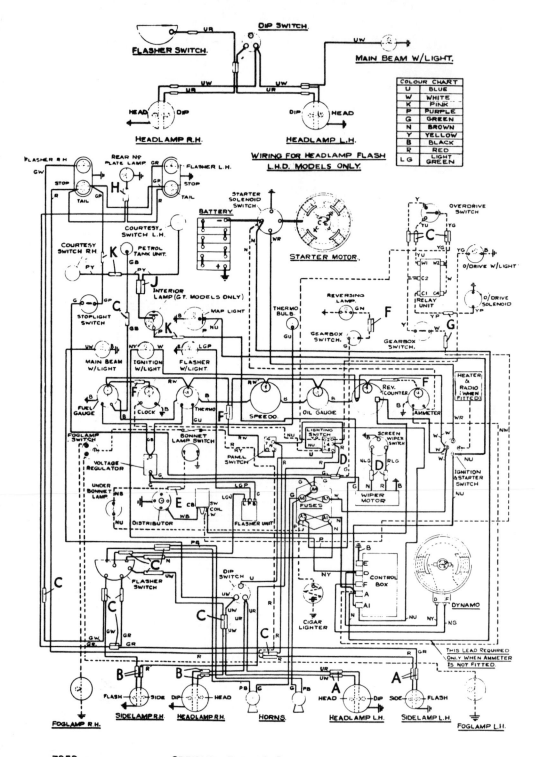

7252   OPTIONAL EXTRAS SHOWN THUS :-----------

FIG 13:4   Wiring diagram for Alpine Series IV Standard and GT models

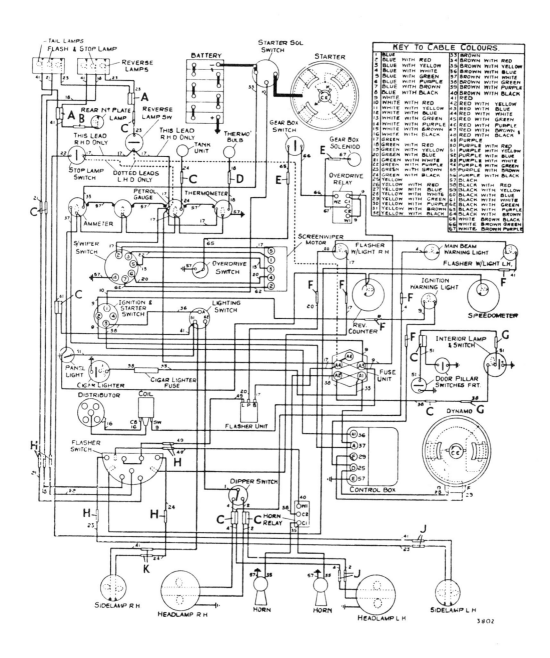

FIG 13:5   Wiring diagram for Rapier Series I—snap connector locations

Key to Fig 13:5   **A** Top lefthand corner of boot
side of car   **D** Adjacent to control box   **E** Adjacent to overdrive relay   **C** Under facia at lefthand   **F** Under facia behind the lamp
G Behind the lefthand side quarterlight trim panel   **B** In boot, under side of rear parcel tray   **H** Under facia in line with steering column   **J** On lefthand side wing
valance   **K** On righthand side wing valance

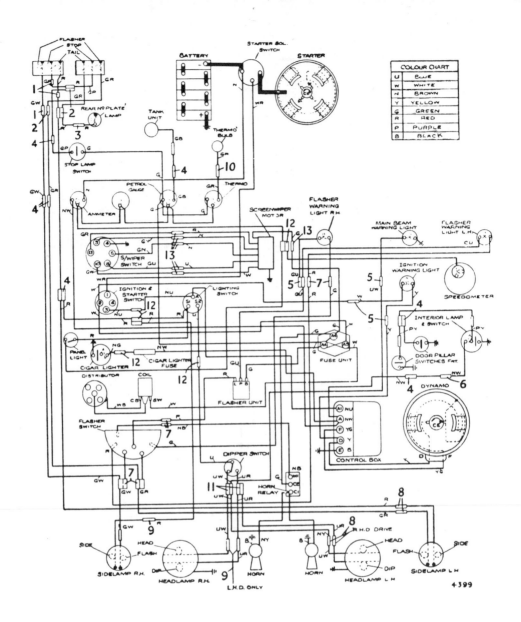

FIG 13:6 Wiring diagram for Rapier Series II—snap connector locations

Key to Fig 13:6   1 Top righthand corner of luggage boot   2 Top lefthand corner of luggage boot   3 In luggage boot under parcel shelf   4 Under facia lefthand side of car   5 Under facia behind warning lights   6 Behind the base lefthand side of quarterlight trim panel   7 Under facia in line with steering column   8 On lefthand side wing valance (front) 9 On righthand side wing valance (front)   10 Adjacent to transmitter on water pump   11 At lefthand wing valance on LHD. At righthand wing valance on RHD   12 Behind facia adjacent to instruments   13 Adjacent to windscreen wiper motor

142

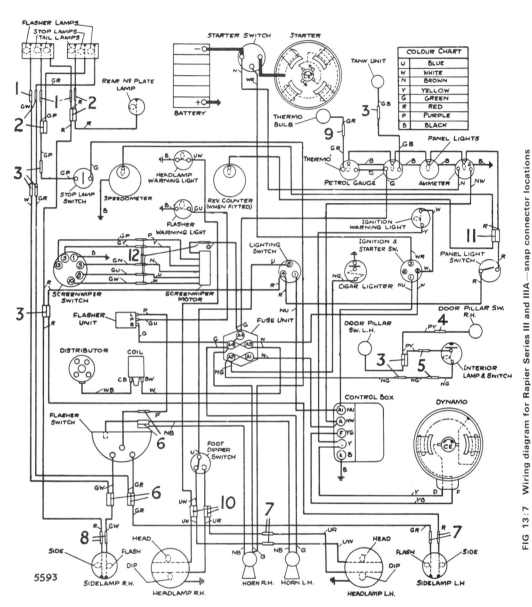

COLOUR CHART

U	BLUE
W	WHITE
N	BROWN
Y	YELLOW
G	GREEN
R	RED
P	PURPLE
B	BLACK

FIG 13:7 Wiring diagram for Rapier Series III and IIIA—snap connector locations

Key to Fig 13:7
1 Top righthand corner of boot   2 Top lefthand corner of boot
3 Under lefthand side of facia   4 Under righthand side of facia
5 Behind lefthand quarter trim pad   6 Under facia in line with steering column   7 On lefthand front wing valance   8 On righthand front wing valance
9 Near thermometer element on water pump   10 LHD at lefthand front wing valance. RHD at righthand front wing valance   11 Behind facia near instruments
12 Near windscreen wiper motor

5593

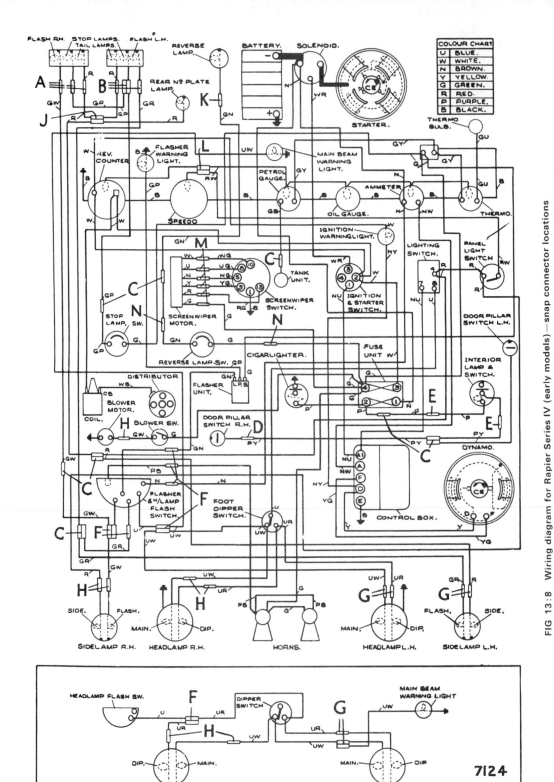

FIG 13:8 Wiring diagram for Rapier Series IV (early models)—snap connector locations

COLOUR CHART	
U	BLUE.
W	WHITE.
N	BROWN.
Y	YELLOW.
G	GREEN.
R	RED.
P	PURPLE.
B	BLACK.

C Beneath lefthand side of facia
J Upper lefthand corner of luggage compartment
N Lefthand wing valance beneath control box

A At rear of righthand tail lamp cluster
D Beneath righthand side of facia
K Adjacent to reversing lamp

B At rear of lefthand tail lamp cluster
F Beneath facia adjacent to steering column
M Adjacent to windscreen wiper motor

E At rear of lefthand quarter trim
L Behind facia in line with instruments

Key to Fig 13:8

WIRING OF HEADLAMPS, W/LIGHT & FLASH SWITCH FOR L.H.D.

7124

144

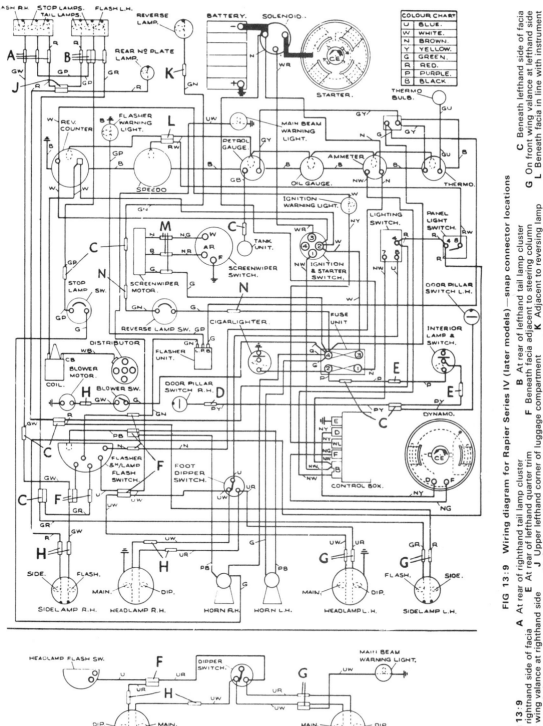

FIG 13:9 Wiring diagram for Rapier Series IV (later models) — snap connector locations

COLOUR CHART	
U	BLUE.
W	WHITE.
N	BROWN.
Y	YELLOW.
G	GREEN.
R	RED.
P	PURPLE.
B	BLACK.

Key to Fig 13:9
A At rear of righthand tail lamp cluster   B At rear of lefthand tail lamp cluster   C Beneath lefthand side of facia
D Beneath righthand side of facia   E At rear of lefthand side   G On front wing valance at lefthand side
H On front wing valance at righthand side   F Beneath facia adjacent to steering column   L Beneath facia in line with instrument
J Upper lefthand corner of luggage compartment   K Adjacent to reversing lamp
M Adjacent to windscreen wiper motor   N On front wing valance at lefthand side beneath control box

7565

WIRING OF HEADLAMPS, W/LIGHT & FLASH SWITCH FOR L.H.D.

Inches	Decimals	Milli-metres	Inches to Millimetres		Millimetres to Inches	
			Inches	mm	mm.	Inches
1/64	.015625	.3969	.001	.0254	.01	.00039
1/32	.03125	.7937	.002	.0508	.02	.00079
3/64	.046875	1.1906	.003	.0762	.03	.00118
1/16	.0625	1.5875	.004	.1016	.04	.00157
5/64	.078125	1.9844	.005	.1270	.05	.00197
3/32	.09375	2.3812	.006	.1524	.06	.00236
7/64	.109375	2.7781	.007	.1778	.07	.00276
1/8	.125	3.1750	.008	.2032	.08	.00315
9/64	.140625	3.5719	.009	.2286	.09	.00354
5/32	.15625	3.9687	.01	.254	.1	.00394
11/64	.171875	4.3656	.02	.508	.2	.00787
3/16	.1875	4.7625	.03	.762	3	.01181
13/64	.203125	5·1594	.04	1.016	.4	.01575
7/32	.21875	5.5562	.05	1.270	.5	.01969
15/64	.234375	5.9531	.06	1.524	.6	.02362
1/4	.25	6.3500	.07	1.778	.7	.02756
17/64	.265625	6.7469	.08	2.032	.8	.03150
9/32	.28125	7.1437	.09	2.286	.9	.03543
19/64	.296875	7.5406	.1	2.54	1	.03937
5/16	.3125	7.9375	.2	5.08	2	.07874
21/64	.328125	8.3344	.3	7.62	3	.11811
11/32	.34375	8.7312	.4	10.16	4	.15748
23/64	.359375	9.1281	.5	12.70	5	.19685
3/8	.375	9.5250	.6	15.24	6	.23622
25/64	.390625	9.9219	.7	17.78	7	.27559
13/32	.40625	10.3187	.8	20.32	8	.31496
27/64	.421875	10.7156	.9	22.86	9	.35433
7/16	.4375	11.1125	1	25.4	10	.39370
29/64	.453125	11.5094	2	50.8	11	.43307
15/32	.46875	11.9062	3	76.2	12	.47244
31/64	.484375	12.3031	4	101.6	13	.51181
1/2	.5	12.7000	5	127.0	14	.55118
33/64	.515625	13.0969	6	152.4	15	.59055
17/32	.53125	13.4937	7	177 8	16	.62992
35/64	.546875	13.8906	8	203.2	17	.66929
9/16	.5625	14.2875	9	228.6	18	.70866
37/64	.578125	14.6844	10	254.0	19	.74803
19/32	.59375	15.0812	11	279.4	20	.78740
39/64	.609375	15.4781	12	304.8	21	.82677
5/8	.625	15.8750	13	330.2	22	.86614
41/64	.640625	16.2719	14	355.6	23	.90551
21/32	.65625	16.6687	15	381.0	24	.94488
43/64	.671875	17.0656	16	406.4	25	.98425
11/16	.6875	17.4625	17	431.8	26	1.02362
45/64	.703125	17.8594	18	457.2	27	1.06299
23/32	.71875	18.2562	19	482.6	28	1.10236
47/64	.734375	18.6531	20	508.0	29	1.14173
3/4	.75	19.0500	21	533.4	30	1.18110
49/64	.765625	19.4469	22	558.8	31	1.22047
25/32	.78125	19.8437	23	584.2	32	1.25984
51/64	.796875	20.2406	24	609.6	33	1.29921
13/16	.8125	20.6375	25	635.0	34	1.33858
53/64	.828125	21.0344	26	660.4	35	1.37795
27/32	.84375	21.4312	27	685.8	36	1.41732
55/64	.859375	21.8281	28	711.2	37	1.4567
7/8	.875	22.2250	29	736.6	38	1.4961
57/64	.890625	22.6219	30	762.0	39	1.5354
29/32	.90625	23.0187	31	787.4	40	1.5748
59/64	.921875	23.4156	32	812.8	41	1.6142
15/16	.9375	23.8125	33	838.2	42	1.6535
61/64	.953125	24.2094	34	863.6	43	1.6929
31/32	.96875	24.6062	35	889.0	44	1.7323
63/64	.984375	25.0031	36	914.4	45	1.7717

UNITS	Pints to Litres	Gallons to Litres	Litres to Pints	Litres to Gallons	Miles to Kilometres	Kilometres to Miles	Lbs. per sq. In. to Kg. per sq. Cm.	Kg. per sq. Cm. to Lbs. per sq. In.
1	.57	4.55	1.76	.22	1.61	.62	.07	14.22
2	1.14	9.09	3.52	.44	3.22	1.24	.14	28.50
3	1.70	13.64	5.28	.66	4.83	1.86	.21	42.67
4	2.27	18.18	7.04	.88	6.44	2.49	.28	56.89
5	2.84	22.73	8.80	1.10	8.05	3.11	.35	71.12
6	3.41	27.28	10.56	1.32	9.66	3.73	.42	85.34
7	3.98	31.82	12.32	1.54	11.27	4.35	.49	99.56
8	4.55	36.37	14.08	1.76	12.88	4.97	.56	113.79
9		40.91	15.84	1.98	14.48	5.59	.63	128.00
10		45.46	17.60	2.20	16.09	6.21	.70	142.23
20				4.40	32.19	12.43	1.41	284.47
30				6.60	48.28	18.64	2.11	426.70
40				8.80	64.37	24.85		
50					80.47	31.07		
60					96.56	37.28		
70					112.65	43.50		
80					128.75	49.71		
90					144.84	55.92		
100					160.93	62.14		

UNITS	Lb ft to kgm	Kgm to lb ft	UNITS	Lb ft to kgm	Kgm to lb ft
1	.138	7.233	7	.967	50.631
2	.276	14.466	8	1.106	57.864
3	.414	21.699	9	1.244	65.097
4	.553	28.932	10	1.382	72.330
5	.691	36.165	20	2.765	144.660
6	.829	43.398	30	4.147	216.990

HINTS ON MAINTENANCE AND OVERHAUL

There are few things more rewarding than the restoration of a vehicle's original peak of efficiency and smooth performance.

The following notes are intended to help the owner to reach that state of perfection. Providing that he possesses the basic manual skills he should have no difficulty in performing most of the operations detailed in this manual. It must be stressed, however, that where recommended in the manual, highly-skilled operations ought to be entrusted to experts, who have the necessary equipment, to carry out the work satisfactorily.

Quality of workmanship:

The hazardous driving conditions on the roads to-day demand that vehicles should be as nearly perfect, mechanically, as possible. It is therefore most important that amateur work be carried out with care, bearing in mind the often inadequate working conditions, and also the inferior tools which may have to be used. It is easy to counsel perfection in all things, and we recognize that it may be setting an impossibly high standard. We do, however, suggest that every care should be taken to ensure that a vehicle is as safe to take on the road as it is humanly possible to make it.

Safe working conditions:

Even though a vehicle may be stationary, it is still potentially dangerous if certain sensible precautions are not taken when working on it while it is supported on jacks or blocks. It is indeed preferable not to use jacks alone, but to supplement them with carefully placed blocks, so that there will be plenty of support if the car rolls off the jacks during a strenuous manoeuvre. Axle stands are an excellent way of providing a rigid base which is not readily disturbed. Piles of bricks are a dangerous substitute. Be careful not to get under heavy loads on lifting tackle, the load could fall. It is preferable not to work alone when lifting an engine, or when working underneath a vehicle which is supported well off the ground. To be trapped, particularly under the vehicle, may have unpleasant results if help is not quickly forthcoming. Make some provision, however humble, to deal with fires. Always disconnect a battery if there is a likelihood of electrical shorts. These may start a fire if there is leaking fuel about. This applies particularly to leads which can carry a heavy current, like those in the starter circuit. While on the subject of electricity, we must also stress the danger of using equipment which is run off the mains and which has no earth or has faulty wiring or connections. So many workshops have damp floors, and electrical shocks are of such a nature that it is sometimes impossible to let go of a live lead or piece of equipment due to the muscular spasms which take place.

Work demanding special care:

This involves the servicing of braking, steering and suspension systems. On the road, failure of the braking system may be disastrous. Make quite sure that there can be no possibility of failure through the bursting of rusty brake pipes or rotten hoses, nor to a sudden loss of pressure due to defective seals or valves.

Problems:

The chief problems which may face an operator are:
1. External dirt.
2. Difficulty in undoing tight fixings.
3. Dismantling unfamiliar mechanisms.
4. Deciding in what respect parts are defective.
5. Confusion about the correct order for reassembly.
6. Adjusting running clearance.
7. Road testing.
8. Final tuning.

Practical suggestions to solve the problems:

1. Preliminary cleaning of large parts—engines, transmissions, steering, suspensions, etc.,—should be carried out before removal from the car. Where road dirt and mud alone are present, wash clean with a high-pressure water jet, brushing to remove stubborn adhesions, and allow to drain and dry. Where oil or grease is also present, wash down with a proprietary compound (Gunk, Tepol etc.,) applying with a stiff brush—an old paint brush is suitable—into all crevices. Cover the distributor and ignition coils with a polythene bag and then apply a strong water jet to clear the loosened deposits. Allow to drain and dry. The assemblies will then be sufficiently clean to remove and transfer to the bench for the next stage.

   On the bench, further cleaning can be carried out, first wiping the parts as free as possible from grease with old newspaper. Avoid using rag or cotton waste which can leave clogging fibres behind. Any remaining grease can be removed with a brush dipped in paraffin. If necessary, traces of paraffin can be removed by carbon tetrachloride. Avoid using paraffin or petrol in large quantities for cleaning in enclosed areas, such as garages, on account of the high fire risk.

   When all exteriors have been cleaned, and not before, dismantling can be commenced. This ensures that dirt will not enter into interiors and orifices revealed by dismantling. In the next phases, where components have to be cleaned, use carbon tetrachloride in preference to petrol and keep the containers covered except when in use. After the components have been cleaned, plug small holes with tapered hard wood plugs cut to size and blank off larger orifices with grease-proof paper and masking tape. Do not use soft wood plugs or matchsticks as they may break.

2. It is not advisable to hammer on the end of a screw thread, but if it must be done, first screw on a nut to protect the thread, and use a lead hammer. This applies particularly to the removal of tapered cotters. Nuts and bolts seem to 'grow' together, especially in exhaust systems. If penetrating oil does not work, try the judicious application of heat, but be careful of starting a fire. Asbestos sheet or cloth is useful to isolate heat.

   Tight bushes or pieces of tail-pipe rusted into a silencer can be removed by splitting them with an open-ended hacksaw. Tight screws can sometimes be started by a tap from a hammer on the end of a suitable screwdriver. Many tight fittings will yield to the judicious use of a hammer, but it must be a soft-faced hammer if damage is to be avoided, use a heavy block on the opposite side to absorb shock. Any parts of the steering system which have been damaged should be renewed, as attempts to repair them may lead to cracking and subsequent failure, and steering ball joints should be disconnected using a recommended tool to prevent damage.

3   It often happens that an owner is baffled when trying to dismantle an unfamiliar piece of equipment. So many modern devices are pressed together or assembled by spinning-over flanges, that they must be sawn apart. The intention is that the whole assembly must be renewed. However, parts which appear to be in one piece to the naked eye, may reveal close-fitting joint lines when inspected with a magnifying glass, and, this may provide the necessary clue to dismantling. Left-handed screw threads are used where rotational forces would tend to unscrew a right-handed screw thread.

Be very careful when dismantling mechanisms which may come apart suddenly. Work in an enclosed space where the parts will be contained, and drape a piece of cloth over the device if springs are likely to fly in all directions. Mark everything which might be reassembled in the wrong position, scratched symbols may be used on unstressed parts, or a sequence of tiny dots from a centre punch can be useful. Stressed parts should never be scratched or centre-popped as this may lead to cracking under working conditions. Store parts which look alike in the correct order for reassembly. Never rely upon memory to assist in the assembly of complicated mechanisms, especially when they will be dismantled for a long time, but make notes, and drawings to supplement the diagrams in the manual, and put labels on detached wires. Rust stains may indicate unlubricated wear. This can sometimes be seen round the outside edge of a bearing cup in a universal joint. Look for bright rubbing marks on parts which normally should not make heavy contact. These might prove that something is bent or running out of truth. For example, there might be bright marks on one side of a piston, at the top near the ring grooves, and others at the bottom of the skirt on the other side. This could well be the clue to a bent connecting rod. Suspected cracks can be proved by heating the component in a light oil to approximately 100°C, removing, drying off, and dusting with french chalk, if a crack is present the oil retained in the crack will stain the french chalk.

4   In determining wear, and the degree, against the permissible limits set in the manual, accurate measurement can only be achieved by the use of a micrometer. In many cases, the wear is given to the fourth place of decimals; that is in ten-thousandths of an inch. This can be read by the vernier scale on the barrel of a good micrometer. Bore diameters are more difficult to determine. If, however, the matching shaft is accurately measured, the degree of play in the bore can be felt as a guide to its suitability. In other cases, the shank of a twist drill of known diameter is a handy check.

Many methods have been devised for determining the clearance between bearing surfaces. To-day the best and simplest is by the use of Plastigage, obtainable from most garages. A thin plastic thread is laid between the two surfaces and the bearing is tightened, flattening the thread. On removal, the width of the thread is compared with a scale supplied with the thread and the clearance is read off directly. Sometimes joint faces leak persistently, even after gasket renewal. The fault will then be traceable to distortion, dirt or burrs. Studs which are screwed into soft metal frequently raise burrs at the point of entry. A quick cure for this is to chamfer the edge of the hole in the part which fits over the stud.

5   **Always check a replacement part with the original one before it is fitted.**

If parts are not marked, and the order for reassembly is not known, a little detective work will help. Look for marks which are due to wear to see if they can be mated. Joint faces may not be identical due to manufacturing errors, and parts which overlap may be stained, giving a clue to the correct position. Most fixings leave identifying marks especially if they were painted over on assembly. It is then easier to decide whether a nut, for instance, has a plain, a spring, or a shakeproof washer under it. All running surfaces become 'bedded' together after long spells of work and tiny imperfections on one part will be found to have left corresponding marks on the other. This is particularly true of shafts and bearings and even a score on a cylinder wall will show on the piston.

6   Checking end float or rocker clearances by feeler gauge may not always give accurate results because of wear. For instance, the rocker tip which bears on a valve stem may be deeply pitted, in which case the feeler will simply be bridging a depression. Thrust washers may also wear depressions in opposing faces to make accurate measurement difficult. End float is then easier to check by using a dial gauge. It is common practice to adjust end play in bearing assemblies, like front hubs with taper rollers, by doing up the axle nut until the hub becomes stiff to turn and then backing it off a little. Do not use this method with ballbearing hubs as the assembly is often preloaded by tightening the axle nut to its fullest extent. If the splitpin hole will not line up, file the base of the nut a little.

Steering assemblies often wear in the straight-ahead position. If any part is adjusted, make sure that it remains free when moved from lock to lock. Do not be surprised if an assembly like a steering gearbox, which is known to be carefully adjusted outside the car, becomes stiff when it is bolted in place. This will be due to distortion of the case by the pull of the mounting bolts, particularly if the mounting points are not all touching together. This problem may be met in other equipment and is cured by careful attention to the alignment of mounting points.

When a spanner is stamped with a size and A/F it means that the dimension is the width between the jaws and has no connection with ANF, which is the designation for the American National Fine thread. Coarse threads like Whitworth are rarely used on cars to-day except for studs which screw into soft aluminium or cast iron. For this reason it might be found that the top end of a cylinder head stud has a fine thread and the lower end a coarse thread to screw into the cylinder block. If the car has mainly UNF threads then it is likely that any coarse threads will be UNC, which are not the same as Whitworth. Small sizes have the same number of threads in Whitworth and UNC, but in the $\frac{1}{2}$ inch size for example, there are twelve threads to the inch in the former and thirteen in the latter.

7 After a major overhaul, particularly if a great deal of work has been done on the braking, steering and suspension systems, it is advisable to approach the problem of testing with care. If the braking system has been overhauled, apply heavy pressure to the brake pedal and get a second operator to check every possible source of leakage. The brakes may work extremely well, but a leak could cause complete failure after a few miles.

Do not fit the hub caps until every wheel nut has been checked for tightness, and make sure the tyre pressures are correct. Check the levels of coolant, lubricants and hydraulic fluids. Being satisfied that all is well, take the car on the road and test the brakes at once. Check the steering and the action of the handbrake. Do all this at moderate speeds on quiet roads, and make sure there is no other vehicle behind you when you try a rapid stop.

Finally, remember that many parts settle down after a time, so check for tightness of all fixings after the car has been on the road for a hundred miles or so.

8 It is useless to tune an engine which has not reached its normal running temperature. In the same way, the tune of an engine which is stiff after a rebore will be different when the engine is again running free. Remember too, that rocker clearances on pushrod operated valve gear will change when the cylinder head nuts are tightened after an initial period of running with a new head gasket.

Trouble may not always be due to what seems the obvious cause. Ignition, carburation and mechanical condition are interdependent and spitting back through the carburetter, which might be attributed to a weak mixture, can be caused by a sticking inlet valve.

For one final hint on tuning, never adjust more than one thing at a time or it will be impossible to tell which adjustment produced the desired result.

GLOSSARY OF TERMS

Allen key   Cranked wrench of hexagonal section for use with socket head screws.

Alternator   Electrical generator producing alternating current. Rectified to direct current for battery charging.

Ambient temperature   Surrounding atmospheric temperature.

Annulus   Used in engineering to indicate the outer ring gear of an epicyclic gear train.

Armature   The shaft carrying the windings, which rotates in the magnetic field of a generator or starter motor. That part of a solenoid or relay which is activated by the magnetic field.

Axial   In line with, or pertaining to, an axis.

Backlash   Play in meshing gears.

Balance lever   A bar where force applied at the centre is equally divided between connections at the ends.

Banjo axle   Axle casing with large diameter housing for the crownwheel and differential.

Bendix pinion   A self-engaging and self-disengaging drive on a starter motor shaft.

Bevel pinion   A conical shaped gearwheel, designed to mesh with a similar gear with an axis usually at 90 deg. to its own.

bhp   Brake horse power, measured on a dynamometer.

bmep   Brake mean effective pressure. Average pressure on a piston during the working stroke.

Brake cylinder   Cylinder with hydraulically operated piston(s) acting on brake shoes or pad(s).

Brake regulator   Control valve fitted in hydraulic braking system which limits brake pressure to rear brakes during heavy braking to prevent rear wheel locking.

Camber   Angle at which a wheel is tilted from the vertical.

Capacitor   Modern term for an electrical condenser. Part of distributor assembly, connected across contact breaker points, acts as an interference suppressor.

Castellated   Top face of a nut, slotted across the flats, to take a locking splitpin.

Castor   Angle at which the kingpin or swivel pin is tilted when viewed from the side.

cc   Cubic centimetres. Engine capacity is arrived at by multiplying the area of the bore in sq cm by the stroke in cm by the number of cylinders.

Clevis   U-shaped forked connector used with a clevis pin, usually at handbrake connections.

Collet   A type of collar, usually split and located in a groove in a shaft, and held in place by a retainer. The arrangement used to retain the spring(s) on a valve stem in most cases.

Commutator   Rotating segmented current distributor between armature windings and brushes in generator or motor.

Compression   The ratio, or quantitative relation, of the total volume (piston at bottom of stroke) to the unswept volume (piston at top of stroke) in an engine cylinder.

Condenser   See capacitor.

Core plug   Plug for blanking off a manufacturing hole in a casting.

Crownwheel   Large bevel gear in rear axle, driven by a bevel pinion attached to the propeller shaft. Sometimes called a 'ring wheel'.

'C'-spanner   Like a 'C' with a handle. For use on screwed collars without flats, but with slots or holes.

Damper   Modern term for shock-absorber, used in vehicle suspension systems to damp out spring oscillations.

Depression   The lowering of atmospheric pressure as in the inlet manifold and carburetter.

Dowel   Close tolerance pin, peg, tube, or bolt, which accurately locates mating parts.

Drag link   Rod connecting steering box drop arm (pitman arm) to nearest front wheel steering arm in certain types of steering systems.

Dry liner   Thinwall tube pressed into cylinder bore.

Dry sump   Lubrication system where all oil is scavenged from the sump, and returned to a separate tank.

Dynamo   See Generator.

Electrode   Terminal, part of an electrical component, such as the points or 'Electrodes' of a sparking plug.

Electrolyte   In lead-acid car batteries a solution of sulphuric acid and distilled water.

End float   The axial movement between associated parts, end play.

EP   Extreme pressure. In lubricants, special grades for heavily loaded bearing surfaces, such as gear teeth in a gearbox, or crownwheel and pinion in a rear axle.

Fade	Of brakes. Reduced efficiency due to overheating.
Field coils	Windings on the polepieces of motors and generators.
Fillets	Narrow finishing strips usually applied to interior bodywork.
First motion shaft	Input snaft from clutch to gearbox.
Fullflow filter	Filters in which all the oil is pumped to the engine. If the element becomes clogged, a bypass valve operates to pass unfiltered oil to the engine.
FWD	Front wheel drive.
Gear pump	Two meshing gears in a close fitting casing. Oil is carried from the inlet round the outside of both gears in the spaces between the gear teeth and casing to the outlet, the meshing gear teeth prevent oil passing back to the inlet, and the oil is forced through the outlet port.
Generator	Modern term for 'Dynamo'. When rotated produces electrical current.
Grommet	A ring of protective or sealing material. Can be used to protect pipes or leads passing through bulkheads.
Grubscrew	Fuly threaded headless screw with screwdriver slot. Used for locking, or alignment purposes.
Gudgeon pin	Shaft which connects a piston to its connecting rod. Sometimes called 'wrist pin', or 'piston pin'.
Halfshaft	One of a pair transmitting drive from the differ ntial.
Helical	In spiral form. The teeth of helical gears are cut at a spiral angle to the side faces of the gearwheel.
Hot spot	Hot area that assists vapourisation of fuel on its way to cylinders. Often provided by close contact between inlet and exhaust manifolds.
HT	High Tension. Applied to electrical current produced by the ignition coil for the sparking plugs.
Hydrometer	A device for checking specific gravity of liquids. Used to check specific gravity of electrolyte.
Hypoid bevel gears	A form of bevel gear used in the rear axle drive gears. The bevel pinion meshes below the centre line of the crownwheel, giving a lower propeller shaft line.
Idler	A device for passing on movement. A free running gear between driving and driven gears. A lever transmitting track rod movement to a side rod in steering gear.
Impeller	A centrifugal pumping element. Used in water pumps to stimulate flow.

Journals	Those parts of a shaft that are in contact with the bearings.
Kingpin	The main vertical pin which carries the front wheel spindle, and permits steering movement. May be called 'steering pin' or 'swivel pin'.
Layshaft	The shaft which carries the laygear in the gearbox. The laygear is driven by the first motion shaft and drives the third motion shaft according to the gear selected. Sometimes called the 'countershaft' or 'second motion shaft.'
lb ft	A measure of twist or torque. A pull of 10 lb at a radius of 1 ft is a torque of 10 lb ft.
lb/sq in	Pounds per square inch.
Little-end	The small, or piston end of a connecting rod. Sometimes called the 'small-end'.
LT	Low Tension. The current output from the battery.
Mandrel	Accurately manufactured bar or rod used for test or centring purposes.
Manifold	A pipe, duct, or chamber, with several branches.
Needle rollers	Bearing rollers with a length many times their diameter.
Oil bath	Reservoir which lubricates parts by immersion. In air filters, a separate oil supply for wetting a wire mesh element to hold the dust.
Oil wetted	In air filters, a wire mesh element lightly oiled to trap and hold airborne dust.
Overlap	Period during which inlet and exhaust valves are open together.
Panhard rod	Bar connected between fixed point on chassis and another on axle to control sideways movement.
Pawl	Pivoted catch which engages in the teeth of a ratchet to permit movement in one direction only.
Peg spanner	Tool with pegs, or pins, to engage in holes or slots in the part to be turned.
Pendant pedals	Pedals with levers that are pivoted at the top end.
Phillips screwdriver	A cross-point screwdriver for use with the cross-slotted heads of Phillips screws.
Pinion	A small gear, usually in relation to another gear.
Piston-type damper	Shock absorber in which damping is controlled by a piston working in a closed oil-filled cylinder.
Preloading	Preset static pressure on ball or roller bearings not due to working loads.
Radial	Radiating from a centre, like the spokes of a wheel.

Radius rod	Pivoted arm confining movement of a part to an arc of fixed radius.
Ratchet	Toothed wheel or rack which can move in one direction only, movement in the other being prevented by a pawl.
Ring gear	A gear tooth ring attached to outer periphery of flywheel. Starter pinion engages with it during starting.
Runout	Amount by which rotating part is out of true.
Semi-floating axle	Outer end of rear axle halfshaft is carried on bearing inside axle casing. Wheel hub is secured to end of shaft.
Servo	A hydraulic or pneumatic system for assisting, or, augmenting a physical effort. See 'Vacuum Servo'.
Setscrew	One which is threaded for the full length of the shank.
Shackle	A coupling link, used in the form of two parallel pins connected by side plates to secure the end of the master suspension spring and absorb the effects of deflection.
Shell bearing	Thinwalled steel shell lined with antifriction metal. Usually semi-circular and used in pairs for main and big-end bearings.
Shock absorber	See 'Damper'.
Silentbloc	Rubber bush bonded to inner and outer metal sleeves.
Socket-head screw	Screw with hexagonal socket for an Allen key.
Solenoid	A coil of wire creating a magnetic field when electric current passes through it. Used with a soft iron core to operate contacts or a mechanical device.
Spur gear	A gear with teeth cut axially across the periphery.
Stub axle	Short axle fixed at one end only.
Tachometer	An instrument for accurate measurement of rotating speed. Usually indicates in revolutions per minute.

TDC	Top Dead Centre. The highest point reached by a piston in a cylinder, with the crank and connecting rod in line.
Thermostat	Automatic device for regulating temperature. Used in vehicle coolant systems to open a valve which restricts circulation at low temperature.
Third motion shaft	Output shaft of gearbox.
Threequarters floating axle	Outer end of rear axle halfshaft flanged and bolted to wheel hub, which runs bearing mounted on outside of axle casing. Vehicle weight is not carried by the axle shaft.
Thrust bearing or washer	Used to reduce friction in rotating parts subject to axial loads.
Torque	Turning or twisting effort. See 'lb ft'.
Track rod	The bar(s) across the vehicle which connect the steering arms and maintain the front wheels in their correct alignment.
UJ	Universal joint. A coupling between shafts which permits angular movement.
UNF	Unified National Fine screw thread.
Vacuum servo	Device used in brake system, using difference between atmospheric pressure and inlet manifold depression to operate a piston which acts to augment brake pressure as required. See 'Servo'.
Venturi	A restriction or 'choke' in a tube, as in a carburetter, used to increase velocity to obtain a reduction in pressure.
Vernier	A sliding scale for obtaining fractional readings of the graduations of an adjacent scale.
Welch plug	A domed thin metal disc which is partially flattened to lock in a recess. Used to plug core holes in castings.
Wet liner	Removeable cylinder barrel, sealed against coolant leakage, where the coolant is in direct contact with the outer surface.
Wet sump	A reservoir attached to the crankcase to hold the lubricating oil.

INDEX

THE AUTOBOOK SERIES OF WORKSHOP MANUALS

Make					Author	Title
ALFA ROMEO						
1600 Giulia TI 1961–67	..	..	..		Ball	Alfa Romeo Giulia 1962–70 Autobook
1600 Giulia Sprint 1962–68	..	..	..		Ball	Alfa Romeo Giulia 1962–70 Autobook
1600 Giulia Spider 1962–68	..	..	..		Ball	Alfa Romeo Giulia 1962–70 Autobook
1600 Giulia Super 1965–70	..	..	..		Ball	Alfa Romeo Giulia 1962–70 Autobook
ASTON MARTIN						
All models 1921–58	..	..	..	..	Coram	Aston Martin 1921–58 Autobook
AUSTIN						
A30 1951–56	..	..	..	..	Ball	Austin A30, A35, A40 Autobook
A35 1956–62	..	..	..	..	Ball	Austin A30, A35, A40 Autobook
A40 Farina 1957–67	..	..	..	..	Ball	Austin A30, A35, A40 Autobook
A40 Cambridge 1954–57	..	..	..		Ball	BMC Autobook Three
A50 Cambridge 1954–57	..	..	..		Ball	BMC Autobook Three
A55 Cambridge Mk 1 1957–58	..	..	..		Ball	BMC Autobook Three
A55 Cambridge Mk 2 1958–61	..	..	..		Ball	Austin A55 Mk 2, A60 1958–69 Autobook
A60 Cambridge 1961–69	..	..	..		Ball	Austin A55 Mk 2, A60 1958–69 Autobook
A99 1959–61	..	....	..		Ball	BMC Autobook Four
A110 1961–68	..	..	..		Ball	BMC Autobook Four
Mini 1959–70	..	..	..	..	Ball	Mini 1959–70 Autobook
Mini Clubman 1969–70	..	..	..		Ball	Mini 1959–70 Autobook
Mini Cooper 1961–70	..	..	..		Ball	Mini Cooper 1961–70 Autobook
Mini Cooper S 1963–70	..	..	..		Ball	Mini Cooper 1961–70 Autobook
1100 Mk 1 1963–67	..	..	..		Ball	1100 Mk 1 1962–67 Autobook
1100 Mk 2 1968–70	..	..	..		Ball	1100 Mk 2, 1300 Mk 1, 2, America 1968–71 Autobook
1300 Mk 1, 2 1968–71	..	..	..		Ball	1100 Mk 2, 1300 Mk 1, 2, America 1968–71 Autobook
America 1968–71	..	..	..		Ball	1100 Mk 2, 1300 Mk 1, 2, America 1968–71 Autobook
1800 Mk 1, 2 1964–71	..	..	..		Ball	1800 1964–71 Autobook
1800 S 1969–71	..	..	..		Ball	1800 1964–71 Autobook
Maxi 1500 1969–71	..	..	..		Ball	Austin Maxi 1969–71 Autobook
Maxi 1750 1970–71	..	..	..		Ball	Austin Maxi 1969–71 Autobook
AUSTIN HEALEY						
100/6 1956–59	..	..	..	..	Ball	Austin Healey 100/6, 3000 1956–68 Autobook
Sprite 1958–70	..	..	..	..	Ball	Sprite, Midget 1958–70 Autobook
3000 Mk 1, 2, 3 1959–68	..	..	..		Ball	Austin Healey 100/6, 3000 1956–68 Autobook
BEDFORD						
CA Mk 1 and 2 1961–69	..	..	..		Ball	Vauxhall Victor 1, 2 FB 1957–64 Autobook
Beagle HA 1964–66	..	..	..		Ball	Vauxhall Viva HA 1964–66 Autobook
BMW						
1600 1966–70	..	..	..	..	Ball	BMW 1600 1966–70 Autobook
1600–2 1966–70	..	..	..	..	Ball	BMW 1600 1966–70 Autobook
1600TI 1966–70	..	..	..	..	Ball	BMW 1600 1966–70 Autobook
1800 1964–70	..	..	..	..	Ball	BMW 1800 1964–70 Autobook
1800TI 1964–67	..	..	..	..	Ball	BMW 1800 1964–70 Autobook
2000 1966–70	..	..	..	..	Ball	BMW 2000, 2002 1966–70 Autobook
2000A 1966–70	..	..	..	..	Ball	BMW 2000, 2002 1966–70 Autobook
2000TI 1966–70	..	..	..	..	Ball	BMW 2000, 2002 1966–70 Autobook
2000CS 1967–70	..	..	..	..	Ball	BMW 2000, 2002 1966–70 Autobook
2000CA 1967–70	..	..	..	..	Ball	BMW 2000, 2002 1966–70 Autobook
2002 1968–70	..	..	..	..	Ball	BMW 2000, 2002 1966–70 Autobook
CITROEN						
DS19 1955–65	..	..	..	..	Ball	Citroen DS19, ID19 1955–66 Autobook
ID19 1956–66	..	..	..	..	Ball	Citroen DS19, ID19 1955–66 Autobook

Make				Author	Title

COMMER

Cob Series 1, 2, 3 1960–65	..	..	..	Ball	Hillman Minx 1 to 5 1956–65 Autobook
Imp Vans 1963–68	..	..	..	Smith	Hillman Imp 1963–68 Autobook
Imp Vans 1969–71	..	..	..	Ball	Hillman Imp 1969–71 Autobook

DE DION BOUTON

One-cylinder 1899–1907	..	..	..	Mercredy	De Dion Bouton Autobook One
Two-cylinder 1903–1907	..	..	..	Mercredy	De Dion Bouton Autobook One
Four-cylinder 1905–1907	..	..	..	Mercredy	De Dion Bouton Autobook One

DATSUN

1300 1968–70	..	..	..	Ball	Datsun 1300, 1600 1968–70 Autobook
1600 1968–70	..	..	..	Ball	Datsun 1300, 1600 1968–70 Autobook

FIAT

500 1957–61	..	..	..	Ball	Fiat 500 1957–69 Autobook
500D 1960–65	..	..	..	Ball	Fiat 500 1957–69 Autobook
500F 1965–69	..	..	..	Ball	Fiat 500 1957–69 Autobook
500L 1968–69	..	..	..	Ball	Fiat 500 1957–69 Autobook
600 633cc 1955–61	..	..	..	Ball	Fiat 600, 600D 1955–69 Autobook
600D 767cc 1960–69	..	..	..	Ball	Fiat 600, 600D 1955–69 Autobook
850 Sedan 1964–70	..	..	..	Ball	Fiat 850 1964–70 Autobook
850 Coupé 1965–70	..	..	..	Ball	Fiat 850 1964–70 Autobook
850 Roadster 1965–70	..	..	..	Ball	Fiat 850 1964–70 Autobook
850 Family 1965–70	..	..	..	Ball	Fiat 850 1964–70 Autobook
850 Sport 1968–70	..	..	..	Ball	Fiat 850 1964–70 Autobook
124 Saloon 1966–70	..	..	..	Ball	Fiat 124 1966–70 Autobook
124S 1968–70		..	..	Ball	Fiat 124 1966–70 Autobook
124 Spyder 1966–70	..	..	..	Ball	Fiat 124 Sport 1966–70 Autobook
124 Coupé 1967–69	..	..	..	Ball	Fiat 124 Sport 1967–70 Autobook

FORD

Anglia 100E 1953–59	..	..	..	Ball	Ford Anglia Prefect 100E Autobook
Anglia 105E 1959–67	..	..	..	Smith	Ford Anglia 105E, Prefect 107E 1959–67 Autobook
Anglia Super 123E 1962–67	..	..	.	Smith	Ford Anglia 105E, Prefect 107E 1959–67 Autobook
Capri 109E 1962		..	..	Smith	Ford Classic, Capri 1961–64 Autobook
Capri 116E 1962–64	..	..	..	Smith	Ford Classic, Capri 1961–64 Autobook
Capri 1300, 1300GT 1968–71		..	..	Ball	Ford Capri 1300, 1600 1968–71 Autobook
Capri 1600, 1600GT 1968–71		..	..	Ball	Ford Capri 1300, 1600 1968–71 Autobook
Classic 109E 1961–62		..	..	Smith	Ford Classic, Capri 1961–64 Autobook
Classic 116E 1962–63		..	..	Smith	Ford Classic, Capri 1961–64 Autobook
Consul Mk 1 1950–56		..	..	Ball	Ford Consul, Zephyr, Zodiac 1, 2 1950–62 Autobook
Consul Mk 2 1956–62		..	..	Ball	Ford Consul, Zephyr, Zodiac 1, 2 1950–62 Autobook
Corsair Straight Four 1963–65		..	..	Ball	Ford Corsair Straight Four 1963–65 Autobook
Corsair Straight Four GT 1963–65		..	..	Ball	Ford Corsair Straight Four 1963–65 Autobook
Corsair V4 3004E 1965–68	..		..	Smith	Ford Corsair V4 1965–68 Autobook
Corsair V4 GT 1965–66	..		..	Smith	Ford Corsair V4 1965–68 Autobook
Corsair V4 1663cc 1969–70	..	..	..	Ball	Ford Corsair V4 1969–70 Autobook
Corsair 2000, 2000E 1966–68	.:		..	Smith	Ford Corsair V4 1965–68 Autobook
Corsair 2000, 2000E 1969–70		..	..	Ball	Ford Corsair V4 1969–70 Autobook
Cortina 113E 1962–66		..	..	Smith	Ford Cortina 1962–66 Autobook
Cortina Super 118E 1963–66	..	..	..	Smith	Ford Cortina 1962–66 Autobook
Cortina Lotus 125E 1963–66	..	..	..	Smith	Ford Cortina 1962–66 Autobook
Cortina GT 118E 1963–66	..	..	..	Smith	Ford Cortina 1962–66 Autobook
Cortina 1300 1967–68	..	..	..	Smith	Ford Cortina 1967–68 Autobook
Cortina 1300 1969–70	..	..	..	Ball	Ford Cortina 1969–70 Autobook
Cortina 1500 1967–68	..	..	..	Smith	Ford Cortina 1967–68 Autobook
Cortina 1600 (including Lotus) 1967–68		..	..	Smith	Ford Cortina 1967–68 Autobook
Cortina 1600 1969–70	..	..	..	Ball	Ford Cortina 1969–70 Autobook
Escort 100E 1955–59	..	..	..	Ball	Ford Anglia Prefect 100E Autobook
Escort 1100 1967–71	..	..	..	Ball	Ford Escort 1967–71 Autobook

Make					Author	Title
Escort 1300 1967–71	..	..	..	..	Ball	Ford Escort 1967–71 Autobook
Prefect 100E 1954–59		..	..	..	Ball	Ford Anglia Prefect 100E Autobook
Prefect 107E 1959–61		..	..	..	Smith	Ford Anglia 105E, Prefect 107E 1959–67 Autobook
Popular 100E 1959–62		..	..	..	Ball	Ford Anglia Prefect 100E Autobook
Squire 100E 1955–59	..	..	..	..	Ball	Ford Anglia Prefect 100E Autobook
Zephyr Mk 1 1950–56		..	..	..	Ball	Ford Consul, Zephyr, Zodiac 1, 2 1950–62 Autobook
Zephyr Mk 2 1956–62		..	..	..	Ball	Ford Consul, Zephyr, Zodiac 1, 2 1950–62 Autobook
Zephyr 4 Mk 3 1962–66		..	..	..	Ball	Ford Zephyr, Zodiac Mk 3 1962–66 Autobook
Zephyr 6 Mk 3 1962–66		..	..	..	Ball	Ford Zephyr, Zodiac Mk 3 1962–66 Autobook
Zodiac Mk 3 1962–66	..	..	..	..	Ball	Ford Zephyr, Zodiac Mk 3 1962–66 Autobook
Zodiac Mk 1 1953–56	..	..	..	..	Ball	Ford Consul Zephyr, Zodiac 1, 2 1950–62 Autobook
Zodiac Mk 2 1956–62	..	..	..	..	Ball	Ford Consul, Zephyr, Zodiac 1, 2 1950–62 Autobook
Zephyr V4 2 litre 1966–70	..	..	..	..	Ball	Ford Zephyr V4, V6, Zodiac 1966–70 Autobook
Zephyr V6 2.5 litre 1966–70	..	..	..	..	Ball	Ford Zephyr V4, V6, Zodiac 1966–70 Autobook
Zodiac V6 3 litre 1966–70		..	..	..	Ball	Ford Zephyr V4, V6, Zodiac 1966–70 Autobook

HILLMAN

Avenger 1970–71		..	..	..	Ball	Hillman Avenger 1970–71 Autobook
Avenger GT 1970–71	..	..	..	..	Ball	Hillman Avenger 1970–71 Autobook
Hunter GT 1966–70	..	..	..	..	Ball	Hillman Hunter 1966–70 Autobook
Minx series 1, 2, 3 1956–59	..	..	..	..	Ball	Hillman Minx 1 to 5 1956–65 Autobook
Minx series 3A, 3B, 3C 1959–63		..	..	..	Ball	Hillman Minx 1 to 5 1956–65 Autobook
Minx series 5 1963–65		..	..	..	Ball	Hillman Minx 1 to 5 1956–65 Autobook
Minx series 6 1965–67		..	..	..	Ball	Hillman Minx 1965–67 Autobook
New Minx 1500, 1725 1966–70		..	..	..	Ball	Hillman Minx 1966–70 Autobook
Imp 1963–68	..	..	..	..	Smith	Hillman Imp 1963–68 Autobook
Imp 1969–71	..	..	..	..	Ball	Hillman Imp 1969–71 Autobook
Husky series 1, 2, 3 1958–65	..	..	..	..	Ball	Hillman Minx 1 to 5 1956–65 Autobook
Husky Estate 1969–71		..	..	..	Ball	Hillman Imp 1969–71 Autobook
Super Minx Mk 1, 2, 3 1961–65		..	..	..	Ball	Hillman Super Minx 1961–65 Autobook
Super Minx Mk 4 1965–67		..	..	..	Ball	Hillman Minx 1965–67 Autobook

HUMBER

Sceptre Mk 1 1963–65		..	..	..	Ball	Hillman Super Minx 1961–65 Autobook
Sceptre Mk 2 1965–67		..	..	..	Ball	Hillman Minx 1965–67 Autobook
Sceptre 1967–70		..	..	..	Ball	Hillman Hunter 1966–70 Autobook

JAGUAR

XK 120 1948–54	..	..	..	..	Ball	Jaguar XK 120, 140, 150 Mk 7, 8, 9 1948–61 Autobook
XK 140 1954–57	..	..	..	..	Ball	Jaguar XK 120, 140, 150 Mk 7, 8, 9 1948–61 Autobook
XK 150 1957–61	..	..	..	..	Ball	Jaguar XK 120, 140, 150 Mk 7, 8, 9 1948–61 Autobook
XK 150S 1959–61	..	..	..	..	Ball	Jaguar XK 120, 140, 150 Mk 7, 8, 9 1948–61 Autobook
Mk 7, 7M, 8, 9 1950–61		..	..	..	Ball	Jaguar XK 120, 140, 150 Mk 7, 8, 9 1948–61 Autobook
2.4 Mk 1, 2 1955–67	..	..	..	..	Ball	Jaguar 2.4, 3.4, 3.8 Mk 1, 2 1955–69 Autobook
3.4 Mk 1, 2 1957–67	..	..	..	..	Ball	Jaguar 2.4, 3.4, 3.8 Mk 1, 2 1955–69 Autobook
3.8 Mk 2 1959–67		..	..	..	Ball	Jaguar 2.4, 3.4, 3.8 Mk 1, 2 1955–69 Autobook
240 1967–69	..	..	..	..	Ball	Jaguar 2.4, 3.4, 3.8 Mk 1, 2 1955–69 Autobook
340 1967–69		..	..	..	Ball	Jaguar 2.4, 3.4, 3.8 Mk 1, 2 1955–69 Autobook
E Type 3.8 1961–65	..	..	..	..	Ball	Jaguar E Type 1961–70 Autobook
E Type 4.2 1964–69		..	..	..	Ball	Jaguar E Type 1961–70 Autobook
E Type 4.2 2+2 1966–70		..	..	..	Ball	Jaguar E Type 1961–70 Autobook
E Type 4.2 Series 2 1969–70	..	..	..	..	Ball	Jagua E Type 1961–70 Autobook
S Type 3.4 1963–68	..	..	..	..	Ball	Jaguar S Type and 420 1963–68 Autobook
S Type 3.8 1963–68	..	..	..	..	Ball	Jaguar S Type and 420 1963–68 Autobook
420 1963–68	..	..	..	..	Ball	Jaguar S Type and 420 1963–68 Autobook
XJ6 2.8 litre 1968–70	..	..	..	..	Ball	Jaguar XJ6 1968–70 Autobook
XJ6 4.2 litre 1968–70	..	..	..	..	Ball	Jaguar XJ6 1968–70 Autobook

Make				Author	Title

JOWETT

Javelin PA 1947–49	..	..	..	Mitchell	Jowett Javelin Jupiter 1947–53 Autobook
Javelin PB 1949–50	..	..	..	Mitchell	Jowett Javelin Jupiter 1947–53 Autobook
Javelin PC 1950–51	..	..	..	Mitchell	Jowett Javelin Jupiter 1947–53 Autobook
Javelin PD 1951–52	..	..	..	Mitchell	Jowett Javelin Jupiter 1947–53 Autobook
Javelin PE 1952–53	..	..	..	Mitchell	Jowett Javelin Jupiter 1947–53 Autobook
Jupiter Mk 1 SA 1949–52	..	..	..	Mitchell	Jowett Javelin Jupiter 1947–53 Autobook
Jupiter Mk 1A SC 1952–53	..	..	..	Mitchell	Jowett Javelin Jupiter 1947–53 Autobook

LANDROVER

Series 1 1948–58	..	..	..	Ball	Landrover 1, 2 1948–61 Autobook
Series 2 1997cc 1959–61	..	..	..	Ball	Landrover 1, 2 1948–61 Autobook
Series 2 2052cc 1959–61	..	..	..	Ball	Landrover 1, 2 1948–61 Autobook
Series 2 2286cc 1959–61	..	..	..	Ball	Landrover 2, 2A 1959–70 Autobook
Series 2A 2286cc 1961–70	..	..	..	Ball	Landrover 2, 2A 1959–70 Autobook
Series 2A 2625cc 1967–70	..	..	..	Ball	Landrover 2, 2A 1959–70 Autobook

MG

TA 1936–39	..	..	..	Ball	MG TA to TF 1936–55 Autobook
TB 1939	..	..	..	Ball	MG TA to TF 1936–55 Autobook
TC 1945–49	..	..	..	Ball	MG TA to TF 1936–55 Autobook
TD 1950–53	..	..	..	Ball	MG TA to TF 1936–55 Autobook
TF 1953–54	..	..	..	Ball	MG TA to TF 1936–55 Autobook
TF 1500 1954–55	..	..	..	Ball	MG TA to TF 1936–55 Autobook
Midget 1961–70	..	..	..	Ball	Sprite, Midget 1958–70 Autobook
Magnette ZA, ZB 1955–59	..	..	..	Ball	BMC Autobook Three
MGA 1500, 1600 1955–62	..	..	..	Ball	MGA, MGB 1955–68 Autobook
MGA Twin Cam 1958–60	..	..	..	Ball	MGA, MGB 1955–68 Autobook
MGB 1962–68	..	..	..	Ball	MGA, MGB 1955–68 Autobook
MGB 1969–71	..	..	..	Ball	MG MGB 1969–71 Autobook
1100 Mk 1 1962–67	..	..	..	Ball	1100 Mk 1 1962–67 Autobook
1100 Mk 2 1968	..	..	..	Ball	1100 Mk 2, 1300 Mk 1, 2, America 1968–71 Autobook
1300 Mk 1, 2 1968–71	..	..	..	Ball	1100 Mk 2, 1300 Mk 1, 2, America 1968–71 Autobook

MERCEDES-BENZ

190B 1959–61	..	..	..	Ball	Mercedes-Benz 190 B, C, 200 1959–68 Autobook
190C 1961–65	..	..	..	Ball	Mercedes-Benz 190 B, C, 200 1959–68 Autobook
200 1965–68	..	..	..	Ball	Mercedes-Benz 190 B, C, 200 1959–68 Autobook
220B 1959–65	..	..	..	Ball	Mercedes-Ben 220 1959–65 Autobook
220SB 1959–65	..	..	..	Ball	Mercedes-Benz 220 1959–65 Autobook
220SEB 1959–65	..	..	..	Ball	Mercedes-Benz 220 1959–65 Autobook
220SEBC 1961–65	..	..	..	Ball	Mercedes-Benz 220 1959–65 Autobook
230 1965–67	..	..	..	Ball	Mercedes-Benz 230 1963–68 Autobook
230 S 1965–68	..	..	..	Ball	Mercedes-Benz 230 1963–68 Autobook
230 SL 1963–67	..	..	..	Ball	Mercedes-Benz 230 1963–68 Autobook
250 S 1965–68	..	..	..	Ball	Mercedes-Benz 250 1965–67 Autobook
250 SE 1965–67	..	..	..	Ball	Mercedes-Benz 250 1965–67 Autobook
250 SE BC 1965–67	..	..	..	Ball	Mercedes-Benz 250 1965–67 Autobook
250 SL 1967	..	..	..	Ball	Mercedes-Benz 250 1965–67 Autobook

MORGAN

Four wheelers 1936–69	..	..	..	Clarke	Morgan 1936–69 Autobook

MORRIS

Oxford 2, 3 1954–59	..	..	..	Ball	BMC Autobook Three
Oxford 5, 6 1959–69	..	..	..	Ball	Morris Oxford 5, 6 1959–70 Autobook
Minor series 2 1952–56	..	..	..	Ball	Morris Minor 1952–71 Autobook
Minor 1000 1957–71	..	..	..	Ball	Morris Minor 1952–71 Autobook
Mini 1959–70	..	..	..	Ball	Mini 1959–70 Autobook
Mini Clubman 1969–70	..	..	..	Ball	Mini 1959–70 Autobook
Mini Cooper 1961–70	..	..	..	Ball	Mini Cooper 1961–70 Autobook

Make				Author	Title
Mini Cooper S 1963–70	..	..	..	Ball	Mini Cooper 1961–70 Autobook
1100 Mk 1 1962–67	..	..	..	Ball	1100 Mk 1 1962–67 Autobook
1100 Mk 2 1968–70	..	..	..	Ball	1100 Mk 2, 1300 Mk 1, 2, America 1968–71 Autobook
1300 Mk 1, 2 1968–71	..	..	..	Ball	1100 Mk 2, 1300 Mk 1, 2, America 1968–71 Autobook
1800 Mk 1, 2 1966–71	..	..	..	Ball	1800 1964–71 Autobook
1800 S 1968–71	..	..	..	Ball	1800 1964–71 Autobook

NSU

Prinz 1000 L, LS 1963–67	..	..	..	Ball	NSU 1000 1963–70 Autobook
Prinz TT, TTS 1965–70	..	..	..	Ball	NSU 1000 1963–70 Autobook
1000 C 1967–70	..	..	..	Ball	NSU 1000 1963–70 Autobook
TYP 110 1966–67	..	..	..	Ball	NSU 1000 1963–70 Autobook
110 SC 1967	..	..	..	Ball	NSU 1000 1963–70 Autobook
1200, C, TT 1967–70	..	..	..	Ball	NSU 1000 1963–70 Autobook

OPEL

Kadett 993 cc 1962–65	..	..	..	Ball	Opel Kadett, Olympia 993 cc, 1078 cc 1962–70 Autobook
Kadett 1078 cc 1965–70	..	..	..	Ball	Opel Kadett, Olympia 993 cc and 1078 cc 1962–70 Autobook
Kadett 1492 cc 1967–70	..	..	..	Ball	Opel Kadett, Olympia 1492 cc, 1698 cc and 1897 cc 1967–70 Autobook
Kadett 1698 cc 1967–70	..	..	..	Ball	Opel Kadett, Olympia 1492 cc, 1698 cc and 1897 cc 1967–70 Autobook
Kadett 1897 cc 1967–70	..	..	..	Ball	Opel Kadett, Olympia 1492 cc, 1698 cc and 1897 cc 1967–70 Autobook
Olympia 1078 cc 1967–70	..	..	..	Ball	Opel Kadett, Olympia 993 cc and 1078 cc 1962–70 Autobook
Olympia 1492 cc 1967–70	..	..	..	Ball	Opel Kadett, Olympia 1492 cc, 1698 cc and 1897 cc 1967–70 Autobook
Olympia 1698 cc 1967–70	..	..	..	Ball	Opel Kadett, Olympia 1492 cc, 1698 cc and 1897 cc 1967–70 Autobook
Olympia 1897 cc 1967–70	..	..	..	Ball	Opel Kadett, Olympia 1492 cc, 1698 cc and 1897 cc 1967–70 Autobook
Rekord C 1.5, 1.7, 1.9 1966–70	..	..		Ball	Opel Rekord C 1966–70 Autobook

PEUGEOT

404 1960–69	..	..	..	Ball	Peugeot 404 1960–69 Autobook

PLYMOUTH

Cricket 1971	..	..	..	Ball	Hillman Avenger 1970–71 Autobook

PORSCHE

356A 1957–59	..	..	..	Ball	Porsche 356A, 356B, 356C 1957–65 Autobook
356B 1959–63	..	..	..	Ball	Porsche 356A, 356B, 356C 1957–65 Autobook
356C 1963–65	..	..	..	Ball	Porsche 356A, 356B, 356C 1957–65 Autobook
911 1964–67	..	..	..	Ball	Porsche 911 1964–69 Autobook
911L 1967–68	..	..	..	Ball	Porsche 911 1964–69 Autobook
911S 1966–69	..	..	..	Ball	Porsche 911 1964–69 Autobook
911T 1967–69	..	..	..	Ball	Porsche 911 1964–69 Autobook
911E 1968–69	..	..	..	Ball	Porsche 911 1964–69 Autobook
912 1582 cc 1965–70	..	..	..	Ball	Porsche 912 1965–70 Autobook

RENAULT

R4L 748 cc 845 cc 1961–65	..	..	..	Ball	Renault R4, R4L, 4 1961–70 Autobook
R4 845 cc 1962–66	..	..	..	Ball	Renault R4, R4L, 4 1961–70 Autobook
4 845 cc 1966–70	..	..	..	Ball	Renault R4, R4L, 4 1961–70 Autobook
6 1968–70	..	..	..	Ball	Renault 6 1968–70 Autobook
R8 956 cc 1962–65	..	..	..	Ball	Renault 8, 10, 1100 1962–70 Autobook
8 956 cc 1108 cc 1965–70	..	..	..	Ball	Renault 8, 10, 1100 1962–70 Autobook
8S 1108 cc 1968–70	..	..	..	Ball	Renault 8. 10. 1100 1962–70 Autobook

Make				Author	Title
1100, 1108 cc 1964–69	..	..	..	Ball	Renault 8, 10, 1100 1962–70 Autobook
R10 1108 cc 1967–69 ..	..	..	..	Ball	Renault 8, 10, 1100 1962–70 Autobook
10 1289 cc 1969–70 ..	..	..	..	Ball	Renault 8, 10, 1100 1962–70 Autobook
16 1470 cc 1965–70 ..	..	..	..	Ball	Renault R16 1965–70 Autobook
16TS 1565 cc 1968–70	..	..	..	Ball	Renault R16 1965–70 Autobook

RILEY

1.5 1957–65 ..	..	..	..	Ball	BMC Autobook Three
Elf Mk 1, 2, 3 1961–70	..	..	..	Ball	Mini 1959–70 Autobook
1100 Mk 1 1965–67 ..	..	..	..	Ball	1100 Mk 1 1962–67 Autobook
1100 Mk 2 1968	..	..	..	Ball	1100 Mk 2, 1300 Mk 1, 2 America 1968–71 Autobook
1300 Mk 1, 2 1968–71	..	..	..	Ball	1100 Mk 2, 1300 Mk 1, 2, America 1968–71 Autobook

ROVER

60 1953–59 ..	..	..	..	Ball	Rover 60–110 1953–64 Autobook
75 1954–59 ..	..	..	..	Ball	Rover 60–110 1953–64 Autobook
80 1959–62 ..	..	..	..	Ball	Rover 60–110 1953–64 Autobook
90 1954–59 ..	..	..	..	Ball	Rover 60–110 1953–64 Autobook
95 1962–64 ..	..	..	..	Ball	Rover 60–110 1953–64 Autobook
100 1959–62	..	..	..	Ball	Rover 60–110 1953–64 Autobook
105R 1957–58	..	..	..	Ball	Rover 60–110 1953–64 Autobook
105S 1957–59	..	..	..	Ball	Rover 60–110 1953–64 Autobook
110 1962–64 ..	..	..	..	Ball	Rover 60–110 1953–64 Autobook
2000 SC 1963–70	..	..	..	Ball	Rover 2000 1963–70 Autobook
2000 TC 1963–70	..	..	..	Ball	Rover 2000 1963–70 Autobook
3 litre Saloon Mk 1, 1A 1958–62	..	..	..	Ball	Rover 3 litre 1958–67 Autobook
3 litre Saloon Mk 2, 3 1962–67	..	..	..	Ball	Rover 3 litre 1958–67 Autobook
3 litre Coupé 1965–67	..	..	..	Ball	Rover 3 litre 1958–67 Autobook
3500, 3500S 1968–70	..	..	..	Ball	Rover 3500, 3500S 1968–70 Autobook

SAAB

95, 96, 1960–64	..	..	..	Ball	Saab 95, 96 Sport 1960–68 Autobook
95(5), 96(5) 1964–68	..	..	..	Ball	Saab 95, 96 Sport 1960–68 Autobook
Sport 1962–66	..	..	..	Ball	Saab 95, 96 Sport 1960–68 Autobook
Monte Carlo 1965–66 ..	..	..	..	Ball	Saab 95, 96 Sport 1960–68 Autobook
99 1969–70 ..	..	..	..	Ball	Saab 99 1969–70 Autobook

SIMCA

1000 1961–65	..	..	..	Ball	Simca 1000 1961–71 Autobook
1000 Special 1962–63	..	..	..	Ball	Simca 1000 1961–71 Autobook
1000 GL 1964–71	..	..	..	Ball	Simca 1000 1961–71 Autobook
1000 GLS 1964–69	..	..	..	Ball	Simca 1000 1961–71 Autobook
1000 GLA 1965–69	..	..	..	Ball	Simca 1000 1961–71 Autobook
1000 LS 1965–71	..	..	..	Ball	Simca 1000 1961–71 Autobook
1000 L 1966–68	..	..	..	Ball	Simca 1000 1961–71 Autobook
1000 Special 1968–71	..	..	..	Ball	Simca 1000 1961–71 Autobook
1100 LS 1967–70	..	..	..	Ball	Simca 1100 1967–70 Autobook
1100 GL, GLS 1967–70	..	..	..	Ball	Simca 1100 1967–70 Autobook
1204 1970 ..	..	..	..	Ball	Simca 1100 1967–70 Autobook

SINGER

Chamois 1964–68	..	..	..	Smith	Hillman Imp 1963–68 Autobook
Chamois 1969–70	..	..	..	Ball	Hillman Imp 1969–71 Autobook
Chamois Sport 1964–68	..	..	..	Smith	Hillman Imp 1963–68 Autobook
Chamois Sport 1969–70	..	..	..	Ball	Hillman Imp 1969–71 Autobook
Gazelle series 2A 1958	..	..	..	Ball	Hillman Minx 1 to 5 1956–65 Autobook
Gazelle 3, 3A, 3B, 3C 1958–63	..	..	..	Ball	Hillman Minx 1 to 5 1956–65 Autobook
Gazelle series 5 1963–65	..	..	..	Ball	Hillman Minx 1 to 5 1956–65 Autobook'
Gazelle series 6 1965–67	..	..	..	Ball	Hillman Minx 1965–67 Autobook

Make				Author	Title
New Gazelle 1500, 1725 1966–70	..		..	Ball	Hillman Minx 1966–70 Autobook
Vogue Mk 1 to 3 1961–65	..	..	..	Ball	Hillman Super Minx 1961–65 Autobook
Vogue series 4 1965–67	..	..	..	Ball	Hillman Minx 1965–67 Autobook
New Vogue 1966–70 ..	..	..	..	Ball	Hillman Hunter 1966–70 Autobook

SKODA

440, 445, 450 1957–69	..	..	..	Skoda	Skoda Autobook One

SUNBEAM

Alpine series 1, 2, 3, 4 1959–65	..	..	Ball	Sunbeam Rapier Alpine 1955–65 Autobook
Alpine series 5 1965–67	..	..	Ball	Hillman Minx 1965–67 Autobook
Alpine 1969–70	..	..	Ball	Hillman Hunter 1966–70 Autobook
Rapier series 1, 2, 3, 3A, 4 1955–65	..	..	Ball	Sunbeam Rapier Alpine 1955–65 Autobook
Rapier series 5 1965–67	..	..	Ball	Hillman Minx 1965–67 Autobook
Rapier H.120 1967–70	..	..	Ball	Hillman Hunter 1966–70 Autobook
Imp Sport 1963–68	..	..	Smith	Hillman Imp 1963–68 Autobook
Imp Sport 1969–71	..	..	Ball	Hillman Imp 1969–71 Autobook
Stilletto 1967–68	..	..	Smith	Hillman Imp 1963–68 Autobook
Stilletto 1969–71	..	..	Ball	Hillman Imp 1969–71 Autobook
1250 1970–71	..	..	Ball	Hillman Avenger 1970–71 Autobook
1500 1970–71	..	..	Ball	Hillman Avenger 1970–71 Autobook

TOYOTA

Corolla 1100 1967–70	..	..	Ball	Toyota Corolla 1100 1967–70 Autobook
Corolla 1100 De luxe 1967–70	..	..	Ball	Toyota Corolla 1100 1967–70 Autobook
Corolla 1100 Automatic 1968–69	..	..	Ball	Toyota Corolla 1100 1967–70 Autobook
Corona 1500 Mk 1 1965–70 ..	..	..	Ball	Toyota Corona 1500 Mk 1 1965–70 Autobook
Corona 1900 Mk 2 1969–71 ..	..	..	Ball	Toyota Corona 1900 Mk 2 1969–71 Autobook

TRIUMPH

TR2 1952–55 ..	..	..	..	..	Ball	Triumph TR2, TR3, TR3A 1952–62 Autobook
TR3, TR3A 1955–62 ..	..	..	..	Ball	Triumph TR2, TR3, TR3A 1952–62 Autobook
TR4, TR4A 1961–67 ..	..	..	..	Ball	Triumph TR4, TR4A 1961–67 Autobook
TR5 1967–69 ..	..	..	..	Ball	Triumph TR5, TR250, TR6 1967–70 Autobook
TR6 1969–70 ..	..	..	..	Ball	Triumph TR5, TR250, TR6 1967–70 Autobook
TR250 1967–69 ..	..	..	..	Ball	Triumph TR5, TR250, TR6 1967–70 Autobook
1300 1965–70	..	..	..	Ball	Triumph 1300 1965–70 Autobook
1300TC 1967–70	..	..	..	Ball	Triumph 1300 1965–70 Autobook
2000 Mk 1 1963–69 ..	..	..	..	Ball	Triumph 2000 Mk 1, 2.5 Pl Mk 1 1963–69 Autobook
2000 Mk 2 1969–71 ..	..	..	..	Ball	Triumph 2000 Mk 2, 2.5 Pl Mk 2 1969–71 Autobook
2.5 Pl Mk 1 1963–69 ..	..	..	..	Ball	Triumph 2000 Mk 1, 2.5 Pl Mk 1 1963–69 Autobook
2.5 Pl Mk 2 1969–71 ..	..	..	..	Ball	Triumph 2000 Mk 2, 2.5 Pl Mk 2 1969–70 Autobook
Herald 948 1959–64 ..	..	..	..	Smith	Triumph Herald 1959–68 Autobook
Herald 1200 1961–68 ..	..	..	..	Smith	Triumph Herald 1959–68 Autobook
Herald 1200 1969–70 ..	..	..	..	Ball	Triumph Herald 1969–71 Autobook
Herald 12/50 1963–67	..	..	..	Smith	Triumph Herald 1959–68 Autobook
Herald 13/60 1967–68	..	..	..	Smith	Triumph Herald 1959–68 Autobook
Herald 13/60 1969–71	..	..	..	Ball	Triumph Herald 1969–71 Autobook
Spitfire 1962–68	..	..	..	Smith	Triumph Spitfire Vitesse 1962–68 Autobook
Spitfire Mk 3 1969–70	..	..	..	Ball	Triumpn Spitfire Mk 3 1969–70 Autobook
Vitesse 1600 and 2 litre 1962–68	..	..	Smith	Triumph Spitfire Vitesse 1962–68 Autobook
Vitesse 2 litre 1969–70	..	..	..	Ball	Triumph GT6, Vitesse 2 litre 1969–70 Autobook
GT Six 2 litre 1966–68	..	..	..	Smith	Triumph Spitfire Vitesse 1962–68 Autobook
GT Six 1969–70	..	..	..	Ball	Triumph GT6, Vitesse 2 litre 1969–70 Autobook

VANDEN PLAS

3 litre 1959–64	..	..	..	Ball	BMC Autobook Four
1100 Mk 1 1963–67 ..	..	..	..	Ball	1100 Mk 1 1962–67 Autobook
1100 Mk 2 1968	..	..	..	Ball	1100 Mk 2, 1300 Mk 1, 2, America 1968–71 Autobook
1300 Mk 1, 2, 1968–71	..	..	..	Ball	1100 Mk 2, 1300 Mk 1, 2, America 1968–71 Autobook

Make					Author	Title

VAUXHALL

Make	Author	Title
Victor 1 1957–59	Ball	Vauxhall Victor 1, 2 FB 1957–64 Autobook
Victor 2 1959–61	Ball	Vauxhall Victor 1, 2 FB 1957–64 Autobook
Victor FB 1961–64	Ball	Vauxhall Victor 1, 2 FB 1957–64 Autobook
VX4/90 FBH 1961–64	Ball	Vauxhall Victor 1, 2 FB 1957–64 Autobook
Victor FC 101 1964–67	Ball	Vauxhall Victor 101 1964–67 Autobook
VX 4/90 FCH 1964–67	Ball	Vauxhall Victor 101 1964–67 Autobook
Victor FD 1599 cc 1967–71	Ball	Vauxhall Victor FD 1600, 2000 1967–71 Autobook
Victor FD 1975 cc 1967–71	Ball	Vauxhall Victor FD 1600, 2000 1967–71 Autobook
VX 4/90 1969–71	Ball	Vauxhall Victor FD 1600, 2000 1967–71 Autobook
Velox, Cresta PA 1957–62	Ball	Vauxhall Velox Cresta 1957–70 Autobook
Velox, Cresta PB 1962–65	Ball	Vauxhall Velox Cresta 1957–70 Autobook
Cresta PC 1965–70	Ball	Vauxhall Velox Cresta 1957–70 Autobook
Viscount 1966–70	Ball	Vauxhall Velox Cresta 1957–70 Autobook
Viva HA (including 90) 1964–66	Ball	Vauxhall Viva HA 1964–66 Autobook
Viva HB (including 90 and SL90) 1966–70	Ball	Vauxhall Viva HB 1966–70 Autobook

VOLKSWAGEN

Make	Author	Title
1200 Beetle 1954–67	Ball	Volkswagen Beetle 1954–67 Autobook
1200 Beetle 1968–71	Ball	Volkswagen Beetle 1968–71 Autobook
1200 Karmann Ghia 1955–65	Ball	Volkswagen Beetle 1954–67 Autobook
1200 Transporter 1954–64	Ball	Volkswagen Transporter 1954–67 Autobook
1300 Beetle 1965–67	Ball	Volkswagen Beetle 1954–67 Autobook
1300 Beetle 1968–71	Ball	Volkswagen Beetle 1968–71 Autobook
1300 Karmann Ghia 1965–66	Ball	Volkswagen Beetle 1954–67 Autobook
1500 Beetle 1966–67	Ball	Volkswagen Beetle 1954–67 Autobook
1500 Beetle 1968–70	Ball	Volkswagen Beetle 1968–71 Autobook
1500 1961–65	Ball	Volkswagen 1500 1961–66 Autobook
1500N 1963–65	Ball	Volkswagen 1500 1961–66 Autobook
1500S 1963–65	Ball	Volkswagen 1500 1961–66 Autobook
1500A 1965–66	Ball	Volkswagen 1500 1961–66 Autobook
1500 Karmann Ghia 1966–67	Ball	Volkswagen Beetle 1954–67 Autobook
1500 Transporter 1963–67	Ball	Volkswagen Transporter 1954–67 Autobook
1500 Karmann Ghia 1968–70	Ball	Volkswagen Beetle 1968–71 Autobook
1600 TL 1965–70	Ball	Volkswagen 1600 Fastback 1965–70 Autobook
1600 Variant 1965–66	Ball	Volkswagen 1600 Fastback 1965–70 Autobook
1600 L 1966–67	Ball	Volkswagen 1600 Fastback 1965–70 Autobook
1600 Variant L 1966–70	Ball	Volkswagen 1600 Fastback 1965–70 Autobook
1600 T 1968–70	Ball	Volkswagen 1600 Fastback 1965–70 Autobook
1600 TA 1969–70	Ball	Volkswagen 1600 Fastback 1965–70 Autobook
1600 Variant A, M	Ball	Volkswagen 1600 Fastback 1965–70 Autobook

VOLVO

Make	Author	Title
121, 131, 221 1962–68	Ball	Volvo P120 1961–68 Autobook
122, 132, 222 1961–68	Ball	Volvo P120 1961–68 Autobook
123 GT 1967–68	Ball	Volvo P120 1961–68 Autobook
142, 142S 1967–69	Ball	Volvo 140 1966–70 Autobook
144, 144S 1966–70	Ball	Volvo 140 1966–70 Autobook
145, 145S 1968–71	Ball	Volvo 140 1966–70 Autobook

WOLSELEY

Make	Author	Title
1500 1959–65	Ball	BMC Autobook Three
15/50 1956–58	Ball	BMC Autobook Three
6/99 1959–61	Ball	BMC Autobook Four
6/110 1961–68	Ball	BMC Autobook Four
Hornet Mk 1, 2, 3 1961–70	Ball	Mini 1959–70 Autobook
1100 Mk 1 1965–67	Ball	1100 Mk 1 1962–67 Autobook
1100 Mk 2 1968	Ball	1100 Mk 2, 1300 Mk 1, 2, America 1968–71 Autobook
1300 Mk 1, 2 1968–71	Ball	1100 Mk 2, 1300 Mk 1, 2, America 1968–71 Autobook
18/85 Mk 1, 2 1967–71	Ball	1800 1964–71 Autobook
18/85 S 1969–71	Ball	1800 1964–71 Autobook

NOTES

NOTES

NOTES

NOTES